D1477792

STOPPING RAPE

Towards a comprehensive policy

Sylvia Walby,
Philippa Olive, Jude Towers, Brian Francis,
Sofia Strid, Andrea Krizsán, Emanuela Lombardo,
Corinne May-Chahal, Suzanne Franzway,
David Sugarman, Bina Agarwal and Jo Armstrong

First published in Great Britain in 2015 by

Policy Press
University of Bristol
1-9 Old Park Hill
Bristol BS2 8BB
UK
t: +44 (0)117 954 5940
pp-info@bristol.ac.uk
www.policypress.co.uk

North America office:
Policy Press
c/o The University of Chicago Press
1427 East 60th Street
Chicago, IL 60637, USA
t: +1 773 702 7700
f: +1 773 702 9756
sales@press.uchicago.edu
www.press.uchicago.edu

British Library Cataloguing in Publication Data
A catalogue record for this book is available from the British Library.

Library of Congress Cataloging-in-Publication Data
A catalog record for this book has been requested.

ISBN 978 1 4473 2209 2 paperback
ISBN 978 1 4473 2212 2 ePub
ISBN 978 1 4473 2211 5 Kindle

Cover design by Qube Design, Bristol
Front cover: image kindly supplied by iStock
Printed and bound in Great Britain by www.4edge.co.uk
Policy Press uses environmentally responsible print partners

Contents

List of abbreviations

A&E	Accident and Emergency
ABS	Australian Bureau of Statistics
ADT	androgen deprivation therapy
BME	black and minority ethnic
CBT	cognitive behavioural therapy
CJS	Criminal Justice System
CPA	cyproterone acetate
CVTV	closed circuit television
DFID	Department for International Development
EIGE	European Institute for Gender Equality
EP	European Parliament
ESF	European Structural Fund
EU	European Union
EWL	European Women's Lobby
FOI	Freedom of Information
FRA	(European Union) Fundamental Rights Agency
GRIP	Greater Rape Intervention Program
HEFCE	Higher Education Funding Council for England
IAFN	checklist for disaster planning
IAPT	Improving Access to Psychological Therapies
IASC	Inter-Agency Standing Committee
IAWG	Inter-Agency Working Group
ICTR	International Criminal Tribunal for Rwanda
ICTY	International Criminal Tribunal for the former Yugoslavia
IMAGE	Microfinance for AIDS and Gender Equality
IRC	International Rescue Committee
ISVA	independent sexual violence advisor
LEA	local education authority
LGBTQ	lesbian, gay, bisexual, trans or questioning
MARAC	multi-agency risk assessment conference
MHPSS	mental health and psychosocial support system
MISP	minimum initial service package
MPA	medroxyprogesterone
NAP	national action plan
NGO	non-governmental organisation
NPA	National Prosecuting Authority

NSOR	National Sex Offender Registry
PATH	Psychological Advocacy Towards Healing
PFA	psychological first aid
PTSD	post-traumatic stress disorder
RCNE	Rape Crisis Network Europe
Roks	Riksorganisationen För Kvinnojourer och Tjejjourer i Sverige
SACT	Sexual Assault Crisis Team
SAME	sexual assault medical examiner
SANE	sexual assault nurse examiner
SARC	sexual assault referral centre
SART	sexual assault response team
SORN	sex offender registration and notification
Star	Southampton Talking About Relationships
SVRI	Sexual Violence Research Initiative
UN	United Nations
UNESCO	United Nations Educational, Scientific and Cultural Organisation
UNHCR	United Nations High Commissioner for Refugees
UNSCR	United Nations Security Council Resolution
VAWG	Violence Against Women and Girls
WHO	World Health Organization
WWC SA	Working Women's Centre South Australia

Notes on authors

Sylvia Walby is Distinguished Professor of Sociology and UNESCO Chair in Gender Research, Lancaster University, UK. She has conducted research on gender-based violence for the UK Home Office, published as *Domestic violence, sexual assault and stalking: Findings from the British Crime* Survey (with Allen, Home Office, 2004); the UK Women and Equality Unit, *The cost of domestic violence* (2004); the UK Equality and Human Rights Commission, *Physical and legal security and the criminal justice system* (with Armstrong and Strid, 2010); Trust for London/ Northern Rock Foundation, *Cuts in public expenditure on services to prevent violence against women* (with Towers, 2012); the European Institute for Gender Equality, *Estimating the costs of gender-based violence in the European Union* (with Olive, 2014); and for the Economic and Social Research Council on the changing rate of domestic violence with Brian Francis and Jude Towers, European Commission on the gender dimension of trafficking in human beings, European Parliament, Council of Europe on the Istanbul Convention, United Nations Division for the Advancement of Women and the United Nations Economic Commission for Europe. She has an OBE for services to equal opportunities and diversity. Further publications include *Sex crime in the news* (with Soothill, Routledge 1991), *Globalization and inequalities: Complexity and contested modernities* (Sage, 2009), *The future of feminism* (Polity, 2011), and an edited special issue of *Current Sociology*, 2013, vol 61, no 2, on 'Violence and society'.

Philippa Olive is Senior Lecturer, Department of Nursing, Health and Professional Practice, University of Cumbria and Senior Researcher affiliated with the UNESCO, and Chair in the Gender Research Group, Department of Sociology, Lancaster University, UK. Philippa's research is concerned with gender-based violence, its impacts and health systems responses, and she recently completed a project with Sylvia Walby on the costs of gender-based violence in the European Union. Philippa's previous research examined the classification of forms of gender-based violence in health systems, and the sociology of domestic violence diagnosis during emergency department consultations.

Her current research projects involve analysis of health systems domestic violence incidence data and the development of better measures of the health impacts of gender-based violence.

Jude Towers is Senior Research Associate in the Sociology Department at Lancaster University, UK. She has a PhD in Applied Social Statistics. Her research concentrates on the measurement of gender-based violence and on exploring the relationship between different forms of gender-based violence within varying economic, social and political contexts. She has worked on research projects on gender-based violence funded by the Economic and Social Research Council, the European Parliament, and the Northern Rock Foundation and Trust for London. Her recent publications include, with Walby, Towers and Francis (2014), 'Mainstreaming domestic and gender-based violence into sociology and the criminology of violence', *The Sociological Review*, vol 62, no S2.

Brian Francis is Professor of Social Statistics, and a member of the Centre for Law and Society at Lancaster University, UK. He has over 30 years' experience of statistical consultancy and applied statistical research, as well as a strong substantive interest in criminology. His recent work has focused on the analysis of criminal careers and issues relating to serious crime, including homicide, kidnap, domestic violence and sex offending, as well as organised crime. He is co-editing the *Oxford handbook of sex offences and sex offending*. His 230 publications span statistics, criminology, health, sociology and psychology. His recent work includes papers on football and domestic violence, the desistance of sex offenders and the statistical modelling of social networks.

Sofia Strid is Senior Lecturer in Gender Studies at Örebro University, Sweden. Her research is both theoretical and policy-oriented, and focuses primarily on violence, intersectionality and civil society in the European Union. Her current projects, funded by the European Commission and the Swedish Research Council, bring key theoretical and methodological strands of feminist intersectional analysis into dialogue, and set up arenas for cross-fertilisations, leading to more comprehensive and transgressive analytical approaches and theoretical understandings of intersectional gender. Sofia is one of the scientific chairs within the GEXCEL International Collegium for Advanced Transdisciplinary Gender Studies and editor of the Nordic *Journal of Gender Studies*.

Andrea Krizsán is Research Fellow at the Center for Policy Studies, Central European University, Budapest, Hungary. Her work focuses on the politics of inequality, and understanding progressive policy change regarding gender equality and gender-based violence, ethnicity and intersectionality issues in Central and Eastern Europe. Her publications include articles in the journals *Violence against Women, Social Politics, European Integration Online Papers, Policy Studies, Ethnic and Racial Studies, Journal for Ethnic and Minority Studies*, and the *European Journal of Women's Studies*, and chapters in several edited volumes. She recently co-edited a volume with Squires and Skjeie on institutionalising intersectionality and the changing nature of European equality regimes, published by Palgrave Macmillan (2012).

Emanuela Lombardo, is Lecturer at the Department of Political Science and Administration II of Madrid Complutense University, Spain. Her research concerns gender equality policies and their intersections with other inequalities, particularly in the European Union and Spain, Europeanisation, gender mainstreaming, and gender and political representation. On these issues she has published articles in peer-reviewed journals and chapters in edited books including the Oxford University Press Handbooks of Gender and Politics and of Feminist Theory. Her last books are *The symbolic representation of gender* (with Meier, Ashgate, 2014), and *The Europeanization of gender equality policies* (edited with Forest, Palgrave, 2012). She is editor (with Meier and Verloo) of the Special Issue on Policymaking forthcoming in the *Journal of Women, Politics and Policy*.

Corinne May-Chahal, Lancaster University, UK, practised as a social worker while conducting research aimed at improving children's participation in services designed to safeguard them. Her early work (*Making a case in child protection*, 1992; *Child* *protection: Risk and the moral order*, 1997; and *Child sexual abuse: Responding to the experiences of children*, 1999) has subsequently had an impact on policy and practice through membership of non-governmental public bodies such as the Family Justice Council, as co-chair of the College of Social Work, and her work with international organisations. She currently researches from a digital world perspective, developing and applying new technologies to create software to aid identity recognition and to facilitate children reporting rape and abuse (see May-Chahal, C., Mason, C., Rashid, A., Walkerdine, J., Rayson, P. and Greenwood, P., 2014, 'Safeguarding cyborg childhoods: Incorporating the on/offline behaviour of children into everyday social work practices', *British Journal of Social Work*, vol 44, no 3, pp 596-614).

Suzanne Franzway is Professor of Sociology and Gender Studies at the University of South Australia, Adelaide. Her research focuses on sexual politics, greedy institutions, gendered violence and citizenship, social movements, and epistemologies of ignorance. Her books include *Challenging knowledge, sex and power: Gender, work and engineering* (Routledge, 2013); *Making feminist politics: Transnational alliances between women and labor* (University of Illinois Press, 2011); *Sexual politics and greedy institutions: Union women, commitments and conflicts in public and in private* (Pluto Press, 2001); and *Staking a claim: Feminism, bureaucracy and the state* (Allen & Unwin, 1989).

David Sugarman is Emeritus Professor of Law at Lancaster University, UK, and Fellow of the Royal Historical Society. He has undertaken research for intergovernmental organisations, government departments and non-governmental organisations, most recently the European Court of Justice, the European Court of Human Rights and the European Union Parliament. Sugarman has written and/or edited 20 books and written over 90 articles and book chapters. He has also published articles in *The Guardian*, *The Times* and *Open Democracy*. Relevant publications include *The handbook of European non-discrimination law* (with Butler, European Union Agency for Fundamental Rights and the European Court of Justice, 2011).

Bina Agarwal is Professor of Development Economics and Environment at the University of Manchester, UK, and former Director of the Institute of Economic Growth, Delhi, India. She has been President of the International Society for Ecological Economics, and President of the International Association for Feminist Economics. Her 9 books and over 75 professional papers include the multiple award-winning book, *A field of one's own: Gender and land rights in South Asia*, and her latest, *Gender and green governance*. In 2005, she catalysed a successful campaign for gender equality in India's Hindu inheritance law. A three-volume compendium of her selected papers is forthcoming from Oxford University Press. In 2008, Agarwal received a Padma Shri from the President of India, and in 2010, the Leontief Prize from Tufts University 'for broadening the frontiers of economic thought'.

Jo Armstrong is Researcher at Lancaster University, UK, working in both the Sociology Department and the Department of Educational Research. Her doctoral research used in-depth interviews to explore the intersections of gender and social class. Jo's interests have since extended into the broader field of inequalities, including gender-based violence, and she has been engaged in projects funded by various organisations (for example, the Equality and Human Rights Commission, European Commission and European Parliament). Her research outputs include contributions to edited collections (for example, *Classed intersections*, edited by Y. Taylor), journals (for example, *Social Policy and Society*) and reports (for example, *Review of equality statistics*, Equality and Human Rights Commission).

Acknowledgements

The research was led by Sylvia Walby at Lancaster University, UK, conducted by members of a research team drawn from around the world – Philippa Olive, Jude Towers, Brian Francis, Sofia Strid, Andrea Krizsán, Emanuela Lombardo, Corinne May-Chahal, Suzanne Franzway, David Sugarman, Bina Agarwal and Jo Armstrong – and assisted with information from people and agencies who were innovating approaches to stopping rape.

We would like to thank the following people for their help and contributions:

The European Parliament, for funding the underlying study, and in particular, Erika Schultz, for assisting with the project, including contributions to the editing of the original report (see Walby et al 2013).

Comprehensive rape crisis services case study: Bobbi Gagne (SACT) and Michelle Barry (Southampton Rape Crisis).

Australia case study: Bec Neill.

Health case studies: Rachel Belk, Research Officer, St Mary's Sexual Assault Referral Centre, Manchester; Jennifer Holly, Stella Project Mental Health Initiative Coordinator, AVA (Against Violence and Abuse), London; Jackie Patiniotis, reVision (formerly The Joint Forum), Liverpool, England; Bill Roberts, Locate Investigations Ltd; Bernie Ryan, Service Manager, St Mary's Sexual Assault Referral Centre, Manchester; Dr Kylee Trevillion, Visiting Postdoctoral Research Fellow, Section of Women's Mental Health, Health Service and Population Research Department, Institute of Psychiatry, King's College, London; Dr Cath White, Clinical Director, St Mary's Sexual Assault Referral Centre, Manchester; Liz Willows, Specialist Mental Health Independent Sexual Violence Adviser, The Haven, Paddington Sexual Assault Referral Centre, London.

Cyber-rape case study: Awais Rashid.

Mexican law case study: Deysi Cheyne, Ana de Mendoza, Ana María Moreno, Lorena Pajares, Guadalupe Portillo and Charo Rubio.

#talkaboutit case study: Gustav Almestad.

For commenting on the draft report, Liz Kelly (Child and Woman Abuse Studies Unit, London Metropolitan University).

Most of all, we would like to thank victim-survivors of rape for their ongoing contributions to our knowledge.

1

Introduction

Rape shatters lives. Its traumatising effects can linger for many years after the immediate pain and suffering. Rape is a consequence and a cause of gender inequality. It is an injury to health; a crime; a violation of women's human rights; and costly to both the economy and society.

Stopping rape requires changes to many policies and practices. There is no simple solution; rather, a myriad of reforms are needed to prevent rape. New policies are being innovated around the world, north and south, which are often intended to prevent rape and to support victims/survivors simultaneously. This book provides an overview of the current best practice from around the world for ending rape.

In order to prevent rape, it is necessary to know what causes rape. The selection of the examples of good and promising practice in this book is guided by a theory of the causes of rape. The causal pathways that lead to rape involve many of society's institutions. These pathways are embedded in the state and public services, including the criminal justice system and healthcare; culture, media and education; in other forms and contexts of violence; and in the economy.

Stopping rape requires the effective mobilisation of all of these actors and institutions. It is not a single institution that needs to change, however: most social institutions need reform, and society needs transforming. Prevention is not a simple matter of changing attitudes such as by 'educating' boys, although every reform makes a contribution. Preventing rape requires reforms in the many institutions that make up the social system. This, in turn, requires the deepening of the gender dimension of democracy, and a reduction in overall gender inequalities.

The enormity of the task of preventing rape does not make it impossible. Stopping rape can be achieved step by step. In order to achieve this goal we need institutions that support the health and welfare of victims, deliver justice, deepen democracy, reduce gender inequalities, and reduce other forms of violence, as well as cultural change. The theories, evidence and practice presented in this book are a contribution to the knowledge base needed to prevent rape.

'What works' to prevent rape?

This book is concerned with 'what works' to prevent rape. It identifies and evaluates recent strategies and policy practices from around the world, including the UK and the European Union (EU), drawing on the international academic and policy literature. Preventing rape requires reforms to policies for major institutions concerned with: strategy, planning and coordination; victim and healthcare services; law and the criminal justice system; conflict zones; culture, media and education; and the economy. Separate chapters of the book address the reforms needed in each of these policy fields.

Strategy, planning and coordination

Strategy is needed to guide effective policy development and its implementation. This requires the development of expertise as to 'what works' to reduce rape, followed by the mainstreaming of this expertise into all relevant fields of public policy. It requires coordination of the actions of a myriad of relevant institutions. It requires research, supported by data and statistics, to build theory about the causes of rape and in order to evaluate the effectiveness of policy practices.

These developments depend on reform of the policy-making apparatus itself through the deepening of gendered democracy, for example, by reducing the gender imbalance in decision-making, from Parliament to the police. The developments concern: strategic planning; coordination; development of specialist services for victim-survivors; research, data and statistics; and deepening gendered democracy.

- *Strategic planning:* Effective interventions to stop rape require strategic planning at international, national and local levels. Countries need National Action Plans to map out the way forward. The strategic development of effective policy to stop rape requires both the development of specialist expertise and for actions by mainstream institutions to be routinely informed by such expertise. The concept and practice of 'gender mainstreaming' was developed when it was recognised that effective policy development for gender equality required both the development of specialist expertise, and also that normal policy actors incorporate these new practices into their mainstream work. There is often a tension between the specialist expertise and the mainstream, but this is, or at least can be, productive of deep positive changes in a broad range of policy developments. The concept of 'mainstreaming' is applied here to the policy and practices needed to stop rape. There needs to be both specialist units focused on the development of expertise in stopping rape, and also the application of this expert knowledge by normal policy actors in a wide range of mainstream policy domains.
- *Coordination of service provision:* the multiplicity of responses from a myriad of specialist and mainstream services requires coordination at national and local level in order to be effective. There is a need for national-level coordination and funding of policies, and also local-level cooperation of the services needed to serve victims. At the local level, services need coordination in order to ensure that a focus on the needs of the victim is achieved. The international and regional levels are important for exchanging best practice.
- *Specialised services for victim-survivors:* The development of specialised services focused on the needs of the victim-survivors is very important.
- *Research, data and statistics:* strategic planning requires a knowledge base to provide the evidence to evaluate policy developments. It requires research, data and statistics. Policies need to be assessed to find out 'what works' best in particular

locations. It is necessary to know how frequent rape is and how it is patterned, which requires population surveys. It is necessary to know how successful services are in their specific contribution to the stopping of rape, which requires relevant administrative data. It is necessary to develop theories, tested against evidence, as to what causes rape in order to help the evaluation of what is effective in preventing rape.

- *Deepening gendered democracy:* the development of a viable strategy to prevent rape requires the deepening of gendered democracy, reducing the gender imbalance in decision-making, so that women as well as men have an effective voice in the myriad of relevant institutions where decisions are made as to policy priorities. This includes the voices of those who have suffered rape. Deepening the gender dimension of democracy is part of the overarching strategy to develop the institutions, policies and practices needed to stop rape. It is unlikely that this can be achieved without a reduction in overall gender inequality.

Victim services and healthcare systems

It is important to look after the victim-survivors. The hurt and harms from rape are considerable and often long lasting. It is possible to mitigate the effects of rape by good practice, speeding healing and recovery. This is potentially offered both by specialised standalone support services and by expert practices based within mainstream health services. The health system is potentially an important source of assistance to victims of rape, helping them to recover, but, if poorly organised, it may exacerbate the problem.

Looking after the victims of rape is not only important in its own right, but it also contributes to the effectiveness of preventative practices, for example, by helping victim-survivors to endure the gruelling processes of the criminal justice system to secure the convictions necessary to remove impunity from rapists. Survivors of rape also have the potential to contribute knowledge to assist the development of the best form of services for victims, to educate the public in the realities of rape, and to contribute to the improvement of policies. Strengthening the ability of victim–survivors to contribute to these processes of deterrence, public education and policy reform is important for the prevention of rape in the future.

Law and the criminal justice system

Rape is illegal in most places in the world, but the implementation of laws against rape is notoriously inadequate and still needs reform. The purpose of the criminal justice system is to stop people from committing crime by deterrence through punishment, and by rehabilitation in prisons and treatment programmes. But most rapists are not convicted, which generates impunity. The deterrent effect of potential punishment depends on rapists being convicted in the courts. This requires reforms of the criminal justice system so that rapists are more usually convicted. This is not to promote a punitive state, but rather the development of a gender-sensitive state, which responds to the concerns of victim–survivors of rape.

Conflict zones

Rape is more common when other forms of violence are more common. Rape is more frequent in zones of conflict than of peace. The use of rape as a weapon of war has consequences for the long-term perpetuation of ethnic hatred and political instability. The absence of effective sanctioning of offenders can be significant in conflict zones, where informal interventions to sanction offenders may also be absent. Attempts to reduce the higher rates of sexual violence in conflict zones have included reducing the gender imbalance in decision-making in peacekeeping forces. Improving the gender balance in decision-making is important in decisional arenas, from peacekeeping to parliaments. Reducing war and other forms of violence is important for reducing rape.

Culture, media and education

The prevention of rape requires the changing of minds so that no man wants to rape. The public declaration that rape is a crime, and hence wrong, offers significant symbolic power, which may be further enhanced by the successful use of criminal sanctions. But contemporary culture is ambiguous and contradictory on the status of rape, not least in the new social media. Aspects of pornography and the commercialisation of sex can contribute to gendered images that can be conducive to rape. Such 'rape culture' can have detrimental effects on the treatment of victims by the police, juries and others. Hence, culture, media and education have become additional sites of action to prevent rape.

Economy

Gender inequalities in the economy matter, since it is hard to recuperate from rape without a stable source of livelihood. In the case of domestic rape, where sexual violence may be part of domestic violence, of a pattern of coercive control by an intimate partner, economic inequalities are complexly entwined with vulnerabilities to rape and other violence. Further, higher rates of violence are in general associated with economic inequality: countries that have reduced rates of economic inequality have lower rates of violence. Hence action to reduce gendered economic inequalities can have immediate effects on the wellbeing and resilience of victim-survivors as well as longer-term effects on the structure of other institutions that could act to prevent rape.

Rape and other forms of violence are linked to the economy. This perspective can be found within both the global north and south. There are at least two major strands to this approach identifying both processes in which violence damages the economy and those in which economic inequality produces violence.

Research for The World Bank has identified violence as a detriment to economic development (Moser and Shrader, 1999). Redwood, a departmental director of The World Bank, notes: 'Crime and violence erode physical, human, natural, and social capital, undermine the investment climate, and deplete the state's capacity to govern. Previously regarded as an issue of criminal pathology or human rights, violence is now recognized as a macroeconomic problem' (quoted in Moser and Shader, 1999, p v). The negative impact of violence on the economy is identified in studies that estimate the cost of violence, in particular the cost of gender-based violence against women, for economy and society. In the EU, this is estimated to be €258 billion a year (Walby and Olive, 2014).

There is also a causal pathway in the reverse direction, which appears to flow from economic inequality to violent crime, as Fajnzylber et al (1998) found in a study for The World Bank. Indeed, there are a multitude of criminological studies, largely based in the global north, finding that economic inequality is linked to violent crime, as in the meta-review of 63 studies by Chiricos (1987) of 34 studies by Hsieh and Pugh (1993), and the meta-analysis of over 200 studies by Pratt and Cullen (2005). This is part of a wider social science literature that links violence to other aspects of society (Walby, 2009, 2013; Ray, 2011; Walby et al, 2014).

Further, reductions in the amount of resourcing for services to prevent violence against women (Towers and Walby, 2012) can have effects on the level of violence. Changes in the financing of services for victim-survivors can have an impact not only on their well-being but also on their ability to respond through engaging in the prosecution of the rapist and in public education about the realities of rape. These wider consequences of the funding of services for victim-survivors can assist the prevention of further rapes.

Gender equality

Each of these fields relevant to rape is shaped by wider gender inequalities in society. Policy interventions to prevent rape are linked to the wider policy field of gender equality. Addressing gendered inequalities in the economy, governance, security and culture can improve the likelihood of successful interventions in specific institutions that contribute to the prevention of rape. In particular, reducing gender imbalance in decision-making improves the quality of the decisions that are taken about priorities for resources.

Violence against women, of which rape is a particularly serious form, is a consequence of gender inequality as well as itself contributing to that inequality (Brownmiller, 1976; Kelly, 1988; Walby, 2009; Brown and Walklate, 2012). This connection operates at several levels: gendered economic and cultural inequalities increase the vulnerability of the victim and the motivation and capacity of the rapist; gendered inequalities in decision-making and politics reduce the likelihood of institutions prioritising rape prevention policies; and the form of the gender regime affects the structuring of gendered institutions and the relations between them.

The development of effective policy requires input from those who have experienced rape and from gender experts, and it requires gender balance in the key decision-making arenas in order to secure this. Making the relevant changes in policies requires the mobilisation of relevant actors. This in turn also requires gender balance in each of the relevant domains of decision-making, from the police to peacekeepers to parliamentarians. The gender imbalance in decision-making means that women's experiences and interests are under-represented when crucial decisions are made in professional bodies, parliaments and conflict zones. Gender inequalities in the governance and practice of culture, media and education have implications for the likelihood that these institutions propagate rather than contest rape myths, which affect juries making verdicts of guilt and innocence in trials.

The significance of reducing gender imbalance in decision-making for reducing sexual violence is further addressed in Chapter 5 on conflict zones. Gender inequalities in decision-making are less likely where other aspects of the gender regime also have reduced gender inequalities. In cross-national comparisons of gender regimes, alignment between the various dimensions of the gender regime is often found (Walby, 2009, pp 303-8).

Other violence

Violence causes other violence. The higher the level of one form of violence, the higher the level of other forms of violence. Walby (2009) found a statistically significant correlation between the level of homicide, expenditure on the military, expenditure on law and order, rates of imprisonment, and the existence of capital punishment. Further, the higher the rate of homicide against men, the higher the rate of homicide against women. Forms of violence are interconnected. If rape and other forms of gender-based violence are to be significantly reduced, this requires a reduction in other forms of violence.

Rethinking 'prevention'

The prevention of rape requires the development of practices that disrupt the causal pathways leading to rape. In order to prevent rape, it is thus necessary to identify the causes of rape. One approach includes 'prevention' within an ambitious attempt to identify the policy architecture needed for effective national strategies to end violence against women, articulated in the 6Ps of 'perspective, policy, prevention, provision, protection and prosecution' (Coy et al, 2008; Kelly et al, 2011), which has contributed to the development of UK national strategy and plans (HM Government, 2009, 2010, 2015). Another approach, led from public health, distinguishes between primary, secondary and tertiary prevention, drawing on an 'ecological model' (Bronfenbrenner, 1977, 1979; Heise, 1998; WHO, 2002, 2014b; Loots et al, 2011; Walden and Wall, 2014). Each of these approaches to 'prevention' contributes important elements to a model of causation of rape, but each has some limitations. Three revisions of two approaches to the theorisation of prevention are proposed.

First, looking after victim-survivors helps to prevent rape. It not only helps to mitigate the harms, but it is necessary: for the proper functioning of the legal and justice system, that rape victims be supported to endure its processes so as to end impunity for rapists; for the education of the public, policy-makers and politicians, that rape victims are supported to speak out; and for the reform of the institutions that engage with rape, that survivors confidently engage in their reform. Services for victims are part of prevention.

Second, prevention concerns more than changes to culture, norms and attitudes. It requires reforms in all major social institutions, not only culture, media and education; changing attitudes is not enough. All the sites of intervention that have been identified are relevant and important, even if of varying importance. Hence it is necessary to have and to improve interventions in: strategic planning and decision-making; specialised victim support; health services; law and the criminal justice system; conflict zones; culture, media and education; and the economy.

Third, the theory of rape that underpins the strategy for prevention should draw on the concept of 'institution' in preference to that of 'risk factor', and connect the components of the analysis using complex systems theory rather than merely statistical correlations. It should draw on social scientific understandings of social institutions and how these constitute the social system that is a society. The model of prevention needs to be able to address both negative and positive feedback loops (for example, the treatment and subsequent conduct of the survivor). The evidence that is included should be all evidence: the field is not yet so maturely developed, and nor is rape the type of phenomenon for which relevant evidence can be restricted to the standards possible in medical science (for example, random control trials and experimental methods written up in peer-reviewed journals). When reviewing the knowledge base in this book, a broad range of evidence is admitted for critical scrutiny.

A more fully developed model or theory of gender-based violence is needed. The effort put into developing an effective approach to 'prevention' (Coy et al, 2008; Kelly et al, 2011; WHO, 2002, 2014b) indicates the importance of this agenda. This new approach to theorising rape is developed during the course of the book, and is found in the concluding chapter.

Definitions of rape

Rape is a very serious form of violence. It is an important form of gender-based violence against women. While all forms of gender-based violence against women are serious, rape is especially hurtful and damaging, and can have long-lasting consequences. Although some men are victims of rape, this is much less common than among women. There are several approaches to defining rape. Definitions have been developed by international bodies, in particular the United Nations (UN) and the World Health Organization (WHO), although these are not always in agreement. There are slight variations in definition between different legal regimes, both those at a national level, and those of international regimes, such as that of the Rome Statute of the International Criminal Court (2011). Popular culture often uses a concept of rape that is narrower than legal definitions, especially as concerns the conduct of the victim. Social science has used a range of concepts of rape and their operationalisation in research. Definitions may also vary by context, for example, depending on whether it takes place in a conflict zone or not.

The UN (2010a) treats violence against women, including rape, as a form of 'gender-based discrimination' as well as 'a violation of women's human rights'. Over the past two decades, violence against women has come to be understood as a violation of women's human rights and as a form of gender-based discrimination. Legislation on violence against women should be in conformity with the UN General Assembly *Declaration on the elimination of violence against women* (Resolution 48/104 of 1993), read together with Article 1 of the *Convention on the elimination of all forms of discrimination against women* (UN, 1979), and general recommendations No 12 (1989) and 19 (1992) of the Committee on the Elimination of Discrimination against Women (UN, 2010a, p 13).

The WHO (2002) treats rape, other forms of sexual violence and violence in general, as issues of public health. WHO Resolution WHA49.25 in 1996 'declares that violence is a leading worldwide public health problem.' Rape is defined as: 'Physically forced or otherwise coerced penetration – even if slight – of the vulva or anus, using a penis, other body parts or an object' (WHO, 2002, p 149).

The legal definition of rape varies slightly between legal regimes. At its core, rape is coerced violation or penetration of the body. The nature of the coercion is variously understood as the absence of consent, the use of force, the threat of use of force, or a wider context of generalised coercion. There are variations in whether the penetration can be with any object or is restricted to the penis; whether the part of the body penetrated can include the mouth or anus, or is restricted to the vagina. In legal terms, variations in the object and orifice determine whether rape is only ever an offence by a man against a woman, or if men can also be victims, or women can also be perpetrators. Legal developments are discussed in more detail in the review of law below.

The popular definition of rape is often more restricted than the legal definition. Not only the general public, but also even survivors of actions that are legally rape are reluctant to use the term 'rape' unless the circumstances are more extreme than the law requires (Walby and Myhill, 2001). This is probably related to the stigmatisation of rape victims in popular culture (Soothill and Walby, 1991). This discrepancy between popular and legal definitions of rape has consequences for the treatment of victims of rape and for the conviction of rapists by courts that use juries.

Social scientific research has investigated the range of meanings attached to the term 'rape', and explored the implications of the different ways in which rape is defined in both law and popular culture. The findings from this research mean that some recent surveys offer behavioural descriptions rather than the summary term 'rape' to respondents, gaining better understanding of the meaning of the act to the survivor (Walby and Allen, 2004; Fisher, 2009). Further research has developed the concept of a 'continuum of sexual violence' so as to capture the way in which small events are connected to create a context that is more threatening than the sum of its parts (Kelly, 1988).

The terms 'victim' and 'survivor' are used interchangeably in this book, although there are different connotations attached to them. The use of the more conventional term, 'victim', has been subject to the criticism that it denies agency to the raped woman, and hence that the term 'survivor' should be used instead to take account of her actions (Kelly, 1988). However, it is also argued that to attribute agency to the person who has been raped is misleading since it might imply that actions by this person could have made a difference, and is thus consistent with victim blaming. This study follows the practice that has developed in the field of using both terms, 'victim-survivor', but when this is overly complex, the term 'victim' is used, while cognisant of its limitations.

Rape occurs in a range of different settings that affect the possibilities for prevention and assisting victim-survivors, since they entail different levels of power and vulnerability of the perpetrator and victim as well as of potential witnesses and other actors. These situations vary across domestic, stranger/ acquaintance, institutions (hospitals, prisons) and conflict zones (during and after militarised conflict). Of particular importance in this book is the distinction between rape in non-conflict zones, such as EU member states, and rape in conflict zones, which might be of particular interest to EU External Affairs in matters such as the development of humanitarian aid packages.

Rape is adjacent to and overlaps with other forms of violence, including sexual violence, domestic violence, sexual abuse of children, forced marriage and trafficking. Practices of pornography and prostitution can also be seen to be linked, although this is subject to debate. The extent and nature of the overlap between rape and other forms of abuse and violence is complex, not least when these are considered as legal categories. Sexual violence takes different forms in different communities, times and places (Abraham, 1999; Gill and Anitha, 2011; Rehman et al, 2013).

The term 'sexual violence' is more frequently used in the literature than that of 'rape', which is the focus of this study – 'sexual violence' is broader in meaning than 'rape'. For example, the WHO (2002, p 149) defines sexual violence as: 'Any sexual act, attempt to obtain a sexual act, unwanted sexual comments or advances, or acts to traffic, or otherwise directed, against a person's sexuality using coercion, by any person regardless of their relationship to the victim, in any setting, including but not limited to home and work.'

Partners and former partners commit a significant proportion of rapes. The British Crime Survey found that nearly half (45 per cent) of the rapes disclosed to the survey in 2001 were perpetrated by a current or former partner (Walby and Allen, 2004), although other national surveys have found lower proportions. This means that the context and policies concerning domestic violence are of direct relevance to rape, since domestic violence can include rape.

The sexual abuse of children may include rape, but the term 'rape' is rarely used in this context, even though sex with children is considered to be without consent, since a child cannot in law consent to sex.

'Forced marriage' might be considered to include rape, since the sex is without consent because the marriage was 'forced'. However, since the coercion into the marriage may be from the family and kin of the woman, rather than from the man she marries, it is not clear that the man, who did not coerce the marriage, is, in law, a rapist. A similar issue arises in the case of trafficking of women for purposes of sexual exploitation, where the sex is without consent since the victim was trafficked, but where the man may be unaware that this is the case and believes the woman to have consented. It is not clear that the man who buys the (coerced) sex is, in law, a rapist. In law, the rapist is a person who knows that he is coercing the woman as he rapes her, but in the cases of forced marriage and trafficking, the coercion is being done by someone other than the person engaging in the sex. Hence, while the man doing the sex in both of these cases is not usually considered in law to be a rapist, from the woman's point of view this is nevertheless sex without consent, because of the coercive context created by others.

The implication of these complex overlapping categories and concepts is that policies to address one field of gender violence will be relevant for others. This is consistent with the argument that the field of gender-based violence against women should be addressed as a whole, in addition to detailed attention to its specific forms.

Significance and scale of rape

In Britain, the Crime Survey for England and Wales (previously called the British Crime Survey) finds that an estimated 4.3 per cent of women had experienced a completed or attempted rape in their lifetime (3.4 per cent experiencing a completed rape). During one year, an estimated 0.3 per cent of women experienced rape. There has been no statistically significant change in the annual prevalence of rape against women in England and Wales between 2004-05 and 2012-13 (ONS, 2014). In 2012/13 there were an estimated 331,000 sexual assaults committed against women (ONS, 2014). In Britain, the National Survey of Sexual Health Attitudes and Lifestyles conducted between 2010 and 2012 found an estimated 9.8 per cent of women aged 16 to 74 had experienced 'non-volitional sex' since the age of 13 (Macdowall et al, 2013).

Rape Crisis England and Wales responded to over 150,000 calls to their telephone lines in 2014, delivered over 300,000 sessions of individual support in 2014, and received over 1.2 million visits to their web-site in one month (Rape Crisis, England and Wales, 2014).

Across the EU, the Agency for Fundamental Rights Survey on Violence Against Women (EU FRA, 2014) found that 5 per cent of women have experienced rape in their lifetime since the age of 15, ranging from 4 to 17 per cent in different states. This means that an estimated 9 million women have been raped since the age of 15, either by a partner or by another person in the EU. In addition, a further 6 per cent of women said they had experienced an attempted rape since the age of 15. Overall, 11 per cent of women in the EU reported experiencing some form of sexual violence by a partner or other person since the age of 15. In the past 12 months, 0.8 per cent of women in the EU have experienced rape, amounting to an estimated 1.5 million women. Over half of the women reporting being raped by their intimate partner had experienced more than one rape; 31 per cent had experienced six or more rapes by the intimate partner. Ten per cent of victims of non-partner rape had also been raped six or more times (either by the same person or by different people) (EU FRA, 2014).

In the US, the National Intimate Partner and Sexual Violence Survey found that an estimated 19.3 per cent of women have been raped in their lifetime; this is more than 23 million women. An estimated 1.6 per cent of women in the US were raped in 2011 – 1.9 million women. An estimated 8.8 per cent of women have been raped by an intimate partner during their lifetime, 0.8 per cent in the past year (CDC, 2014b).

Globally, 7 per cent of women have experienced sexual violence from someone other than an intimate partner in their lifetime, where sexual violence is defined as any sexual act, attempt to obtain a sexual act, unwanted sexual comments or advances, or acts to traffic, or otherwise directed against a person's sexuality using coercion, by any person regardless of their relationship to the victim, in any setting including but not limited to home and work (WHO, 2014b, pp 76-7). Male self-reported rape of women (in their lifetime) varies across global regions, from 10 per cent in Bangladesh (urban) to 62 per cent in Bougainville, Papua New Guinea. Partner rape was almost always more commonly reported than non–partner rape; 70-80 per cent of men reporting they had raped women were motivated by their belief in their sexual entitlement regardless of whether or not consent had been given. Half the men reporting perpetrating rape of women had first done so as teenagers (UN, 2013).

The occurrence of rape during wartime is reportedly massive. In the Second World War, rapes by American GIs, German and Russian soldiers occurred during and after conflicts, with more than a million women thought to have been raped. In Pakistan, it is reported that more than 200,000 Bengali women were abducted into military brothels and subjected to gang assaults during the conflict of 1971. In Vietnam, both South Vietnamese and American soldiers were widely reported as committing rape (of Indigenous women) during the Vietnam conflict. In El Salvador, Guatemala and Peru, countless crimes against women occurred during civil wars where soldiers and rebels were left unpunished. In Croatia and Bosnia-Herzegovina during 1992 and 1995, the estimates of women raped and sexually violated vary between 10,000 and 60,000. In the 1994 civil war and genocide in Rwanda, between 250,000 and 500,000 women and girls survived rape (Ward, 2013).

Evaluating policy and practices

This book is based on a review of the international literature on policy developments to prevent rape, together with investigation of case studies of best practice. Experts in each of the relevant policy fields conducted the review of literature, using both systematic approaches and their own knowledge of developments in these fields. The case studies used a variety of methods, including interviews with key actors, original data analysis and a review of documents and literature.

The study draws on reports and policies from major transnational governmental bodies, including the European Parliament, European Commission, European Institute for Gender Equality (EIGE), EU FRA, Council of Europe, UN Beijing Platform for Action, UN Secretary-General, UNiTE to End Violence against Women (UNiTE), UN Women and the WHO. These developments have drawn on the work of third sector or non-governmental organisations (NGO), mainly women's groups and groups representing victim-survivors, which have long been at the heart of innovative ways of addressing this long-standing issue.

The evaluation of the practices requires the identification of the causes of rape and of the intended and actual contribution of each of the interventions. The detailed evaluation of specific practices and the exact scale of their contribution are ongoing rather than complete. In broad outline, the set of policies needed to prevent rape and to assist victims is well established. This includes both the development of specialised areas of expertise and also the diffusion of this expertise through normal policy actors, as is usual in the practice of gender mainstreaming. However, the full set of policies that has been identified as necessary in the literature and by practitioners has never been fully implemented. In order to know what would prevent rape, it is necessary to know what causes rape. It is important to build a map of the various causal pathways leading to rape, and to establish the various points at which interventions might contribute to its prevention. Preventing rape and assisting victims of rape are not separate processes but interconnected. The evaluation of innovative practices to prevent rape and assist victim-survivors requires a programme of research. Preventing rape depends on developing capacity and mobilising a wide range of relevant actors.

A wide range of practices is reviewed in the international literature using a wide variety of different means of assessment. In some areas of policy, such as medicine, there are established evaluation methodologies, including 'systematic review', such as those developed by Cochrane and Campbell (Ashman and Duggan, 2004), and 'cost-effectiveness'. However, since rape policy is newly developing, a wider range of methodologies of assessment is appropriate.

There is a need for more research to improve the knowledge to evaluate policies. There is a need for national surveys of the extent of rape in the population, with methodologies sensitive to the special needs of the subject group (Walby and Myhill, 2001). Interventions are usually aimed at addressing one small part of the causal pathways to rape or mitigating one part of its effects, so they need to be assessed in relation to that intended step, rather than in relation to the larger aim of stopping rape. Measuring changes in intermediate policy outcomes, such as the conviction rate or rate of 'attrition' in the criminal justice system (Lovett and Kelly, 2009; Walby et al, 2012; Hester, 2013), and recidivism rates calculated from registers of offenders, are ways forward here. There is a need for further social scientific research in this field.

In order to secure policy development and implementation it is necessary to engage and mobilise all the relevant actors. The motivation for each is likely to be slightly different and dependent on their context. It is relevant to consider the different motivations that are relevant to the actors that need to be mobilised in order to secure policy development and implementation. These include the goals of reducing gender inequality, reducing violations of human rights, reducing the cost to business and the economy, preventing impairments and injuries to victims, reducing crime, increasing security, and increasing wellbeing and health. They are each valid in their context. The relevant actors in this field are usually considered to be governmental bodies, but they also include the third sector and NGOs as well as private bodies and employers.

Promising practices

The book selects a number of case studies of promising practice to illustrate the best of the interventions that are being developed. They were selected using criteria derived from the international literature and reflections on it (EIGE, 2011). These practices are innovative, are proven to have made a difference, and are models for development elsewhere. They are pitched at different levels: both at a high level that is pertinent to many of the services, and at more detailed levels that are pertinent to specific policy practices. The criteria include victim-survivor-centred; gender-expert and gender-sensitive; participation of survivors; trained personnel; skilled specialised centres that act as beacons of good practice to the mainstream; built-in monitoring and evaluation so as to constantly improve practice; interagency working collaboratively with other agencies; and part of a comprehensive package of policies to combat violence against women that is strategically coordinated.

The book offers a range of policy interventions in the chapters, related to relevant policy fields:

- planning, coordination and research, including gender balance in decision-making;
- specialised services for victim-survivors, including healthcare;
- law and the criminal justice system to remove impunity from perpetrators;
- conflict zones;
- culture, media and education to engage with rape myths; and
- economic inclusion and economic inequality.

The 10 examples of promising practice are as follows:

- developing coordinated and integrated services in Australia (Chapter 2)
- coordinated community responses – in the US and other countries (Chapter 2)
- comprehensive rape crisis services sexual assault crisis team (SACT) – US (Chapter 2)

- health-based services in a non-conflict zone – in the UK (Chapter 3)
- integrating a better understanding of rape within the law – in Mexico (Chapter 4)
- identifying potential perpetrators of rape in cyberspace – in the EU (Chapter 4)
- specialised sexual offences courts – in South Africa (Chapter 4)
- health-based services in a conflict zone (Chapter 5)
- sexual relations education – in the UK (Chapter 6)
- talking about consent and coercion – in Sweden (Chapter 6).

The policies and practices analysed vary according to the context of the rape, the agent carrying out the practice and the target of the intervention. Interventions are produced and implemented by diverse types of agencies: governmental – international, national or local; private/public service provider; and civil society/NGO/third sector. Policies vary in their focus on different actors and institutions, including victims (such as advocacy, practical and emotional support, counselling, centres and shelters); perpetrators (for example, identifying perpetrators, prosecution, and treatment programmes); situational (such as monitoring and structuring space, as in CCTV and city design); professionals (for example, training, improving the criminal justice system, improving health services, gender composition of decision-makers, and coordination of agencies); and wider society (such as education and awareness-arising, scientific knowledge base, engagement with media, and women's empowerment).

Structure of the book

The book has eight chapters. Each of the next six chapters concerns a specific field of policy development, focused on analysis of the best emerging policies and practices there. The concluding chapter then offers suggestions for further improvements to policy and practice to prevent rape.

2

Strategy, planning and coordination

Introduction

Preventing rape requires policies that affect many aspects of society. No single intervention is sufficient. This is because many of the causes of rape lie deep in the structures and systems of society. The details of these various interventions are addressed in the chapters that follow. The focus in this chapter is on: the strategic planning for a comprehensive set of policy practices; the coordination of multiple services; the initial development of specialist services for victim-survivors; and the data and research needed to evaluate policy developments.

Strategic planning is taking place at multiple levels: the UN, the Council of Europe, the EU and individual states. The creation of 'national action plans' (NAPs) that are regularly reviewed and evaluated has been an important part of the development of strategic planning. The development of strategic planning and the evaluation of policies require research, data and statistics. It is necessary to know how much rape there is, its patterns, and the quality of the performance of the institutions that are supposed to be addressing the problem.

There are a myriad of services and practices that might potentially be useful to victim-survivors and to changing the environment that produces rape. Coordination of multiple services for victim-survivors not only has a national component but also regional and local aspects. The specialised services for victim-survivors can be either standalone services or integrated into generic services. This chapter discusses the development of standalone services, while Chapters 3 and 4 on health and on justice discuss specialised victim services that are developed within these mainstream service providers.

These strategies, coordination and services develop more effectively under some conditions than others. This is most effective when the voices of women and survivors are included in decision-making, from services such as the police, to consultative platforms, to political forums such as parliaments. The reduction of the gender imbalance in decision-making is part of the changes in the wider environment that promotes more effective policy development. This means deepening the gender dimension of democracy, which is more likely to occur when other gender inequalities are also reduced.

Strategic planning

Strategic planning is taking place at the international, European, regional, national and local levels. Within the UN there are several relevant bodies: the UN Secretary-General, UN Women, the WHO, the UN Security Council, and the UN Office of Drugs and Crime. The Council of Europe has taken important initiatives for its 47 member states; the EU is developing resources to assist its 28 member states; and many states have developed NAPs.

These strategic plans usually embed rape, or more broadly, sexual violence, within a wider concern for gender-based violence against women. An example of a strategic plan is that of UN Women's (2011) '16 steps policy agenda'. A second example is that of the Council of Europe's (2011) *Istanbul Convention on preventing and combating violence against women and domestic violence.*

United Nations

The UN named violence against women as one of the 12 critical areas for action in the Beijing Platform for Action (UN, 1995), following this with the in-depth report on violence against women, including rape, by the Secretary-General to the General Assembly (UN Secretary-General, 2006), and the UN campaign, UNiTE, to end violence against women including rape (UNiTE, 2011).

UN Women (2011) recommends a '16 steps policy agenda' based on the pillars of 'prevention, protection and provision' for member states. These steps are:

1. Ratify international and regional treaties (for example, the Committee on the Elimination of Discrimination against Women)
2. Adopt and enforce laws
3. Develop national and local action plans
4. Make justice accessible to women and girls
5. End impunity towards conflict-related sexual violence
6. Ensure universal access to critical services
7. Train providers of frontline services
8. Provide adequate public resources
9. Collect, analyse and disseminate national data
10. Invest in gender equality and women's empowerment
11. Enhance women's economic empowerment
12. Increase public awareness and social mobilisation
13. Engage the mass media
14. Work for and with young people as champions of change
15. Mobilise men and boys
16. Donate to the UN Trust Fund to end violence against women.

Council of Europe

The Council of Europe's (2011) Istanbul Convention constitutes a strategic plan to prevent and combat violence against women and domestic violence. Its many articles address a similar range of actions as recommended by UN Women. The similarity between the UN and Council of Europe strategies suggests that there is an emerging consensus on the best strategy for ending rape. In both cases, the focus is the broader one of violence against women, rather than the narrower one of rape. The Convention has been signed by 46 states and ratified by sufficient states for it to have come into force on 1 August 2014.

National Action Plans

NAPs are examples of strategic planning at the level of specific countries. There has been a discussion of their objectives and content over the last two decades at both national and international levels. NAPs are widely recommended by many international bodies, including various entities within the UN.

NAPs and associated coordination mechanisms are considered key elements in the implementation of laws and policies in reports commissioned by the UN, Council of Europe and European Commission. The UN *Handbook for legislation on violence against women* (UN, 2010a) considers them to be the main guarantee for a comprehensive and coordinated approach to the implementation of relevant legislation. The Council of Europe (2006) notes the importance of a national level coordinating mechanism to which all stakeholder ministries, agencies and criminal justice actors can join together with women's rights and victims' rights advocates. At the national level, NAPs and related national coordination mechanisms are instruments of efficient, victim-centred implementation of anti-rape laws, which also keep victims' and women's interests at the core of policies addressing rape in the implementation stages. National coordination mechanisms play a role in monitoring and reviewing laws and policy and improving the accountability of actors involved in the implementation process. The goals of national planning mechanisms are to: be a deliberative forum for democratic and professional debate; ensure gender-sensitive implementation processes; ensure the centrality of the needs of the victim-survivors; develop a common understanding of violence; develop policies, protocols, referral systems and data collection systems in a way that develops a common understanding among the agencies and actors involved; aid accountability, monitoring and evaluation of the policy and law in place and aid review of policy if needed; serve efficient policy coordination; and to provide a participatory policy mechanism for addressing gender violence including rape (UNIFEM, 2010).

Kelly et al (2011, pp 23-4) consider that there has been a progressive development of NAPs, beginning with the UN Beijing Platform for Action, and developed by UNIFEM, the Committee on the Elimination of Discrimination against

Women, and the Council of Europe, and that the best guidelines now include: developing an integrated, holistic approach to address the range of interrelated needs and the rights of women survivors, ensuring that both responses to, and prevention of, violence against women is encompassed in all relevant policies and programmes; building multisectoral approaches, specifying the respective roles of state and non-state organisations; setting out principles, costed concrete goals and actions; timelines and actors/agencies with responsibility and competence to carry out the actions; and monitoring and accountability mechanisms.

End Violence Against Women (EWAW) set out six objectives for inclusion in NAPs (Kelly et al, 2011, p 24):

"Perspective", by which is meant underpinning principles of gender equality, human rights, due diligence and non-discrimination;

"policy" refers to an integrated strategy that addresses all forms of VAW [violence against women] and intersections between them; an agreed definition; research and disaggregated statistics; analysis of causes of VAW; and mainstreaming VAW into all policy areas;

"prevention" which encompasses education, work with perpetrators, public awareness and self-defence for women and girls;

"provision" includes the specialised women's sector, women's centres, including services for rural women, black and minority ethnic women, and the statutory sector;

"protection" which likewise includes provision but also encompasses support networks, civil law, safety in public places, and non-discrimination;

"prosecution", holding perpetrators accountable, European models of good practice, procedural justice for victim-survivors, and, again, non-discrimination.

Comparisons of countries have found that the adoption of NAPs contributes to the implementation of policies on violence against women (Kelly et al, 2011; Weldon and Htun, 2012). NAPs have been developing recently across the member states of the EU and Council of Europe. Reviews of these plans find some weaknesses, such as not being sufficiently comprehensive (for example, an undue emphasis on domestic violence at the expense of rape and other forms of sexual assault); vague general statements; absence of indicators, monitoring and follow-up; and a lack of allocated budgets (Council of Europe, 2006, 2014a; Kelly et al, 2011). This means that further developments are needed to improve the quality of these NAPs.

Coordination of service provision

Coordination is a necessary component of good policy responses in order to effectively deliver services from multiple agencies to victim-survivors. There is potentially a wide range of disparate interventions involving several state and non-state, public and private actors: the police, courts, prosecutors, healthcare and mental health providers, crisis centres and helplines. In the absence of effective coordination between the different actors involved, interventions may be inefficient, not act in the victim's interests, or aggravate the harm through re-victimisation (Pence and Shepard, 1999; Martin, 2005, 2007; Stark, 2007). The need for coordination and cooperation between actors is important for the victim-centred implementation of policies to address rape.

At the local level, good coordinated responses aim to provide efficient, victim-centred services. Effective coordination ensures that diverse stakeholders, including women's and victims' rights advocates, work together towards a mutual understanding of the problem of rape, and implement policies accordingly. These are most effective when led from the experiences of survivors and informed by gender expertise. The importance of coordination across multisector agencies to help service providers to better address the legal, medical, mental health needs and other needs of the victim-survivor is often noted (Campbell and Ahrens, 1998; Campbell et al, 2001; Council of Europe, 2006; Morrison et al, 2007; Home Office, 2014).

Coordinated community responses have been devised, implemented and evaluated in the US for three decades. The most famous model is the 'Duluth' model (see www.theduluthmodel. org/), which was developed in relation to domestic violence, and has, to a lesser extent, been extended to rape. Coordinated community responses have been introduced in some European countries but have not yet become a widespread practice (Council of Europe, 2006, 2014a). Coordinated community responses have been favourably compared with fragmented interventions. It is widely argued that coordinated community responses should include all relevant service providers, criminal justice system agents and victims' rights advocates (Martin, 2007; Mallios and Markowitz, 2011), while noting that serious problems can arise if there is imbalance between the participating services, as has sometimes occurred with a disproportionately strong criminal justice lead.

The objectives of coordinated community responses include: improving the efficiency of responses to victims' needs and preventing the risk of further secondary victimisation; contextualising rape and thus improving the community understanding and response to rape; and continuous monitoring and evaluation and improvement of the functioning of rape intervention schemes.

There are several modes of operation for coordinated community (or local) responses. Some are more formalised than others. Potentially, they provide several advantages. They offer a single entry point for victims to the system: one contact point often means one contact person for the victim to avoid re-victimisation. Referrals from the contact point will secure the possibility of multidisciplinary responses, flow of information and coordination of responses. Sustained interagency consultation allows for the identification of a shared philosophical framework on sexual violence, a shared understanding of the roles played by the different actors, and an up-to-date understanding of gaps in the system. Interagency consultation may concern more general matters, but most often discusses specific cases, such as the US sexual assault response teams (SARTs). This potentially allows for openness to the (cultural) context of rape and opportunities to include specific attention for victims coming from particular subgroups (minority ethnic groups, people with disabilities). Coordination aids the development of standardised victim-centred policies, procedures and protocols for intervention across all actors. It aids the development of the appropriate training and professional development of all involved.

The inclusion of women victims' rights advocates and victim-survivors can secure continuing deliberation about objectives, and ensure that the victim-survivor as an individual and the group-level problem of violence against women remain at the centre of the intervention. However, there has been criticism from women's rights groups in the US that cooperation between women's autonomous groups and states carries the risks of entrenching them within a punitive justice and service model, leading to deleterious changes in the initial objectives (Bumiller, 2008). Criticism of some forms of coordination has also occurred in the UK in relation to multi-agency risk assessment conferences (MARACs) (for cases of domestic violence) if women become turned into 'an object of concern' when their cases are discussed without their consent or presence (Coy et al, 2011). Some hope that the deliberative potential of coordinated community response models may overcome these drawbacks by conscious and organised efforts to transform state intervention modes. Bumiller (2008) argues that too much emphasis on criminalisation has been eroding the original objective of the women's movement, leading to a loss of focus on women victims' interests. Protecting women, she argues, means enabling and empowering women, sustaining fundamental rights and dignity, since this is the most efficient long-term approach to fight violence against women. Yet routine forms of state control, by turning the issue into a 'treatable social problem', can lose sight of the victim's perspective (Bumiller, 2008). Coordination is a potential route to a solution to this problem, if it brings together grassroots organisations, victims' rights advocates, service providers and agents of the criminal justice system in a common platform.

Best practice criteria for coordination practices found in the literature include: inclusiveness *vis-à-vis* relevant agencies, criminal justice actors and women's or victims' rights advocates; spelled-out common understanding of gender violence including rape; working cooperatively towards development of policies, guidelines, referral and data collection mechanisms; led from gender expertise and the experiences of survivors; and accountability mechanisms and some independence from the state. Successful protection for women is dependent on improving victims' treatment within mainstream organisations. The objective is to avoid re-victimisation at the hands of agencies working on addressing sexual violence. Martin (2005, 2007), on the basis of decades of rape work in the US, points to the failures of mainstream organisations and their personnel to 'own rape', that is, to see addressing rape and placing its victim in the centre as a primary objective of their organisation. Rather than bad intentions, conflict between other work objectives (for example, efficiency, transparency) and rape victims' priorities can result in weak and inefficient responses. Interagency cooperation and cooperation with victim advocates is a route to spell out and address some of these conflicts, and to bring the victim's perspective back to the centre in a way that is necessary to ensure the intervention becomes truly supportive and empowering (Martin, 2007; Mallios and Markowitz, 2011).

In conclusion, local coordination of service provision is important in order to avoid fragmentation and to enable the victim-survivor to be at the centre of the provision of the necessarily multiple services. It is, however, a challenge to ensure that the victim-survivor remains at the centre of the process in the face of competing pressures from bureaucratic and other forces.

Specialised services for victim-survivors

The provision of a comprehensive set of specialised services for victim-survivors is important in order to assist victims and can make a significant contribution to prevention. Specialised rape crisis centres have developed that offer expert provision to victim-survivors and expert engagement in policy development. Specialised services to survivors of domestic violence, such as refuges and shelters, are relevant to rape, since domestic partners commit a significant proportion of rape. In addition, specialised services have developed within mainstream health and humanitarian, as well as criminal justice, services.

Typically, early developments were in standalone institutions, with their mainstreaming occurring later. Finding the best balance between the development of specific expertise, which may require separate institutional development, and ensuring that expert services are available for all in need, which may require attention to mainstream services, is an ongoing issue within many policy fields concerning gender issues (Walby, 2005a), including gender-based violence against women (Kelly, 2005) and that of preventing rape. The location of the boundary between specialist and mainstream services varies according to circumstances. In some policy domains at some times, services for victims are best provided by free-standing specialist services, while in other domains and times, services can be delivered as an integral and normal part of mainstream work. This depends on the extent to which the mainstream service itself has been transformed through the integration of policies to stop rape.

Wasco et al (2004) note the challenges in evaluating services in this area (for example, the potential impact of research on the welfare of victim-survivors). Nevertheless, their study points to the effectiveness of rape crisis services (a hotline, counselling and advocacy) in terms of providing support and information, and helping women understand their options and to make decisions. Further, Westmarland and Alderson (2013) have demonstrated the positive impact of counselling on the welfare of rape victim-survivors. Macy et al (2011) offer a list of six sets of services considered necessary in the US: crisis services; legal advocacy; medical advocacy; support groups; individual counselling; and shelters. Shelters are a specific form of service provision, and are used by groups of women with particular needs.

The Council of Europe's (2011) Istanbul Convention includes a widely recognised list of minimum standards for support services to victims of violence against women and domestic violence, including sexual violence and rape. The minimum services recommended are: free 24-hour helplines; support and advocacy services; accessible services for socially excluded women, especially recent migrants, refugees, women from minority ethnic groups, and women with disabilities; access to financial support, housing, residence rights education and training; networking between specialist NGOs; multi-agency coordination; training curricula for professionals addressing the continuum of violence against women within a human rights framework; work with perpetrators rooted in women's safety and prevention; and safe shelters.

The Istanbul Convention makes specific reference to the services needed by victims of sexual violence in Article 25, which states:

> Parties shall take the necessary legislative or other measures to provide for the setting up of appropriate, easily accessible rape crisis or sexual violence referral centres for victims in sufficient numbers to provide for medical and forensic examination, trauma support and counselling for victims.

Health services are developing significant services. (Health-based services are more fully addressed in Chapter 4, on health.) There needs to be coordination between health-based and non-health-based services for victim-survivors of rape: for example, responses to recent rape are most often addressed in sexual assault referral centres (SARCs), while rape crisis centres more often respond to historic rape.

There are further needs in conflict zones (addressed further in Chapter 6). The UN High Commissioner for Refugees (UNHCR) has developed a set of guiding principles for service provisions to refugee victims of rape (2003). They underline the importance of any service provision programme to: engage the refugee community fully; ensure equal participation by women and men, girls and boys, in planning, implementing, monitoring and evaluating programmes; ensure coordinated, multisectoral action by all actors; strive to integrate and mainstream actions; and ensure accountability at all levels. On the individual level, all actions and interactions with individuals should ensure the physical safety of the victim; guarantee confidentiality; and respect the wishes, the rights, and the dignity of the victim; and consider the best interests of the child (UNHCR, 2003, p 28).

Specialist centres

The development of specialist centres of expertise to provide services to victim-survivors of rape has been central within this policy field. These centres sometimes take a physical form, although sometimes they offer services by phone. There are different needs for women who have recently experienced rape and those for whom it happened some time earlier. Shelters are important for victims of rape by an intimate partner, where the sexual violence is part of a wider pattern of coercive control made up of different kinds of violence and threat. They are also important in locations where communities might reject women victims of rape, offering a route to alternative forms of livelihood and independence.

Rape crisis centres provide a range of services including crisis hotlines, emergency contraception, abortion, victim advocacy, job training, research, education and re-education, policy work, training of police, prosecutors and health staff, community outreach, housing, medical assistance, psychological assistance, legal assistance, pre-court training, and awareness-raising. They have been at the forefront of challenging mistaken views about rape in the wider society, and are important institutions, sites through which women have been enabled to engage in transformative actions.

There were 84 rape crisis centres in England and Wales in 2014. These run telephone helplines, deliver individual sessions of individual support, run a widely accessed website, and provide information for the public, journalists and policy-makers (Rape Crisis England & Wales, 2014).

Most shelters provide for emergency needs, including food, clothing, medical and mental health referrals (for example, Haven in the US), while others engage actively in wider issues of gender equality and feminist politics (for example, Rape Crisis Network Europe, RCNE and Riksorganisationen för Kvinnojourer och Tjejjourer i Sverige, Roks, Sweden). Other interventions focus on helping women through the criminal justice system (for example, the Greater Rape Intervention Program, GRIP, in South Africa).

Shelters/refuges offer a short-term refuge for women and children from violent relationships, which may include sexual as well as physical violence. They allow an abused woman to separate from the perpetrator and help the woman locate social services, find transitional and permanent housing, legal aid and access alternative means of livelihood. However, lack of long-term funding for shelters is a problem raised in much of the literature (Macy et al, 2011; Kulkarni et al, 2012).

In both non-conflict and (post)-conflict zones, shelters are especially needed by women who lack other means to find safety and security. Literature from the non-conflict zones of the global north often name the consideration of intersecting inequalities as conditions for good practice, whereas the literature on shelters in (post)-conflict zones of the global south more often name services that provide education and empowerment resulting in reintegration into society as good practice. There are a lot of different models, with varying degrees of quality.

Centres can be transformative. In many instances the vision underpinning the rape crisis movement is that, while they are intended to protect and assist women in moments of extreme duress, they are also intended to be the bases of practices of social transformation, to engage with the society that produced rape to effect changes such that rape would not occur again. Centres sometimes have the goal of transformation of the society that produced the rape, rather than simply reintegrating women back into a rape-producing society (Zaidi, 2002; Fantini and Hegarty, 2003; Critelli, 2012; Kulkarni et al, 2012). By promoting women's independence and economic self-reliance, centres, shelters and service programme providers may help in changing women's perceptions of themselves (UNHCR, 2003). Such interventions, particularly important in (post)-conflict zones, include offering literacy programmes; providing vocational training; developing income-generating and micro-credit projects; and ensuring balanced representation of women on refugee management and assistance delivery committees (UNHCR, 2003).

Rape Crisis Network Europe (2015) suggests that best practice involves thinking about the interaction between victim and service provider as if it were between equals who cooperate to remove the threat of violence. It states that including women who themselves have experienced sexual violence is an important element of good practice. RCNE argues for 'a flexible approach', that only the victim knows what she might need. However, it may take some time to discover these needs in the trauma following rape, including 'wartime rape' (Mertus, 2004). The goal is to enable and empower the victim to become aware of her own needs, and to meet those needs. In some cases, however, traumatisation due to sexual abuse can leave some victims incapacitated for a period of time. For example, Zimmerman et al (2006) found that in some cases of trafficking for sexual exploitation, a victim potentially needs 90 days to recover cognitive functioning to a level where she can reach informed decisions about her future and her role in the prosecution of the perpetrator(s). The knowledge and experience of the service provider enables them to offer alternatives and a range of possible interventions to the victim-survivor.

RCNE offers a guide to best practice for services for rape survivors in Europe. Good practice includes educating, empowerment and awareness-raising in the wider society. RCNE suggests that centre staff's expertise could be used to influence the media to carry out campaigns and to engage in coalitions and cooperation with other organisations, not only shelters. Some shelters publish case studies of women victims and distribute them to other women victims, while others participate in television and radio programmes, press conferences, and produce printed materials that are disseminated to governmental and non-governmental organisations and institutions active within the policy domains of health, education, law and immigration. The development of effective social and political responses to rape requires that service providers have the resources to engage in education, awareness-raising, advocacy work and lobbying.

In South Africa, GRIP offers victims of rape both immediate assistance and ongoing support. GRIP's Court Intervention Program South Africa is an example of services extending beyond immediate care. There are court care rooms, where GRIP staff provide support to victims throughout the trial (Neudorf et al, 2011). Established in the Nelspruit area in South Africa in 2000 as a response to the high levels of sexual violence and HIV, it is a multisector programme with cooperation between the South African Police Service, the Department of Health, the Department of Justice, the National Prosecuting Authority (NPA), and the Department of Social Development. GRIP provides 29 Care Rooms located in police stations, hospitals and courtrooms staffed by volunteers who are trained to provide victims with police and medical attention, emotional support, and courtroom assistance.

Research, data and statistics

In order to assess whether policy innovations are working it is necessary to have relevant data analysed by research. Research on rape has grown in depth and sophistication, from early iconic studies, such as that by Brownmiller (1976) on rape through history, to new forms of conceptualisation, such as Kelly's (1988) 'continuum of sexual violence', to the rich variety of work today, as found in collections such as that put together by Brown and Walklate (2012).

The Council of Europe's (2011) Istanbul Convention states the need for data and research very clearly. There is a need for population surveys of the extent and character of the violence; administrative statistics of the extent to which public services engage effectively with gender-based violence; and research to investigate the causes of the violence and the effectiveness of the measures taken. Article 11 of the Convention states:

1. For the purposes of the implementation of this Convention, Parties shall undertake to:
   a) collect disaggregated relevant statistical data at regular intervals on cases of all forms of violence covered by the scope of this Convention;
   b) support research in the field of all forms of violence covered by the scope of this Convention in order to study its root causes and effects, incidences and conviction rates, as well as the efficacy of measures taken to implement this Convention.
2. Parties shall endeavour to conduct population-based surveys at regular intervals to assess the prevalence of and trends in all forms of violence covered by the scope of this Convention.
3. Parties shall provide the group of experts, as referred to in Article 66 of this Convention, with the information collected pursuant to this article in

order to stimulate international co-operation and enable international benchmarking.

4. Parties shall ensure that the information collected pursuant to this article is available to the public.

Large nationally representative surveys have reported on the extent of violence against women in general, but the information on the extent of rape is limited (see Chapter 1 for details). These surveys include the Crime Survey for England and Wales, the US National Intimate Partner and Sexual Violence Survey, the WHO surveys on violence against women and the EU FRA survey on violence against women. Indeed, 52 per cent of countries have conducted a survey on sexual violence at some point (WHO, 2014b), although there are limitations. The WHO surveys do not distinguish between physical and sexual violence within their concept of domestic violence, only reporting on rape from non-intimate partners. Very few countries have repeated these surveys in a way that allows changes in the rate of rape to be measured. With the exception of the US and UK, it is usually not possible to discover changes in the rate of rape from national surveys.

While there are administrative records of the rapes reported to and recorded by the police and of those convicted by the courts, these underestimate the extent of rape in the population so few people report rape to the police (EIGE, 2014). Further, it is hard to identify the extent to which those rapes reported to the police lead to convictions in the courts.

Research to investigate the cause of rape and what works to prevent it is developing, but the field is not well funded. The Daphne programme (European Commission, 2015), funded under the public health remit, has been a well-regarded programme that assists the exchange of information about best practice in the policy field of gender violence including rape across the EU.

Criteria for rigor of scientific evidence

The entry of medical science into the construction of the knowledge base needed for the prevention of violence has had mixed results. Traditional standards for evidence used by medical science have more usually been devised with the testing of drugs and treatments than with understanding complex social behaviour. The 'gold standard' for medical science typically involves trials with randomised controls or experimental methods that are published in peer-reviewed journals. But these are not suitable for the investigation of many social issues, for both ethical and practical reasons. Social science has a broader range of methodologies that reach an accepted standard of rigor and a broader range of acceptable forms of publication (as used, for example, in assessment for the Higher Education Funding Council for England, HEFCE, Research Excellence Framework). Hence it is not appropriate to restrict research for systematic review in the field of gender-based violence to those that meet the standards of medical science. Excluding studies that do not meet these standards will unreasonably exclude significant forms of evidence and knowledge. It will have the implication that the findings of systematic review will suffer the equivalent of omitted variable bias. It will produce a distorted impression of the contours of the actually existing research field.

Several of the reviews of literature that have adopted the formal procedures of 'systematic reviews' have omitted very important evidence that does not meet these stringent criteria, even when this evidence has been subject to reasonable critical review and reached 'consensus' level among practitioners and academic experts. This has meant that some reviews have been seriously imbalanced, omitting important, relevant, consensus-held knowledge. The omissions are too important to be tolerable; the resulting reviews are not credible. A different balance needs to be found among the criteria for reviews. Until the field is properly funded and studies conducted, it will be necessary to include a wider range of evidence within reviews than is traditional for medical science, and to use other methods to ascertain its credibility and scientific adequacy given the state of development of the field.

In the long run, it is to be hoped that the quality of the evidence should reach higher standards, but this will require adequate resourcing as well as time. The field is increasing its scale, scope and quality, but more slowly than would be the case if adequate funding were supplied. Insufficient resources are currently allocated to this field to facilitate more than a slow increase in its quality. The scope and quality of the research base could be improved if more resourcing were made available.

In 2015, the evidence to support the development of the theory of rape should be inclusive and not restricted to randomised control trials and experiments, since the field is not appropriate nor resourced nor sufficiently mature for such a narrowing of the evidence to be appropriate. When reviewing the knowledge base in this book, a broad range of evidence is admitted for critical scrutiny.

Conditions under which effective strategy, coordination and services develop

The development of effective strategy, coordination and services is more likely to occur when the voices of victim-survivors are included, there are consultative platforms so that expertise in civil society can contribute to government, gender imbalances in decision-making are narrow, and where there is greater depth of gendered democracy.

Weldon and Htun (2012) found that the most important factor in the development of effective policies on gender-based violence was the strength of feminist engagement. Walby (2009) found that those countries that had a higher proportion of women among members of parliament (MPs) had a lower rate of homicide of women than when there were smaller proportions of women. Indeed, there are further studies finding positive associations between the extent of feminist politics and the reform of laws concerning rape (Frank et al, 2009; McMahon-Howard, 2011). The process of Europeanisation has contributed to the development of national-level policies to address rape and other forms of gender-based violence (Krizsán and Popa, 2010).

The inclusion of victim-survivors and service users in planning, strategy and policy-making improves their quality and effectiveness, by incorporating their knowledge from their experience of abuse and service use. This contribution depends on the healing and resilience of victim-survivors, in which specialised and mainstream services have an important role.

Consultative platforms are important in engaging the expertise in civil society. Those that include gender experts and women's organisations in the development of plans and coordination mechanisms at national and local levels are recommended. Victim-survivors' interests should be at the centre of planning and coordination.

Reducing gender imbalance in decision-making means that the voices and perspectives of those most affected by rape and other forms of gender-based violence are routinely included and consequently improve the knowledge base on which decisions are made. The decision-making forums include cabinets/executives, Parliament, civil service, police, judges, other law enforcement, medical managers, research managers (in universities, and research funding councils/bodies), and financial and economic decision-making.

The use of gender budgeting techniques in ministries of finance, combined with research on the cost-benefit analysis of interventions to prevent rape and other forms of gender-based violence, so as to make visible the benefit of reducing gender-based violence within the arena of financial decision-making, can improve the quality of decision-making.

An 'epistemic community' has been created, in which researchers, expert NGOs, victim-survivors, specialised governmental bodies, international actors and others concerned with gender equality all contribute (Walby, 2011; Ertürk and Purkayastha, 2012). This has led to the generation of a significant body of research. It is a coalition (Ferree, 2012), an alliance (Franzway and Fanow, 2011), and transnational network (Keck and Sikkink, 1998; Moghadam, 2005), with potentially far-reaching consequences (Kelly, 1988; Dobash and Dobash, 1992; Weldon, 2002; EVAW, 2011; Walby, 2011).

The deepening of gender democracy improves the quality of decision-making in relation to rape and other forms of gender-based violence. This is more likely to occur when the level of inequality in the overall system of gender relations, the gender regime, is reduced. Reducing gender inequality contributes to the environment in which the deepening of gender democracy can occur.

Conclusion

Strategic planning and coordination make important contributions to preventing rape and assisting victim-survivors of rape. These take varying forms at international, EU, national and local levels. There is scope for greater strategic planning and coordination at these different levels, and for the greater development of strategy and action plans to combat rape, including a directive on either rape or gender-based violence; for the strengthening of NAPs by each country in which coordination between various actors is a key component of policy implementation; for the enhanced development of data collection through surveys and administrative sources to aid research to assist planning; and the signing, ratification and implementation of the Council of Europe's Istanbul Convention. Consultation platforms at national and local levels that include gender experts and women's organisations in the development of plans and coordination mechanisms are recommended. And victim-survivors' interests should be at the centre of planning and coordination.

We now offer three case studies as promising practices, and to illustrate the complexity of the issues involved in their development. The first is an account of the long and uneven process of the development of strategic planning and service provision in Australia. The second is an example of the development of local coordination and integration of services in the US. The third is an example of a comprehensive rape crisis response in a mobile sexual assault crisis team in the US.

Developing coordinated and integrated services in Australia

Australia has had formal commitments to interventions to prevent rape and to the provision of support services for almost 40 years. Planning and coordination occurs at national and state levels, as well as at local community levels. The quality of the planning depends on valid data, appropriate legislation, enabling mechanisms and resources. This case study of promising practice in Australia first describes the process of development of a coordinated and integrated service, and then focuses on one example of best practice, an integrated rape crisis service in Yarrow Place, South Australia.

More than 30 years of feminist campaigning has done much to improve legislation, increase respect for victim-survivors of rape, establish support services and develop education programmes for professionals working in the field (for example, the police, legal services and health workers). A national plan has been developed from the growing push to work towards a better integration of services so that victims' experiences of the diverse relevant services are smooth and timely (COAG, 2010).

Rape and violence against women became a focus of the Australian women's movement from the early 1970s. Campaigns increased public awareness of the impact on all women, and debated the race and gender politics of rape and sexual violence. Feminist advocacy for the prevention of violence against women persuaded national, state and territory governments in the 1980s that sexual and other forms of violence against women required an organised and coordinated policy approach to meet the needs of victims and to challenge victim-blaming attitudes (Carmody, 1992; Weeks, 1994).

A rape crisis group and voluntary counselling phone service were first set up in Melbourne in 1973. Rape crisis centres and women's refuges were established in most large cities, supported by some funding from state and federal governments. More recently, services have been mostly funded through governments' health portfolios. A number of specialist services have been established to respond to sexual assault and family and domestic violence (Olle, 2005; Astbury, 2006). These services accumulated evidence for the development of campaigns and to inform the improvement of support practices. In addition, there have been major changes to the law concerning sexual offences in every state and territory. Australian law is founded in the English common law tradition. Campaigns to reform rape laws sought to criminalise rape in marriage (first in New South Wales in 1981; see Lake, 1999, p 241), and to redefine 'lack of consent' claimed as a first in the common law world (Scutt, 1998). In 1981 the law on rape was extended to include rape in marriage. As definitions of rape were expanded with rape law reform, the term 'sexual violence' became more common in the research literature as well as in policy development (see Dean et al, 1998; Rowntree, 2010).

A strong knowledge base has been built. There have been specific national surveys of women's experiences of violence undertaken by the Australian

Bureau of Statistics (ABS) and published (1996, 2006, 2013). In addition, national surveys of community attitudes are conducted as part of the national plan to reduce violence against women (VicHealth, 2014). These surveys, together with the survey conducted as the Australian component of the International Violence against Women Survey (Mouzos and Makkai, 2004), inform significant aspects of research about sexual violence across a range of research disciplines.

Australian research suggests that one in five women and one in twenty men over the age of 18 have been 'forced or frightened into unwanted sexual activity' across their lifetimes, many of them having experienced coercion when aged under 16 (de Visser et al, 2003, p 200). A high proportion of sexual assaults against women are perpetrated by male intimate partners (Heenan, 2004; VicHealth, 2014). The 2012 Personal Safety Survey reported that there was no reduction in the prevalence of violence against women between 2005 and 2012 (ABS, 2013). The production of the *National standards of practice manual for services against sexual violence*, developed in consultation with over 80 services throughout the country, was a milestone in 'represent[ing] the first Australian effort to document the nature of the professional response to which women, children and men are entitled following sexual violence' (Dean et al, 1998, p i).

Aboriginal women argue it is inappropriate and oppressive to universalise women's oppression, and that the complex conditions for all women must be confronted if policy is to be relevant for all communities (Pettman, 1992; Behrendt, 1993; Lake, 1999; Moreton-Robinson, 2002; Phillips, 2008). At the same time, evidence suggests that sexual assault of Indigenous women by both Aboriginal and non-Aboriginal men is endemic (Lievore, 2003; VicHealth, 2014). Various task forces and inquiries commissioned by state, territory and federal governments have yielded qualitative information about sexual and family violence through consultation with Indigenous women and organisations involved in their welfare. In the last decade, attention has shifted to focus on child sexual assault, with the Mullighan (2008) inquiry conducted on Anangu Pitjantjatjara Yankunytjatjara, a large Aboriginal local government area located in the remote north west of South Australia. The Wild and Anderson (2007) report was dramatically adopted in the last months of the Howard federal government to justify highly intrusive interventions into Aboriginal communities in the Northern Territory in the name of child protection.

Gains in policy and service provision came under attack with the election of a Conservative federal government (1996-2007). Phillips (2008) argued that women's organisations and the politics of social policy were directly challenged by a hostile, anti-feminist environment and a neoconservatism that denied gender in its approaches to violence against women. Neoliberal social policies shifted focus to individuals and their responsibility for risk avoidance (O'Malley and Sutton, 1997; Hogg and Brown, 1998; Culpitt, 1999). The capacity of Australian women's policy interventions was undermined as government agencies were restructured, resources severely cut and women's advocacy organisations were excluded from policy governance at the national level (Chappell, 2002; Sawer, 2002; Summers, 2003; Hamilton and Maddison, 2007). The UN Committee on the Elimination of Discrimination Against Women reported an apparent reversal in Australian women's policy, particularly in relation to gender equity and human rights for women. In addition, the Howard federal government refused to sign the protocol to the Convention on the Elimination of Discrimination Against Women.

The change of government at the federal level in 2007 to a less socially conservative leadership allowed for renewed effort at national level. Sexual assault services and domestic violence services were extended, working with other government and non-government agencies to provide flexible, innovative, inclusive and integrated services. However, the incoming Labor federal government retained interventionist policies in Aboriginal communities in the Northern Territory. The change of government did allow the National Council to Reduce Violence against Women and their Children to produce the report, *Time for action*, based on extensive consultation (National Council to Reduce Violence against Women and their Children, 2009). It recommends a series of strategies across six fields for improvement, described as 'outcome areas'. These include: safety in the whole community; access to appropriate high-quality services; the legal system to treat women with dignity and to hold the perpetrator accountable for his behaviour; the perpetrator to accept responsibility for changing his behaviour; and preventative measures to be available to ensure he does not repeat his violence; the success of the action plan hinges on the success of the sixth outcome area, which is that the entire system joins seamlessly and all its parts work together. These strategies were encapsulated in the *National plan to reduce violence against women and their children 2010-2022* (COAG, 2010). This provides policy settings and standards for State and Territory agencies to establish their own programmes and services. With a strong emphasis on coordination, the plan led to the establishment of Our Watch (formerly the Foundation to Prevent Violence against Women and their Children) and Australia's National Research Organisation for Women's Safety (ANROWS). Our Watch is aimed at cultural and attitudinal change, while ANROWS supports and promotes research.

The most recent research finds some improvement in the attitudes of young men towards violence against women. However, there has been an increase, from three in ten in 2009 to over four in ten in 2013 who believe that rape results from men not being able to control their need for sex (VicHealth, 2014). Overall, the level of victimisation of women from all forms of violence has not changed since 2005, despite considerable efforts (ABS, 2013).

Every jurisdiction, both state and federal, has created distinct legislation on sexual offences. As a result, Australia offers significant opportunities to consider which laws work most effectively and why (Heath, 2005; Daly and Bouhours, 2010). Most Australian jurisdictions have also undertaken evaluation of this legislation (Heenan and McKelvie, 1997; Stubbs, 2003). The law relating to adult sexual offences has moved a long way from its history in a legal tradition that saw women as the property of their husbands or fathers, and treated rape as a violation of male property rights. The modern law of rape focuses much more strongly on sexual autonomy. However, the past exercises an intense pull on the law in a range of ways. Myths about sexual assault remain prevalent within Australian culture (Friedman and Golding, 1997; Xenos and Smith, 2001). Legal changes to laws and judicial processes on rape and sexual assault in the state of South Australia were proclaimed in December 2008 (Government of South Australia, 2013). These changes aim to increase consideration for victims during the judicial process. Sexual offences committed since this date will be prosecuted under the Criminal Law Consolidation (Rape and Sexual Offences) Amendment Act 2008. Offences committed prior to the legal changes will be prosecuted under the Criminal Law Consolidation Act (Sexual Offences) 1978. The laws have been strengthened to provide a clearer definition of offences, and what constitutes consent. The reforms require a person's agreement to sexual activity to be free and voluntary. Rape is also defined as a situation in which a person withdraws their consent after initially agreeing to sexual intercourse and the other party continues regardless. Courts will also have to make special arrangements for victims of rape and sexual assault giving evidence.

Daly and Bouhours warn that conviction estimates and rates of attrition depend on when and where research is conducted, types of offences and the age of victims (Daly and Bouhours, 2010, p 618). Their comparative study of five countries nevertheless shows an overall decline in conviction rates, which in Australia reportedly reduced from 17 per cent to 11.5 per cent over the last three decades (2010, p 602). Heath (2005) calculates that convictions have not risen above 3.1 per cent of reports in any year in the previous decade. These figures are all the more disturbing since at least 85 per cent of sexual offences are never reported to the police (McLennan, 1996; Cook et al, 2001; de Visser et al, 2003; Lievore, 2003; Larcombe, 2011). Alternative models have been proposed. In particular, 'restorative justice' approaches are being examined for their applicability to sexual assault and domestic violence. These approaches bring together people who have been affected by criminal activity and aim to achieve a reintegration of the offender into the broader community. Restorative justice processes take a large number of forms with widely varying relationships to usual criminal justice processes (Stubbs, 2004).

Evaluation of family conferencing of sexual offences committed by young people in South Australia has shown that while a substantial proportion of offenders whose cases go to court are never held responsible for their conduct, family conferencing may produce better outcomes for victim-complainants (Daly, 2011). Family conferences resulted in more apologies to victim-complainants as well as more undertakings to do community service, and more undertakings to participate in therapeutic counselling from offenders than court processes. By contrast, the few custodial sentences imposed in court were almost all suspended (Daly et al, 2003; Daly, 2005). However, critics question whether restorative justice approaches adequately address power imbalances and provide safety for victim-complainants (Stubbs, 2004). While appropriate restorative justice processes may provide a valuable alternative choice within the context of the criminal justice system, the current failures of the criminal law still need to be effectively addressed (Heath, 2005, p 6).

The Yarrow Place Rape and Sexual Assault Service (www.yarrowplace. sa.gov.au) was established in 1993 by merging the SARC, based in a city hospital, with the community-based, feminist rape crisis centre. Funded by the state government, Yarrow Place works with and for victims of both sexes who were over the age of 16 at the time of the assault. Yarrow Place is the leading public health agency responding to rape and sexual assault in South Australia, with a state-wide mandate. It provides a lead agency role in South Australia. This includes advocacy in relation to key issues, public policy, planning and service delivery in the area of sexual violence against adults. It provides resources for other agencies to provide services to victim-survivors. It works to prevent rape and sexual assault. In addition, Yarrow Place has Aboriginal sexual assault workers who provide counselling to Aboriginal people who have experienced sexual assault/ abuse, and training and community education regarding issues of sexual violence in Aboriginal communities. The Yarrow Place service is designed to ensure that women's forensic and longer-term healthcare needs can adequately be met on site, regardless of when the assault occurred. Hence, women victim-survivors, who may, months or even years after the assault, endeavour to seek medical support, especially in terms of gynaecological care, can continue to access the service and be assured of seeing a doctor who is both sensitive and aware of the effects of sexual violence. This is in contrast to those services that focus on acute or crisis care responses that can result in less attention being given to the potential for longer-term or lifespan health effects of sexual violence for individuals (Olle, 2005). This shift in focus is only now beginning to recognise the need for responses over time or over lifespans. This is of particular value for those for whom no initial acute response was possible or desirable, or for those for whom no response was historically available.

Yarrow Place is an example of best practice in the delivery of services to victim-survivors because it provides integrated services that are victim-centred, time- and cost-effective for victims and providers, and is integrated with services beyond crisis services.

Services such as Yarrow Place are victim-centred, with a long-term service provision focus, designed to integrate medical and counselling services (with, for example, health agencies such as Dale Street Women's Centre). The formal integration policy implemented through such services involves trialling and implementing restorative and interrogative justice approaches, as well as feminist approaches to sexual assault victim services. It is also important that service providers are able to work under supportive conditions with high-level workplace standards.

Yarrow Place is an exemplar of integrated service delivery models. The model has been most effective in streamlining the extent to which victim-survivors are obliged to repeat the details of their abuse. These integrated health models offer forensic and counselling services on the same premises, either attached to, or close by, hospitals, where emergency departments can provide medical treatment for serious injury. Pregnancy and testing for sexually transmitted infections, and the provision of prevention and amelioration measures such as emergency contraception counselling services, follow-up medical care and short-term counselling for acute or recent sexual assault, are all provided in an environment of relative security and comfort (Olle, 2005).

Such a model provides a cost-effective means to prevent delays in forensic examinations, increase the availability of female forensic examiners, and has the potential to enhance professional standards (Regan et al, 2004, p 1). Nurses have previously been able to access specialist forensic training in Australia. Yarrow Place currently delivers training in forensics where some of the participants in the course have been nurses (some from remote areas).

Women's needs extend beyond the immediate health and legal services. Informed advice and advocacy are also necessary in education, employment and safety. Yarrow Place connects with the Working Women's Centre SA (WWC SA) to provide assistance to those who need support around workplace issues that may be affected by rape or sexual assault. The WWC is a non-profit NGO that provides advocacy information and support on the following issues: discrimination and sexual harassment in the workplace, unfair dismissals, workplace bullying, and how to negotiate with employers. Informal networks contribute to the integration of services both local and across state borders, involving state government-funded women's agencies, as well as advocacy groups, government-funded NGOs, women's service organisations and the National Council for Single Mothers and their Children.

Several lessons can be learned from Yarrow Place for implementation elsewhere. Rape crisis services need to be founded in comprehensive legislation dealing with the diversity of sexual offences. This is necessary, but not sufficient. Services need to incorporate cultural and ethnic awareness. Funding for services needs to be adequate and predictable. Formal integration of services (from legal, to health and counselling) overcomes obstacles such as legal delay to best practice. Informal sustainable networks between and across services and agencies encourage flexibility and responsiveness to emerging issues, such as the impact of economic insecurity and policy changes.

Coordinated community responses, in the US and other countries

Coordination at the community level is important for the delivery of policies to prevent rape. Early examples came from the US, but are now found elsewhere. Coordinated community responses first developed in the US for domestic violence intervention. However, similar coordinated responses were used for rape and sexual assault intervention from the 1970s, when rape crises centres first started to coordinate action with hospitals, including developing common protocols for interventions (Advocates for Human Rights, 2009). Other countries, including within the EU, have also developed coordination practices.

The variety of actors involved depends on local contexts and community needs. It may include law enforcement, prosecution, judiciary, healthcare, as in Dodge, Fillmore and Olmsted County in Minnesota, but can also involve mental health providers, victim advocacy, crises centres, social services and other specifically concerned community actors (Roy and Martin, 2002). For example, the sexual assault response teams in Fresno, California, include sexual assault nurse examiners, and their monthly meetings are extended to include participants representing district attorney's office, hospitals, the rape counselling centre and local child protection services. The sexual assault response team (SART) in Montgomery, Alabama, has a multidisciplinary team that also involves representatives from the local domestic violence programme and the

Alabama Crime Victims' Compensation Board. Site-specific stakeholders are often included. Accordingly, communities with minority populations include minority women's crises centres in responding to rape; communities including large university campuses also involve university representatives in developing responses.

US practice in using coordinated community responses highlights eight aspects of activities that make coordinated community intervention more efficient. Of primary importance is the work on the development of a common philosophical framework, a common way of understanding sexual assault, accepted by the various participant organisations in the coordinated community response. Based on this understanding, the first step undertaken is to develop model protocols that guide all further coordinated intervention to prevent and address sexual assault. A series of protocols developed in various communities across the US is available from the National Sexual Violence Resource Centre's website (see www. nsvrc.org/). A further task of importance for coordinated community responses is to monitor and track individual cases and to ensure the accountability of practitioners in dealing with these cases. Furthermore, such responses play a major role in coordinating the exchange of information and interagency communications between those involved in responding to rape. They make sure that the provision of resources and services to victims, of sanctions, restrictions and services for offenders, are smooth and efficient. Finally, a core role of coordinated community responses is the ongoing evaluation of the coordinated justice system response from the victim's perspective (Littel et al, 1998).

The main objective of coordination is to avoid fragmentation and to keep the interests of the victim at the centre of all responses (Allen, 2006). This takes various forms, some more formalised and with more implications for policy development, others less formalised and geared towards a more efficient engagement with individual victim-survivors. The focus on the victim-survivor can also benefit from cross-agency reflexivity and learning. An important objective is to include victims' advocates among the coordinating actors, and to ensure that they have a role in shaping responses. Furthermore, coordinated community responses can address the tendency to fragmentation among services, while also adapting national policies to local contexts and changes in the local environment.

This example from the US shows that the best practice of coordinated community responses can bring benefits to addressing rape in four ways. First, they can enhance the autonomy of the individual victim-survivor. Second, they can place priority on the safety of the victim-survivors rather than focusing on the 'case'. Third, they can promote institutional change within systems (law enforcement, legal, medical or social services etc) to improve response to victim-survivors. Finally, they can promote community-wide response to reduce violence against women, rather than sector-specific responses (Littel et al, 1998).

Coordinated community responses in the US take various forms – community partnering, community organising, councils and task forces, community intervention and training are just some (Littel et al, 1998). While community partnering and community organising are more informal, councils and task forces and interventions are more formalised, with resources (both financial and human) allocated for facilitating coordination and taking initiative. At their core is 'meeting face-to-face, planning, developing policies and protocols, cross training of staff, appearing in educational panels, and communicating about victims' (Martin, 2007).

Formal councils and task forces are the more formalised kind: these are platforms that allow for all involved agencies and actors to meet on a regular basis, to undertake common larger-scale projects, and to monitor and amend policies according to flaws identified in the practice. They are often better resourced than other forms of coordination, but they may also lack independence for a genuinely critical voice. Councils develop model protocols for responses to sexual assault. The Sexual Assault Interagency Council in Dodge, Fillmore and Olmstead is a good example here.

Another form of a platform for coordination is provided by independent community-based victims' advocacy organisations. In such cases there is a stronger emphasis on monitoring and critical evaluation and oversight of activity by stakeholders.

The generally positive experience with coordinated community responses is supported by numerous evaluations and pieces of analysis (see the review by Martin, 2007). Martin argues, however, that while all coordination is good for addressing violence against women, some forms are nevertheless better than others. Weaknesses that emerge can be linked to resource problems and particularly to the lack of staff dedicated specifically to running the coordination exercise. The issue of independence has also been raised as problematic. Independent monitoring along quality criteria supporting the victim's perspective had best been secured in coordinated community responses that were led by victims' advocacy organisations or other autonomous platforms (for example, the Fresno Rape Counselling Centre is a comprehensive sexual assault victim service programme that is a major facilitator of coordinated community responses in Fresno), rather than by hospitals, the police or other stakeholders. Coordination led by victims' advocacy groups is also advantageous for developing a common understanding of objectives acceptable across different agencies that reflects a gender sensitive victim-centred approach and facilitates all participants to 'own rape'. Interference by local politics has also been noted as problematic: convincing political actors as well as peer groups of the need to cooperate can prove difficult (Martin, 2007). Finally, dilemmas around the cooptation of the objectives of women's rights and victims' advocacy groups deriving from the coordinating activity with various public actors have repeatedly been raised (Martin, 2007).

Coordinated community responses are good practices because they provide channels for integrating victims' advocates into developing, implementing and monitoring policy responses to rape. Another related aspect that makes them good practice is that by the integration of victims' rights advocates into coordination, they facilitate the maintenance of the primary focus of intervention on protecting the victim-survivor and on responding to the perpetrator. Finally they also improve the efficiency of the intervention and improve the accountability of the numerous actors involved in responding to rape. Coordinated community responses are transferable. They are now common in Europe, especially in the realm of domestic violence interventions. Countries where this is taking place include Austria (oral communication with Rosa Logar) and Albania (supported by UNDP, 2009, oral communication with Raluca Popa). However, no evaluation is available at this point about how these pilots work in practice. The example of MARACs in the UK points towards the difficulties that arise when the police are the coordinators of community responses, rather than victims' advocates.

Comprehensive rape crisis services: sexual assault crisis team in the US

Specialist services to support victim-survivors of rape are a necessary part of the best practice response, with the potential to mitigate the long-lasting harms inflicted. In supporting the victim-survivors, these services also act to prevent rape, through supporting the victim in challenging the impunity of rapists through the criminal justice system. There are a variety of components to these services and their coordination so that the victim-survivor receives the best support. SACT (Sexual Assault Crisis Team) practice is an example of best practice in the provision of these services.

SACT is a rape crisis shelter intervention in the US that provides residential-based support for victim-survivors of rape, sexual assault and sex trafficking, including those in the immediate aftermath of a rape; those coming to terms with historic rape experiences, including as a child; and those who have returned to the area to testify at trial. SACT has been identified as an example of best practice by a 2011 resource-sharing project for the National Sexual Assault Coalition (see www.nsvrc. org/organizations/84).

The shelter was established in 2002, and serves around 20-30 victim-survivors in its shelter overnight. Unlike many domestic violence shelters, all residential accommodation is in solo rooms to accommodate the specific need for privacy of many rape victim-survivors. The shelter works with both female and male victims of rape and sexual violence. It is designed to have two completely separate sides, allowing female and male victim-survivors' privacy. Clients are also less likely to have young children with them compared with those staying in domestic violence shelters. Importantly, the board that oversees SACT is made up of people from the communities it serves. The average stay in the shelter is three to five days, although individuals who are looking for new housing options or who have other needs might stay longer. There is no limit to the time SACT permits a survivor to stay; as long as they are working towards their goals, they can keep their residential place (Bein and Hurt, 2011). As well as residential accommodation, SACT provides a 24-hour sexual assault hotline answered by trained advocates, and a range of advocacy services for both residential and non-residential clients, including hospital advocacy, legal advocacy, attorney consultation through a specialist law project, education, training and support programmes, information and training on date rape, stranger rape, surviving incest, inner child workshops, ritualised or sadistic abuse, different types of harassment, support groups, for profit, worship, or group/gang-related sexual violence and criminal activity, and school and community safety programmes. SACT is now certified to provide bystander training and offers an on-site campus office at the local military academy, adding prevention programming to all aspects of the SACT programme (SACT, 2013). SACT is a non-profit organisation staffed by personnel with over 40 hours of initial training in sexual violence, and ongoing training in supporting victim-survivors of rape and sexual assault. Recipients are female victim-survivors of rape and sexual assault and male victim-survivors of rape and sexual and domestic assault. As well as serving the local community, referrals to SACT have also come from across the country, including California, Connecticut, New York and Boston.

The goal of SACT is to provide comprehensive services to victim-survivors of sexual violence, including emergency shelter and transitional housing for female victims of sexual violence and male victim-survivors of sexual or domestic violence, legal and medical advocacy, crisis services, support groups and educational forums. To address the problem of sexual violence in the community, these services are designed to meet the needs of both female and male victim-survivors, and services are also available to victim-survivors' non-offending family members and support networks (SACT, 2013). SACT's vision is that 'the shelter serves every non-offending human being' (2013). SACT is designed to provide immediate support to victim-survivors of rape, including accessing health and legal services; to re-build victim-survivors' self-esteem and self-confidence; and to come to terms with what has happened to them no matter when the rape occurred (that is, SACT works with victim-survivors in the immediate aftermath of a rape and with those who were raped longer ago, including those adults who experienced rape or sexual abuse as children). In addition, SACT provides training around prevention, dating violence and healthy relationships to help prevent re-victimisation in the future by enabling victim-survivors, non-offending family members, high schools and colleges, the community at large, and other professionals to better understand the nature of sexual violence, and to develop access to independent living through education and training.

Prior to the opening of the shelter, SACT was already providing outreach services, but was having difficulty finding appropriate shelter for victim-survivors of rape. While the local domestic violence shelter would certainly take in female sexual assault victim-survivors, the shelter's massive workload prevented the development of specific services to support rape and sexual assault victim-survivors in their recovery. SACT already had this expertise from running the 24-hour hotline and outreach services for victim-survivors of rape, and therefore the shelter was conceived of to fill an identified need using the knowledge and skills already available in the local rape and domestic and sexual assault support community (Bein and Hurt, 2011).

In keeping with its vision (to serve every non-offending human being), SACT provides residential services to male victims of rape, sexual and domestic violence, as well as female victims of rape and sexual violence. This enables SACT to address a gap in local provision because the local domestic violence shelter was not able to house men, so male clients were being housed in hotel rooms that did not enable a good model of support and recovery to be delivered, and created additional concerns around client safety and client-advocate meetings (Bein and Hurt, 2011). The shelter ensures issues of privacy and personal safety are taken very seriously. For example, they recognised that the shelter would need to offer bathrooms and showers that individuals could use privately, and that shelter residents would need to be able to lock their doors and be alone whenever they chose. All bedrooms are designed for solo occupation, unless there is a non-offending partner whom the survivor chooses to accompany them. While many of these requirements are similar to those for domestic violence victim-survivors, other 'rules' that work well in these types of shelters need to be adapted to support victim-survivors of rape. SACT also houses family members of victim-survivors who have come to town to provide support in the immediate aftermath of a rape, as well as victim-survivors who are returning to town to deal with legal processes and trials. SACT works collaboratively with organisations across the country, which enables it to meet the needs of diverse range of recipients. For example, through collaborative work with the state-wide Vermont Pride Center, SACT provides specialised services to the lesbian, gay, bisexual, trans or questioning (LGBTQ) community, especially the transgender community and bias/hate crime victims. Their needs for safe housing and shelter are for longer periods of time as the violence often occurs in the home or they are already on the streets and cannot return to their home of origin. They must re-establish their lives in a different location. SACT also works in collaboration with the local children's advocacy centre, for child victims and non-offending parents or guardians, and receives referrals from mental health agencies, therapists, other community programmes such as the Council on Aging, as well as other shelters and network programmes when they have reached capacity. SACT also provides shelter and services for victim-survivors and the professionals who are involved in the work of stopping human sex trafficking, including law enforcement, attorneys and both state and federal professionals.

SACT has been identified as an example of best practice in shelter-based interventions for victim-survivors of rape by the National Sexual Assault Coalition Resource Sharing Project (see www.resourcesharingproject.org). Best practice criteria are the generic features found by scrutinising the SACT intervention that aims to assist victim-survivors of rape through the provision of safe and supported residential accommodation while also contributing to rape prevention by educating and empowering women and men to recognise and resist rape and sexual abuse. This draws on the review of best practice shelter and sexual violence interventions by Bein and Hurt (2011) for the National Sexual Assault Coalition Resource Sharing Project. The Project was created to help US state sexual assault coalitions across the country access the resources they need in order to develop and thrive. It is designed to provide technical assistance, support, and to facilitate peer-driven resources for all state-wide sexual assault coalitions, and is funded by the US Department of Justice, Office on Violence Against Women (see www.resourcesharingproject.org).

SACT can be considered a best practice case study for a number of reasons. Evidence shows that safe and secure shelter in the aftermath of a rape is essential for victim-survivors. SACT addresses this need by providing shelter that is specifically designed to meet the needs of victim-survivors of rape and sexual assault. It was developed and established to respond to identified unmet need for specialist residential shelter for victim-survivors of rape and sexual assault. SACT is collaborative, working with the local domestic violence shelter, and draws on the knowledge and expertise of its outreach arm. SACT multifunctions, providing safe shelter for victim-survivors, but also providing access to a comprehensive range of education, training and support programmes designed to enable residents to identify, work toward, and achieve goals in order to move on from the shelter accommodation.

SACT utilises its expert knowledge in working with victim-survivors of rape and sexual assault in order to establish and run the residential shelter in such a way that specifically identifies and addresses the needs of victim-survivors of sexual violence. It is not only innovative, but its practice is also transferable to other settings where there is an identified need for expert rape-specific residential shelter interventions, and where coalitions can be developed that incorporate expertise on shelter-based interventions and working with victim-survivors of rape.

A number of recommendations are made for the future development and implementation of shelter-based rape prevention projects based on this case study and wider research.

• *Interventions should be led from the needs of the victim-survivor:* projects should address an identified need for victim-survivors of rape that is not being met in that location or context. Assistance should include a range of functions: interventions to assist rape victim-survivors should address crisis intervention, advocacy, support and accessing other services and/ or agencies such as health and criminal justice.
• *Outreach:* best practice interventions reach out beyond the immediate environment through interagency relationships to help develop or facilitate additional resources such as 'safe lists' or accreditation schemes for landlords and organisations/business who install locks and other security devices.
• *Interventions require expert knowledge:* expertise is needed in dealing with the needs and support of victim-survivors of rape across a range of contexts, covering recent and historic experiences of rape; assistance for adults as well as children; dealing with individuals with chronic mental health or substance abuse or homelessness problems; and rape within intimate partnerships, within the family, or in the course of working in the sex industry, including having been trafficked for work in the sex industry. This includes specialist expertise in the issues concerning rape, specialist professional knowledge and gender expertise.
• *Cooperation and collaboration with other agencies:* assistance to victim-survivors should be ensured by collaboration across agencies with

different objectives so that expertise is shared and joint services are, where appropriate, developed and delivered. Best practice interventions should incorporate input and expertise from a range of agencies, including health, criminal justice, housing, local government, landlord tenants, unions and women's organisations. Interagency sharing and strengthening of expertise, knowledge and skills makes the search for help less burdensome for the victim-survivor.

• *Evidence-based:* best practice shelter-based interventions should be designed and implemented with reference to what has been demonstrated to work, and to avoid what has been shown to be detrimental to achieving the outcomes and overall aims of/for the intervention. Best practice interventions should therefore build in comprehensive evaluations from the start; this will require dedicated data collection systems that enable the aims of evaluation to be comprehensively assessed while adhering to high standards of confidentiality, and ensuring ethical principles for working with individuals who have been subject to rape or sexual violence are met.

3

Victim services and healthcare systems

Introduction

The provision of immediate assistance to victim-survivors of rape is the central contribution of the health sector to the mitigation of the harms of rape and to rape prevention. The development of standalone specialised services by feminist activists in the 1970s has been followed by the development of professional care as part of the work of health services. In some locations, such as the UK, both forms of care for victim-survivors of rape co-exist.

The health consequences of rape involve both physical and mental trauma, and require a range of interventions, flexible in response to victim-survivor choices. The improvement in access to and quality of health services for victim-survivors of rape includes mental, sexual and reproductive health services. There have been important innovations in health services addressing actual and potential health issues, and in the use of the diagnosis of post-traumatic stress disorder (PTSD). These health services are differently organised in response to rape in different contexts (Lovett et al, 2004; Wang and Rowley, 2007; WHO, 2013a).

This chapter is focused on establishing current best practices for health sector-led interventions for women who have been raped in non-disaster zones and in humanitarian emergencies. It begins by outlining the health impacts of sexual violence and rape; this is followed by identification of how best practices have been established; and then the minimum and current best practice standards for health interventions for victim-survivors of rape and sexual violence in non-disaster zones and in humanitarian emergencies are explicated and presented. Healthcare for victim-survivors is important in both non-disaster zones and disaster zones, where it is an essential component of humanitarian programmes.

Best practice standards for health interventions for victim-survivors of rape and sexual violence in humanitarian emergencies can be regarded as the core minimum standards for health interventions for victim-survivors of rape and sexual violence in non-disaster zones. This core of minimum standards is then supplemented with reference to further international literature to identify best practices for health interventions for victims of rape and sexual violence in non-disaster zones. Practice standards can be identified in six domains: capable and care conducive environment; health and medical care; forensic examination and evidence collection; community and social support; specialist referral and follow-up care; and quality and monitoring. Best practice is a health-led, multisectoral 'one-stop shop' unit, housed in a hospital or primary healthcare facility with a separate entrance, and providing health interventions, forensic evidence collection, advocacy and counselling.

There are still gaps in provision, including in the medium and long-term care for the mental health consequences of rape (and indeed, of other forms of gender-based violence). This requires further commitment to the prioritisation of violence against women, as well as sustained funding.

Health impacts of rape

Wide-ranging health impacts from rape and other forms of sexual violence have been documented in clinical case studies and research reports (WHO, 2013a, 2013b). Syntheses of sexual violence and health literature (Jewkes et al, 2002; WHO, 2013a) have reported the health impacts experienced by women who have been raped as: sexual and reproductive health problems including unwanted pregnancy and sexually transmitted diseases; mental health problems and health risk coping strategies; physical injuries and fatal outcomes; and social stigmatisation and/or ostracisation.

Rape may result in pregnancy and gynaecological impacts (trauma, bleeding, infection, pain, genital irritation, urinary tract infections, pelvic pain, painful intercourse, and decreased sexual desire), and victim-survivors of rape and sexual violence may have been exposed to HIV and other sexually transmitted diseases (Jewkes et al, 2002) including Hepatitis B. Women of reproductive age subjected to rape are at risk of unwanted pregnancy (WHO, 2013a). The risk of unwanted pregnancy and sexually transmitted disease is uncertain because very few studies have been undertaken (WHO, 2013a). The likelihood of unwanted pregnancy following rape is, however, significant. In a survey of over 4,000 women undertaken in the US, the estimated pregnancy rate following rape was found to be one in twenty (5 per cent), equating to 32,101 rape-related pregnancies in one year in the US alone (Holmes et al, 1996). Within situations of intimate partner sexual violence and rape, McFarlane et al (2005) found that 20 per cent of women had a rape-related pregnancy, and 15 per cent reported contracting at least one sexually transmitted disease. The risk of HIV infection following rape is uncertain, and although generally regarded as low, local HIV prevalence and multi-perpetrator rape will affect transmission risk (WHO, 2013a).

Following rape, victim-survivors may express fear, anger, or sadness, or may control and subdue emotions (Wang and Rowley, 2007). Onset of acute stress reactions is often quick, developing during, or in the immediate aftermath of, a traumatic event. Common signifiers of acute stress reactions are experiences of 'anxiety, low mood, emotional ups and downs, poor concentration, wanting to be alone, recurrent dreams or flashbacks, avoiding anything that will trigger traumatic event memories, feeling numb and detached from others, reckless or aggressive behaviour, palpitations, nausea, chest pain, headaches, stomach pains, and breathing difficulty' (Lawson, 2013, p 1; NICE, 2013). Victim-survivors of rape have also reported enduring psychological distress, further mental health sequelae that have been diagnosed as anxiety, or depression, and panic and obsessive-compulsive disorders (Wang and Rowley, 2007). Many victim-survivors of rape and sexual violence experience nightmares, flashbacks, heightened arousal and/or numbness, all of which are symptoms associated with PTSD (Wang and Rowley, 2007). Indeed, PTSD diagnosis is more likely for victim-survivors of sexual violence than other types of trauma (Regehr et al, 2013). At least one third of rape survivors will develop PTSD (SVRI, 2011).

The diagnostic criteria for PTSD involve the ongoing experience of a number of stress responses for a period of time. A diagnosis of PTSD is often reserved for those experiencing severe PTSD symptoms or symptoms that last for more than one month (Knott, 2013). Research into acute psychological stress responses following sexual violence or rape often has employed measures of PTSD symptoms to capture both early and longer-term victim-survivor experiences. Rothbaum et al (1992), reporting on a prospective, longitudinal study using a measure of PTSD criteria, found that 94 per cent of 95 women victim-survivors of rape met symptom criteria for PTSD at 12 days (mean) following rape, that 65 per cent met PTSD symptom criteria at one month (mean 35 days), and 47 per cent met symptom criteria for PTSD at three months (mean 94 days). Nearly all of the women (95 per cent) in Rothbaum et al's (1992) study reported severe acute psychological stress responses, of which approximately half of the women continued to experience symptoms that met PTSD diagnostic criteria at three months. PTSD-associated symptoms frequently increase over the first three weeks, and then resolve within three months for approximately half of rape victim-survivors (SVRI, 2011).

There is no clear evidence to suggest that there are distinctions in the severity of mental health sequelae based on the victim-perpetrator relationship, but greater prevalence of PTSD has been associated with life-threat and severity of physical injury during the sexual assault (Wang and Rowley, 2007). Indicators of likely development of enduring PTSD symptoms have been identified as persistent dissociation, rumination, self-blame, disorganised memories of the trauma, maladaptive coping strategies, substance abuse, depression, physical reminders of the attack and severity of symptoms (SVRI, 2011). In addition to PTSD, rape and sexual violence is also associated with greater risk of depression, suicidal thoughts and suicide attempts (Jewkes et al, 2002). In a systematic review and meta-analysis, Devries et al (2013) found a relationship between intimate partner physical and/or sexual violence against women and depressive symptoms and suicide attempts. Women subject to rape and sexual violence are also at risk from health risk coping strategies, which are further associated with poor health outcomes (Campbell, 2002). A recent systematic review (WHO, 2013b) identified on meta-analysis of data that women subject to non-partner sexual violence were 2.3 times more likely to use alcohol problematically and 2.6 times more likely to have depression or anxiety than women who had not reported being subject to sexual violence. Rape-associated social fears and stigma may evoke experiences of social isolation (Jewkes et al, 2002), and may exacerbate psychological stress.

The extent of traumatic physical injuries will depend on the severity of violence simultaneously perpetrated during an assault. In conflict and post-conflict zones, the severity of violence is more often extreme (Kippenberg et al, 2009) and associated with severe traumatic injuries. Vaginal fistulae are not uncommon for many women victim-survivors of rape and sexual torture and slavery (Bourke, 2014). Extreme sexual violence, as any daily newspaper will evidence, is not the preserve of conflict/post-conflict zones. Indeed, severe violence against women in non-conflict zones is often allied with sexual violence. Death may result from suicide, HIV infection, murder (Jewkes et al, 2002), so-called honour killing because of rape, pregnancy complications, or unsafe abortion (WHO, 2012a). A child born of rape may be at risk of infanticide (WHO, 2012a). Sexual violence and rape is also frequently perpetrated without extreme physical violence, and therefore there may not be any observable physical injuries (Sugar et al, 2003), or there may be limited injuries in the form of superficial wounds, soft tissue and/or musculoskeletal trauma (Fehler-Cabral et al, 2011).

The harms from rape and sexual violence have important impacts for women's morbidity (health state) and mortality (premature death) (WHO, 2012a, 2013a, 2013b). Research has shown that women subjected to rape used general and mental healthcare services much more than women who had not been raped (Golding et al, 1988). The causal pathway from being subject to rape and sexual violence to harms experienced may be direct and obvious, for example, immediate injury, unwanted pregnancy, disease exposure, or it may be more complex, mediated by social, cultural and economic factors (Murray and Lopez, 1999), psychological and physiological stress, and behavioural, health risk coping strategies (WHO, 2013b). This causal pathway complexity creates challenges for research evidencing the longer-term and wider health impacts of rape and sexual violence and likely accounts, in part, for the limited number of robust, population-based longitudinal studies of harms of sexual violence undertaken. Still, research has identified statistically significant associations between forms of gender-based violence (intimate partner violence, sexual violence and stalking) and greater incidence of long-term, cardiovascular and respiratory, conditions (Black et al, 2011) and mental ill health (Black et al, 2011; Breiding et al, 2014). While ground breaking in the field, this research conflates multiple forms of gender-based violence (physical, sexual, psychological), disaggregating only by victim-perpetrator relationship and not by form of violence. The range and complexity of health impacts in the immediate and longer term remains undetermined (Walby and Olive, 2014), and further research is required. Nevertheless, a recent study did make clear the cost to society of gender-based violence; Walby and Olive (2014) estimated that in the UK alone, the cost of the physical and emotional, and health service impacts of rape and sexual violence, was €12.8 billion in 2012, and that the societal cost of gender-based violence against women in the EU was €226 billion. Even though uncertainties remain regarding the full extent of its impact, the health burden of sexual violence and rape is immense; it is frequently assessed, in terms of morbidity and mortality, as being more harmful than other public health priorities (García-Moreno and Watts, 2011).

Rape and sexual violence occurs in diverse contexts. It is perpetrated by intimate partners, by family members, by acquaintances, and by strangers. It is perpetrated in conflict and post-conflict zones, during humanitarian crises and non-conflict, more stable contexts. In all these different contexts, one commonality is that sexual violence and rape is an abuse of power, and often intended to harm and control its subject. Gender inequality is the root of power imbalances that create contexts conducive to the perpetration of rape and sexual violence, often also with impunity. Comprehending rape and sexual violence as an abuse of power in gender-unequal regimes is important for understanding its health impacts, impacts that simultaneously hold psychological and physiological complexity, and for designing health services to respond. It is therefore important to remain mindful of this complexity and likely co-occurrence of multiple health impacts, and the implications this has for service provision, as interventions and programmes of care will need to be flexible to adapt to individual experiences and harms suffered (Wall and Quadara, 2014).

Establishing best practices in non-disaster zones and in humanitarian emergencies

The WHO report on violence and sexual health (Jewkes et al, 2002) detailed health interventions for victims of rape under the terms: 'psychological care and support', 'medico-legal services', 'prophylaxis for HIV infection', and 'comprehensive care centres' and 'training for health professionals'. Since this first report, and in response to the growing body of research, a number of systematic research reviews (Wang and Rowley, 2007; SVRI, 2011; Regehr et al, 2013; WHO, 2013b), policy guidelines and practice standards have been produced. The WHO emphasises the importance of randomised controlled trials or quasi-experimental designs through which comparisons for *effectiveness* of an intervention can be made against a non-intervention control group (WHO and LSHTM, 2010; WHO, 2014a). However, confidently associating intervention and outcome is often fraught with difficulty in real-world complex social systems, such as health sector responses for assisting victim-survivors, and preventing rape and sexual violence in different contexts, a field which, as well as complex, is still under-researched. Nevertheless, there have been many effective systems responding to violence against women, developed locally in low, middle and high income countries (Kelly et al, 2006), around which a body of expert practice knowledge and research is growing. In these diverse contexts, with varied sources of underpinning knowledge, evidence-informed policy-making requires the synthesis of both scientific knowledge and expert judgement.

Evidence-informed best practice standards for health sector-led interventions for rape and sexual violence in different contexts were developed for this chapter through a synthesis of information (systematic reviews, evaluation studies, expert recommendations and policy documents) found through a search of international data repositories.

Non-disaster zones

Health sector-led rape and sexual violence services have been developing for over 30 years, and have developed globally in non-disaster zones in largely similar ways, differing only in the operational formation of standalone units versus mobile on-call teams.

SARCs commonly operate in the UK, the US, Canada and Australia as standalone units providing on-site crisis intervention, forensic examinations, immediate medical care, follow-up tests and short-term counselling (Lovett et al, 2004). These units are often close to or located within hospital buildings. In England, SARCs can be accessed by contacting a police service, presenting at an emergency department, contacting a victim helpline, or by self-referral. On-call SARTs operate in North America and Australia, and provide a similar service to SARCs, but are activated through victim-survivor contact with a police service or emergency department, and may have designated units or provide mobile services. Similarly, SARCs may also provide outreach services to victim-survivors who are medically unfit to attend the centre.

In recognition, on the one hand, that in non-disaster zones, health-led services for victim-survivors of rape and sexual violence can be offered in a broader and more sustainable way and, on the other hand, that victim-survivors may present and disclose during a consultation at other health services, it is recommended that all health services have a service-relevant policy and protocol to respond to such disclosures, and refer victim-survivors to specialist services as required (WHO, 2003; 2013a). An example of such a non-specialist sexual violence and rape health service policy is the UK national guidelines for genitourinary medicine/sexual health clinics on the management of adult and adolescent complainants of sexual assault (Cybulska et al, 2012). Furthermore, given the high incidence and prevalence of victim-survivors of sexual violence in health populations, it is recommended that first-line support for sexual violence is integrated into the pre-qualification education and training curricula for all healthcare providers, although this is especially important for nurses, midwives and doctors (WHO, 2013a). In the US, addressing the marginalisation of violence and abuse in health professionals' education has been mobilised by the Academy on Violence and Abuse (AVA, 2011), which has produced core competencies for health systems, higher education institutions and practitioners.

Humanitarian emergencies

The term 'humanitarian emergency' is used here to encompass the range of types of 'disasters' globally associated with natural hazards, man-made hazards, or complex political emergencies (including armed conflict). 'Disaster' is defined as 'a serious disruption of the functioning of a community or a society causing widespread human, material, economic or environmental losses which exceed the ability of the affected community or society to cope using its own resources' (UNISDR, 2009, p 9; WHO, 2013c). The terms 'disaster', 'emergency', 'crisis' and 'humanitarian emergency' are used interchangeably in this chapter.

Health services for survivors of rape and sexual violence are essential and crucial in disaster zones (WHO, 2004b, 2005b, 2007a; IASC, 2005; IAWG, 2010; The Sphere Project, 2011); they are a 'human rights and public health imperative' (SVRI, 2013, p 1), in which the protection and safety of women must be central. This chapter addresses health services for victim-survivors of rape and sexual violence in disaster contexts, whether associated with natural or man-made hazards, or complex political (armed conflict) emergencies. This work is principally concerned with best practice for women-survivors of rape and sexual violence, and as such does not include specific consideration of child and adolescent rape services. However, humanitarian actors should be familiar with local legislation in relation to the age of consent, who can give legal consent for clinical care of minors, and requirements and procedures for safeguarding children and young people.

Disaster situations pose new and increased threats to women. Sexual violence in the midst of disasters arising from natural hazards has been reported worldwide in Australia, the Philippines and Central and North America (IASC, 2005). Levels of gender-based violence against women increase as women are displaced, separated from rape and sexual violence preventative social systems, and where perpetrator distancing becomes less possible (WHO, 2005b). In Klein's (2006) review of rape and sexual violence during Hurricane Katrina in the US, women reported being raped while waiting for emergency rescue in life-threatening situations, and while seeking refuge in official evacuation shelters and non-official shelters. Incidents of sexual violence and rape continued as women tried to rebuild their lives in new environments. An online survey identified more than 100 reports of sexual violence made to agencies in the aftermath of Hurricane Katrina – 95 per cent were disaster victims, and 93 per cent were women (Klein, 2006). In the aftermath of Hurricanes Katrina and Rita, a study of sexual assaults found that nearly a third (31 per cent) of sexual assaults were perpetrated at an evacuation site or other shelter (NSVRC, 2006). Displaced women in refugee camps have also reported sexual violence (WHO, 2005b), and in official disaster shelters women are often unprotected.

In complex emergencies, the risk of rape and sexual violence against women is significantly heightened, and sexual violence is perpetrated as a weapon of war (IASC, 2005). The Inter-Agency Standing Committee (IASC) Task Force on Gender and Humanitarian Assistance (2005) document the extent of reported rape and sexual violence experienced by women in the conflict zones of Sierra Leone, Rwanda and Bosnia and Herzegovina, and, as reported by Human Rights Watch (Kippenberg et al, 2009), in the Democratic Republic of Congo. In the chaos of disasters, perpetration of sexual violence and rape against women increases and sexual violence services, if they existed, are often disrupted (IASC, 2005). Social structures are often destabilised and weakened (Spangaro et al, 2013).

Jewkes et al (2014) clearly convey the fragility of state institutions experienced while undertaking sexual violence research in post-conflict contexts and which have an impact on women's safety, service providers and women's access to services. In conflict/post-conflict zones, incidence increases of rape and sexual violence are exploitatively opportunistic, for example, as women are displaced or subjected to abuse by peacekeepers (Spangaro et al, 2013). The scale of conflict-related displacement is huge – the International Rescue Committee (IRC) (2014) reported that by the end of 2013, in Syria alone, more than 2.3 million people had sought refuge in neighbouring countries (Lebanon, Jordan, Turkey and Iraq), and 7 million people were internally displaced.

In conflict zones and humanitarian crises, men and boys are also at an increased risk of sexual violence and rape (Spangaro et al, 2013). In war, rape and sexual violence against men are understood as strategies of emasculation, feminisation, homosexualisation and stigmatisation, and, as also for women, are often combined with genital and anal mutilations (Russell et al, 2011). Rape and sexual violence against women and men constitutes a violent performance of hegemonic, heteronormative masculinity that mobilises subordination and gendered inequality. In this context, men may find disclosure difficult, and healthcare workers will need to be alert to ask about sexual violence in sensitive and non-shaming ways. The person-centred principles of sexual violence and rape healthcare for men are largely similar to those for women.

Minimum standards for primary health services for victim-survivors of rape and sexual violence in disaster zones can be extracted from a review of international policy documents (WHO, 2004b, 2005b, 2007, 2013a; IASC, 2005; IAWG, 2010; The Sphere Project, 2011). Minimum standards, although by no means considered best practice, nonetheless provide key information for service commissioners, leverage for service providers to secure resources from government, and a consistent, minimum set of service provision for service users (Kelly and Dubois, 2008). These minimum standards extracted from international policy documents, together with practice recommendations from the synthesis of literature, have been differentiated into the following six domains of best practice for rape and sexual violence healthcare: capable and care conducive environment; health and medical care; forensic examination and evidence collection; community and social support; specialist referral and follow-up care; and quality and monitoring.

Capable and care conducive environment

The domain 'capable and care conducive environment' is about creating the environment for women to be able to knowingly and safely access integrated and competent health services for care after rape and sexual violence that will make a positive difference to their health and wellbeing. A service environment that is women-centred is critical for sexual violence health services. The WHO (2013a) attributes 'women-centred care' as care that is private and confidential, asks about violence (but does not pressure), listens, validates what the person is saying, responds (but does not intrude on the person's autonomy), offers comfort and help to reduce anxiety, enables access to information, offers practical options, aids mobilisation of support systems, and is non-judgmental. Healthcare providers of frontline care to victim-survivors of sexual violence and rape should receive training in how to ask about and respond to sexual violence, relevant local laws and services, and how to challenge sociocultural victim-blaming practices (WHO, 2013a). It is of central importance that the care people receive is by informed choice (Lovett et al, 2004; NHS England, 2013), and that risks of harm and the options available are accurately represented and explored (WHO, 2013a).

Situations of humanitarian emergencies

In some regions, health services designated as specifically for rape and sexual violence may be stigmatising for women (Wang and Rowley, 2007), and may pose risks of further violence for victim-survivors accessing services, communities hosting services and service providers (WHO, 2007). In light of the incidence of rape and sexual violence against women in disaster zones, potential displacement of women and disruption of travel, health services for rape and sexual violence should be available at all primary health facilities, and accessible to women in the immediate and acute phases of natural hazard and complex emergencies, and included in emergency planning for humanitarian responses to disasters (The Sphere Project, 2011).

It is widely accepted that multisectoral programmes are 'best practice' for gender-based violence services in disaster settings; multisectoral models entail mutually collaborative relationships with an affected community, and are interdisciplinary and interorganisational, bringing together health, legal, psychological and security services (IAWG, 2010; The Sphere Project, 2011). Emergency planning should take account of the configuration of sexual violence health services in the event of disasters (IASC, 2005) in collaboration with local and Indigenous populations (Peate and Mullins, 2008). However, it is likely that in some territories, emergency planning may be absent, or the event may be unforeseen. In the immediate first response in these situations, it is likely that no services will be available, and first-response relief teams will need to work with local women and women leaders to establish the extent of functioning services, and work to restore and/or create sexual violence services (IASC, 2005; The Sphere Project, 2011), for which building relationships and fostering trust and goodwill with affected communities is critical (Jewkes et al, 2014).

Wall and Stathopoulos (2012) nuance the impact of culture for the way that services are best configured in diverse contexts, and clearly evidence the importance of culturally sensitive, innovative and flexible service models. People from affected communities may have had many roles (victim, aggressor, combatant, refugee, detainee or service provider) during times of conflict and post-conflict (Jewkes et al, 2014), which adds layers of complexity in social relations, and for systems responding to and preventing rape and sexual violence.

Basic care and support must be in place before any activities are instigated that may lead to individuals disclosing rape (WHO, 2007; WHO, 2013a). As a minimum response in the midst of emergencies, specific psychological and social considerations should be included in the provision of general primary healthcare (IASC, 2007). Health service staff being prepared for disaster and emergency work should be trained in cultural and linguistic competency and culturally appropriate clinical care for survivors of gender-based violence (IASC, 2007). An example of cultural competency training is the online learning programme for first responders in disaster situations delivered through the US Department of Health and Human Services, Office of Minority Health (no date).

The IASC Global Health Cluster (GHC) (2010) advocates removing user fees and assessing accessibility for primary healthcare services during humanitarian crises. This proposal is based on the humanitarian principle that intervention in crises should be 'based on needs alone' and 'accessible without discrimination'. The removal of user fees is intended to ensure that the poorest and most vulnerable disaster-affected populations are not further disadvantaged or financially prevented from accessing health services. The IASC GHC (2010) recognises that, in parallel with possible increased demand for health services during humanitarian emergencies, any removal of existing fees will impose an additional financial burden on services; consequently, the implications of and solutions to such a move should be considered in emergency plans.

Services for victims of rape in non-disaster zones

SARCs are provided in healthcare settings in addition to rape crisis centres outside of healthcare settings that address historic abuse, discussed earlier in Chapter 2. They may be compared with attempts to care for survivors outside either of these specialised settings. In the first UK evaluation of SARCs, Lovett et al (2004) found that, in comparison with the provision of care to survivors of rape in non-specialised sites, SARCs' more integrated services provided more consistent services; more effectively balanced the needs of the victim-survivor with the needs of the legal system; increased access to health services for victim-survivors of rape who did not wish to report to the police; provided greater access to female medical examiners; facilitated greater victim-survivor control of the examination; encouraged take-up of support services; had more embedded referral systems to a greater range of supports; provided case-tracking services to support victim-survivors through the criminal justice system; and provided procedural justice. In response to victim-survivor service user evaluations, Lovett et al (2004) concluded that SARCs should develop advocacy services and more flexible and practical support. For minimum standards for violence against women advocacy services, see Kelly and Dubois (2008).

SARTs are found in the US. They are on-call teams comprising a police officer, a victim advocate, a SANE or SAME, and a prosecutor. Victim-survivors of rape can mobilise a SART by contacting a police service, presenting at an emergency department, or calling the victim helpline. Experiences of victim-survivors are overall positive (for SANEs, see Fehler-Cabral et al, 2011; for victim advocacy services, see Campbell, 2006). However, victim-survivors presenting at an emergency department for healthcare often did not have life- or limb-threatening physical injuries, and reported long waits to be seen after being triaged as 'non-urgent' (Wang and Rowley, 2007). While victim-survivors who accessed a SANE service valued being given thorough explanations, being able to make choices during their examination, and receiving compassionate care, some had negative experiences, such as not having enough explanation or choice, or their examiner being cold and distant (Fehler-Cabral et al, 2011). Specialist training is important – in a recent systematic review, victim-survivors accessing a SANE service were significantly more likely to receive pregnancy prophylaxis and non-HIV sexually transmitted infection prophylaxis than those accessing a non-SANE health professional (Toon and Gurusamy, 2014).

Even though victim-survivor rather than legal system-centred, both SARCs (Lovett et al, 2004) and SARTs (Campbell et al, 2008) also improve outcomes for victim-survivors of rape and sexual violence proceeding through the criminal justice system. A disadvantage of standalone SARCs is the potential marginalisation of victim-survivors who do not associate their experience of rape and sexual violence with SARC services, or who may be concerned about social stigma associated with rape and sexual violence. Conversely, mobile SARTs, with a geographically spread service network, may be difficult for victim-survivors to navigate.

Kelly et al (2006) identify ethical principles for services for gender-based violence against women that reflect the human rights principles of dignity and bodily integrity, and provide a welcoming environment and a climate of belief and validation. Services should offer privacy and confidentiality, while openly acknowledging the limits of confidentiality, and communication and information should be delivered at the victim-survivor's pace (Kelly et al, 2006; WHO, 2013a). Care should also include checking for risks to current safety, contacting a friend or family member if desired, providing information about the options available, and practical and emotional support (Kelly et al, 2006; WHO, 2013a).

Minimum standards for SARCs have been extracted from a number of reports, and on comparison, they are largely consistent. One difference found, however, was the recommendation for the sex of the examiner – some advocated that the examiner should be female 'wherever possible' (WHO, 2003; DH, 2009), while others advocated that examiners should be female 'unless the service user specifies otherwise' (Kelly and Dubois, 2008, p 51). A study of examiner gender preference by Chowdhury-Hawkins et al (2008) found that most victim-survivors of rape voiced a preference for a female examiner, and perhaps more significantly, that nearly 50 per cent of the women respondents indicated that they would not have proceeded with an examination if they had no choice but to see a male examiner. Templeton et al (2010) contest Chowdhury-Hawkins et al's (2008) assertion that most victim-survivors prefer a female examiner, on the grounds that no respondents had been examined by a male examiner. Based on the current best evidence, examiners for women victim-survivors should be female, unless otherwise requested by the victim-survivor.

In their model framework for mandated NAPs, UN Women (2012a) recommend that healthcare systems be supported to provide integrated multisectoral services, to identify victim-survivors of gender-based violence against women, and to provide services without charge. Lovett et al (2004) propose that health-led integrated rape and sexual violence services should be funded by statutory services. In their sexual assault services commissioning guidance, NHS England (2013) describes an integrated, person-centred model for sexual violence and rape services as one that can:

> ... integrate care pathways in a seamless way for victims, so they tell their story once and can choose care journeys to access crisis support, assessment, specialist clinical interventions, options for forensic medical examination, support, counselling and where needed mental health and other physical health services such as gynaecology. SAS [Sexual Assault Services] enables co-ordination with wider health and care, third sector specialist sexual violence support and criminal justice processes, to improve health and well-being, as well as justice outcomes. Robust partnership working is therefore vital for the care and criminal justice outcomes that service users and victims want. (NHS England, 2013, pp 5-6)

This model articulates the importance of a mutually collaborative and coordinated approach across and within sectors. For the health sector this means clear mutual referral pathways, in terms of integrated first-line responses, immediate and continuing care, and across specialist third, social and criminal justice sectors. Diverse local contexts mean that there is not one best model for health sector sexual violence services. However, health-led specialist, 'one-stop shop' sexual violence services are key for their level of expertise and contribution to advancing knowledge and research in the field to improve health and wellbeing (and criminal justice) outcomes. Often covering a relatively large geographic area, regional health-led specialist sexual violence services may also offer formal and informal support to dispersed mainstream health services that are first-line access points and/ or providers of immediate and longer-term care. Configured in this way, fluid hub (specialist lead centres) and spoke (supported mainstream health services) sexual violence service models emerge, which mutually adapt in response to and are driven by dynamic local geographic and sociocultural contexts.

Mobile technologies are transforming sexual violence reporting and responding practices (Radford, 2014). With mobile phone reach averaging 79 per cent in low to middle income countries, and 87 per cent in high income countries (ITU, 2011), mobile health technologies (mHealth) are rapidly transforming health service delivery globally, emerging dynamically in response to local contexts (WHO, 2011a). Free smartphone apps with geo-location technologies to report sexual violence and/or to access information about local sexual violence services, including opening times and directions, have proven successful in Brazil, Haiti and India (Radford, 2014). UN Women and Microsoft have collaborated on the Safe Cities Global Mapping Project that explores women and girls' experience of mobile phone access and use in prevention, recording and responses to sexual violence in public spaces (UN Women, 2014). Mobile technologies and social media are likely to play an increasing role in women's access to rape and sexual violence health services, and it is therefore important that mHealth and eHealth systems, such as smartphone apps, are responsive to any reconfigurations of sexual violence services or systems for reporting sexual violence.

Best practice health-led sexual violence services are 'one-stop shop' units housed in health facilities providing health interventions, forensic evidence collection, advocacy and counselling (WHO, 2003, 2013a; Kelly et al, 2006), and support to dispersed mainstream service providers accessed by people who have been subjected to sexual violence. Gender-sensitive sexual assault services should be available at a regional level at all times (WHO, 2013a). For the purposes of this book, the term 'SARC' is used to denote this best practice concept of a one-stop, health-led rape and sexual violence service, but which may be known by other terms in other regions of the world. From the review of literature, hospital-based, one-stop shop SARCs have been identified as the most effective for improving outcomes for victim-survivors.

The best practices for rape and sexual violence healthcare in disaster zones form the core practice standards for services in non-disaster zones. The best practice standards for health-led rape and sexual violence services in non-disaster zones that follow on are additional to the best practice standards for disaster zones; together they form the best practice standards for health-led rape and sexual violence services.

Best practice standards of capable and care conducive environments

The service is delivered with respect to the core principles of The Sphere Project's (2011) *Humanitarian charter*, and is woman-centred; established and developed through a multisectoral approach that strengthens established services in collaboration with local populations rather than developing new ones where possible; provides and distributes information (once the service is established) for women and communities about the service and why, when and where to access it via multimedia platforms and mobile technologies; is accessible and available at a healthcare facility that is safe for women to access, to travel to and free from user fees; has sufficient supplies and equipment; is delivered by workers skilled and trained in how to ask about and respond to sexual violence, local laws and services, cultural competence and culturally appropriate care for survivors of sexual violence and rape; has male and female service providers (or chaperones, if not possible) fluent in local languages; offers a private consultation area, is confidential and ensures victim survivors' safety and dignity; and has lockable, secure files for records.

In humanitarian emergencies, treatment and interventions can be started without a medical examination if the victim-survivor chooses. Service providers should communicate supportively at the victim-survivor's pace, listen actively, and provide accurate information and compassionate, non-judgmental care. Providers are able to give PFA (IASC, 2007) to victim-survivors of rape and sexual violence as part of their usual care. ('Psychological first aid', or PFA, is explained in the following mental health best practice standards.)

Additional best practice standards possible in non-disaster zones include that all health services (that is, services that are not specifically for rape and sexual violence) should have a service-relevant policy and protocol to respond to disclosures of rape and sexual violence and refer victim-survivors to specialist services as required. Services for rape and sexual violence should be health-led, multisectoral, 'one-stop shop' units, housed in health facilities with a separate entrance, and offering/providing health interventions, forensic evidence collection, advocacy and counselling. Referral pathways should avoid emergency departments unless fast-track mechanisms for victim-survivors of rape and sexual violence are in place. A skilled crisis support worker should greet the victim-survivor on arrival, and stay with her, at least until the forensic examiner arrives. Medical/forensic examiners should be female, unless the victim-survivor specifies otherwise. Education and training on first-line support for sexual violence and rape should be integrated into pre-qualification curricula across all healthcare professions.

Health and medical care

Health and medical care is concerned with attending to victim-survivors' immediate health needs, assessment of harm and risks, and planning for longer-term care. Some regions require healthcare practitioners to report cases of sexual violence to legal authorities. Such a legal framework, as seen in a study of health sector responses in Central America (McNaughton Reyes et al, 2012), will limit reporting and work to deny women access to healthcare for the risks and harms from sexual violence. Women should normally be able to disclose sexual violence to healthcare providers without fear of breach of confidentiality, unless there is wider public safety risk of serious harm.

After immediate physical stabilisation, reproductive and sexual healthcare is a cornerstone of post-rape health-sector led intervention. A review by the Sexual Violence Research Initiative (SVRI, 2013) reported that while prophylaxis for sexually transmitted diseases such as HIV is often initiated, emergency contraception was less often provided. Emergency contraception is available in most countries, yet women's access is often blocked by (i) lack of on-site availability, (ii) lack of referral systems, or (iii) 'conscientious objection' by healthcare providers and/or depending on sociocultural context. Access to emergency contraception following rape is a 'human rights imperative', and lack of access may result in subsequent unsafe abortions (SVRI, 2013). Similarly, in countries where women's reproductive rights are constrained by anti-abortion moral norms, women's access to legal abortion post-rape may be blocked by moral policing by health practitioners of women's claims of rape, and limited service provision (Diniz et al, 2014).

Situations of humanitarian emergencies

There are a number of resources with information about necessary supplies for emergency health services. A supplies checklist for medical and forensic examination minimum standards of care can be found in IASC's *Guidelines for gender-based violence interventions in humanitarian settings* (2005, p 68). The Inter-Agency Working Group (IAWG) on reproductive health field manual (2010), and WHO's (2013a) clinical and policy guidelines for responding to sexual violence against women, provide information on regimens for emergency contraception, sexually transmitted infection treatment, HIV post-exposure prophylaxis and Hepatitis B vaccination. The IAWG-designed 'interagency reproductive health (RH) kit block 1' contains the medical supplies necessary for a minimum initial service package (MISP) delivery of clinical care to survivors of rape and sexual violence. The RH kit complements the *Interagency emergency health kit* (WHO, 2011b). These kits collectively have the supplies needed to implement MISP, and are designed to supply community and primary healthcare for a population of 10,000 for three months.

Victim-survivors of rape may often need mental health interventions. Standalone mental health services for rape survivors can create fragmented systems, whereas integrated systems are likely to be accessed by more people, be more sustainable, and less stigmatising (IASC, 2007). The IASC (2007), in its guidelines for minimum mental health and psychosocial support systems (MHPSS), recommends that mental health services in emergency settings be integrated into wider systems of general health services and community support networks.

For the IASC (2007), MHPSS are overlapping, layered tiers of support. At the first level are basic services and security for mental and physical wellbeing. In the second tier people find support from family and community and social networks. The third tier provides focused but non-specialised support services facilitated by trained responders, for example, PFA and basic mental healthcare by primary healthcare workers. PFA, rather than being a specific psychiatric intervention, is 'a humane, supportive response to a fellow human being who is suffering' (IASC, 2007, p 119). Many of the components of PFA practice

(IASC, 2007, pp 119-20) are contained within the capable and conducive care context domain. In addition to those listed there, PFA expressly includes protection from further harm, the right to refuse to discuss events, respect of the wish not to talk, identifying basic practical needs and ensuring these are met, asks about people's concerns and tries to address these. PFA discourages negative and health-risk ways of coping, encourages participation in normal daily routines and positive coping methods, encourages (but does not force) company from family or friends, offers the possibility of return for further support, and referral to local appropriate and available support. It is also recommended that, if it is safe to do so, written information about stress responses and coping strategies should be provided (WHO, 2013a). The final, fourth tier of mental health support systems comprises specialised services for people who are experiencing difficulty in day-to-day functioning; if such specialised services do not exist, primary healthcare practitioners should receive further training for the longer-term support of this population.

Some physical and mental health outcomes from sexual violence or rape are more easily directly attributed to an assault than others. For longer-term health sequelae, the association is indirect and more complex, related to long-term stress responses and coping strategies (Campbell, 2002). Distinctiveness and causality of longer-term health risks for victims of sexual violence and rape in isolation is unclear, and much research on the health consequences of gender-based sexual violence is focused on or combined with sexual violence in intimate partner violence, and appropriately so, as much sexual violence and rape takes place within intimate relationships. In a national, cross-sectional study of reported health outcomes and exposure to violence, Black et al (2011) found statistically significant ($p<0.001$) higher prevalence of adverse physical and mental health outcomes for nine out of the ten measured health outcomes in women with a history of rape, stalking or physical violence by an intimate partner in comparison with women with no reported exposure to these forms of gender-based violence. The health outcomes measured in Black et al's (2011) study were: asthma, irritable bowel syndrome, diabetes, high blood pressure, frequent headaches, chronic pain, difficulty sleeping, activity limitations, poor physical health and poor mental health; the only measured outcome with non-significant difference was high blood pressure.

Therefore, it is likely that early intervention to address both physical and psychological consequences from rape and sexual violence can limit, if not prevent, both immediate and longer-term adverse mental and physical health sequelae associated with rape and sexual violence.

Services for victims of rape in non-disaster zones

As in humanitarian contexts, healthcare, crisis intervention and advocacy should be available at the initial consultation, irrespective of the victim-survivor's decision to pursue legal recourse (Lovett et al, 2004; UN Women, 2012a). A nurse-led integrated health service for rape healthcare, which was developed in an existing health service in a rural South African community, resulted in significantly increased rates of post-exposure prophylaxis and completion of treatment, and a reduced time gap between assault and treatment (Kim et al, 2007a). The literature indicates that nurses or medical practitioners with appropriate training can provide sexual violence health (and forensic) services.

Most of the immediate mental health interventions for rape and sexual violence services are included in the core best practice interventions. In addition to these, service providers should provide mental healthcare by helping victim-survivors to understand their reactions as normal, explaining what to expect, giving information so that they can take control and make informed choices, assessing suicidality and responding as needed, and addressing victim-survivor self-blame or guilt (SVRI, 2011).

Emotional support and counselling are more often readily available to victim-survivors of rape and sexual violence through the networks of services globally modelled on rape crisis centres, SARCs and SARTs.

Many mental health therapies have been used to address the mental health sequelae following rape (Wang and Rowley, 2007). For victim-survivors whose mental health symptoms endure, a diagnosis can sometimes help to validate and/or make sense of experiences (SVRI, 2011). Although still limited, the current evidence base indicates that cognitive behavioural therapies (CBT) are effective in reducing symptoms of PTSD, depression and anxiety for victim-survivors of rape and/or sexual violence (Regehr et al, 2013; WHO, 2013a). Debriefing is no longer recommended; rather, victim-survivors control what and when they disclose to whom (SVRI, 2011; WHO 2013a).

Mental health symptoms arising from rape or sexual violence resolve for approximately half of victim-survivors within three months, and the WHO (2013a) recommends 'watchful waiting' during this period, which 'involves explaining to the woman that she is likely to improve over time' while offering regular follow-up appointments and support (WHO, 2013a, p 32). Rape crisis centres, and an increasing number of SARCs, are able to provide emotional support and further counselling programmes to support victim-survivors with longer-term needs for an indeterminate period of time. However, victim-survivors who experience incapacitating, enduring and/or severe mental health consequences may require referral to specialist mental health services for assessment of mental health and arrangement of additional models of psychotherapy, such as CBT by a healthcare provider that has a good understanding of sexual violence (WHO, 2013a) (see WHO, 2013a, for specific guidance for immediate, up to three months, and post-three months psychological/mental health intervention).

There are mixed reports from service users with enduring and/or severe mental health problems about their experiences of mental health services for victim-survivors of rape and sexual violence. While there are some reports of good local practices, women repeatedly express dissatisfaction with statutory mental health services. In the UK, commonly reported insensitivities include minimising or not believing women's experiences; practitioner responses that illustrate a lack of comprehension of violence against women; poor access to female practitioners; and a lack of safe, women-only services (WNC, 2010). Women in the Women's National Commission (2010) study also reported too much emphasis on statutory mental health services in a model of care concerned with treating the symptom and pharmaceutical intervention rather than attending to the underlying experiences of abuse and violence.

Holly et al (2012), reporting on the availability of domestic violence support within mental health service provision in England, illustrate that despite national initiatives to address the mental health sequelae of violence against women, the embeddedness of violence against women strategies in mental health organisations, and access to good services for victim-survivors of rape and sexual violence with enduring mental health problems, remains sparse and variable. In their study of mental health services in England, Holly et al (2012) report that only three (7 per cent) of the 42 (75 per cent) mental health trusts responding to a Freedom of Information (FOI) request offered specialist group therapy for victim-survivors of domestic violence, and only 19 (45 per cent) could refer victim-survivors of domestic violence to specialist abuse trauma therapeutic services.

Lack of specialist mental health support services is not unique to England; Hager (2011) reports that women with mental health problems in New Zealand and Australia also have limited access to domestic violence services, and in Canada, where psychological support services are available, waiting lists are long and incur fees (Morris, 2008). Advances have been made in the provision of systematically available and accessible psychological talking therapies free at the point of delivery in some territories, such as those supported by the Improving Access to Psychological Therapies (IAPT) programme in England (DH, 2011, 2012). However, the ways in which these generalist services link with specialist rape and sexual violence services or support victim-survivors of rape and sexual violence is unclear.

Best practice standards of physical health interventions

The service offers/provides treatment and documentation of physical injuries, wound care and tetanus prevention. It offers/provides sexual and reproductive healthcare that includes: emergency contraception and prevention of unwanted pregnancy with unbiased counselling; safe abortion care (where abortion is legal); prevention of diseases; and treatment for sexually transmitted infections including Hepatitis B and post-exposure prophylaxis for HIV. Treatment and interventions can be commenced without medical examination, if the victim-survivor prefers this. The medical history and physical examination are conducted with victim-survivor understanding and consent, and the history should include time since sexual assault and type of assault, health risks (injury, pregnancy, HIV or sexually transmitted infections), and mental health assessment. Pre-printed forms are used to guide the process, with thorough documentation, and 24-hour/seven-days-a-week referral mechanisms in place for care that is beyond the scope of the primary facility.

Best practice standards of mental health interventions

In humanitarian emergencies, service providers are able to give PFA to victim-survivors of rape and sexual violence as part of their usual care. Victim-survivors should have access to immediate and follow-up emotional and psychological support and counselling. Minimum standards for counselling services addressing violence against women have been identified by Kelly and Dubois (2008). Mental healthcare is integrated into the sexual violence and rape health service. Sexual violence and rape health services should have 24-hour/seven-days-a-week referral systems to specialist mental health services beyond the scope of primary healthcare provision of PFA and basic mental healthcare. Training for more complex mental healthcare management should be provided for primary sexual violence healthcare providers if fourth-tier specialised mental health services do not exist.

Additional best practice standards possible in non-disaster zones include that, during the initial consultation, victim-survivors of rape and sexual violence should be assessed for suicidality and responses developed as appropriate. An assessment for PTSD should be included in the initial assessment for victim-survivors with a delayed first access.

Victim-survivors should be supported to understand their responses to their experiences as normal. 'Watchful waiting' is advised for the first three months after an assault, unless the person is incapacitated by symptoms. Victim-survivors who experience incapacitating, enduring and/or severe mental health consequences should be referred to specialist mental health services for assessment and additional models of psychotherapy, such as CBT. Mental health services should have systems in place so that services are provided by female practitioners, if the victim-survivor chooses. Service providers should give information so that victim-survivors can take control and make informed decisions. They should also address victim-survivor expressions of self-blame or guilt.

Mental health services and practitioners should be sensitive to gender and gender-based violence, and offer holistic, comprehensive advocacy services. They should offer women-only specialist group therapies. Those providing psychological therapies should have practitioners sub-specialising in rape and sexual violence. They should have formalised referral pathways to and from rape and sexual violence services, and to specialist violence and abuse trauma therapeutic services. They should have a strategic vision (in addition to policies) for addressing and responding to victim-survivors of rape and sexual violence. They should evaluate thresholds for access and referral pathways to services, so that early intervention in terms of low and/or high intensity interventions and onward referral as appropriate becomes formalised and standard for victim-survivors of rape and sexual violence.

In recognition of the lack of an identifiable comprehensive and formalised system of a nation-wide mental health service provision specifically focused on victim-survivors of rape and sexual violence experiencing enduring mental health problems, an example of a site of mental health service best practice is not provided here. However, there are a number of localised examples of best practice in the UK that are embedded in other statutory and voluntary sectors worthy of note, and which could form part of an integrated system of interconnected primary and secondary mental health services for victim-survivors of rape and sexual violence, and these are listed below:

Specialist mental health independent sexual violence advisor (ISVA) (The Haven, Paddington and Westminster Mind, no date). This specialist mental service at The Haven's SARC in Paddington provides integrated mental health and sexual violence support and advocacy for people with severe and enduring mental health needs who have been victims of sexual violence in the preceding 12 months. This specialist role is the only one of its kind in England. It provides one-to-one emotional support and advocacy, and offers holistic assessment and support for all aspects of people's lives, to support them to navigate and be fully linked with all services.

The PATH (Psychological Advocacy Towards Healing) project. This is a randomised control trial pilot project, in which independent domestic violence advocates are trained to become specialist psychological advocates, and provide weekly psychological advocacy intervention alongside usual advocate intervention for victim-survivors of domestic violence (Brierley et al, 2013).

The Emma Project (nia, no date) provides refuge services for women escaping gender violence who use substances problematically, and who are commonly excluded from other forms of refuge service provision.

Missing Link provides tiered mental health and housing services for women (2015). It has three arms to its services – Missing Link, Next Link and Safe Link. Missing Link provides floating, outreach mental health support and housing services for women, to help those with mental health problems maintain tenancy and develop skills to become independent. Next Link provides domestic violence advocacy services, and Safe Link provides rape and violence services, sexual crisis support and advocacy services. Configured in this way, Missing Link facilitates women's access to a range of integrated and gender-sensitive primary mental health, housing, domestic violence and sexual violence services.

Forensic examination and evidence collection

The main purpose of a medical examination after rape and sexual violence is to identify the healthcare needs of the rape victim-survivor – forensic examination and evidence collection is secondary (WHO, 2004b). However, forensic evidence can be helpful for the prosecution of perpetrators, which may limit the extent to which they act with impunity. Evidence collection, in the form of documentation and investigation, is an important component of justice (FCO, 2014). Although this varies by context (Spangaro et al, 2013), nonetheless, important information about the assault and perpetrator identity can be established by forensic investigation, which, because of its 'epistemic weight', has, in some contexts, sociocultural significance for victim credibility (Quadara et al, 2013). In Brazil (and elsewhere), DNA databases have aided the identification of otherwise unknown perpetrators and serial rapists for criminal investigations (Ferreira et al, 2013).

The options available for forensic examination and evidence collection should be communicated to victim-survivors, and only undertaken with informed consent by a practitioner trained in sexual assault forensic examination (WHO, 2004b; FCO, 2014). Forensic examination and evidence collection involves the accurate documentation of events and injuries on pre-printed forms with pictograms to guide thorough documentation; diagrams, photographs and videos provide valuable supplementary evidence. Evidence collection of materials such as clothes and samples such as hair, blood, saliva or sperm should only be taken if they can be used and processed according to available laboratory and legal requirements; if this is not possible, then samples should not be taken (WHO, 2004b; IASC, 2005). For gathering evidence of sexual violence as an international crime (that is, as a war crime, a crime against humanity, or an act of genocide), the *International protocol on the documentation and investigation of sexual violence in conflict* (FCO, 2014) provides comprehensive guidance for the sensitive and ethical development of non-maleficent evidence collection for recent and historic sexual violence in conflict-affected regions.

Situations of humanitarian emergencies

In the provision of sexual violence and rape services in evacuation shelters, Klein (2006) recommends that each shelter be staffed with a trained sexual assault crisis worker (Kelly and Dubois, 2008, provide information for minimum standards for advice and advocacy services), and a sexual assault forensic examiner with the necessary equipment to conduct a forensic examination. Forensic examinations should only be conducted in a private and safe space. Any materials and samples taken should be collected and stored in appropriate and locked storage pending transport, in accordance with local legal and laboratory protocols (Klein, 2006). In addition to the standards and resources previously identified, a SANE checklist for disaster planning (International Association of Forensic Nurses, 2011) is available from VAWnet.org's (2011) *Special collection: Disaster and emergency preparedness and response.*

Services for victims of rape in non-disaster zones

Forensic evidence collection should include colposcope examination, and SARCs should support continuing professional development of forensic examiners to develop services in accordance with new technologies (Lovett et al, 2004). Lovett et al (2004) advocate that in addition to no-report storage of forensic evidence, victim-survivors should have the option for anonymised samples to be passed on to the police for intelligence purposes. Ferreira et al (2013) illustrate how, in Brazil, DNA intelligence databases have proved important in identifying serial rapists and their subsequent successful prosecution.

Best practice standards for forensic examination and evidence collection

In disaster zones where there are pre-existing forensic examination services, emergency shelters must be prepared to be able to provide sexual violence healthcare services including forensic examination in accordance with local standards and local emergency protocols, and be staffed with a trained sexual assault crisis worker and sexual assault forensic examiner.

Forensic examination should only be undertaken with the full understanding and consent of the victim-survivor in a private and safe space by a trained SANE or SAME. Materials and samples should only be taken if they can be used, stored and processed in accordance with local protocols and legal requirements. The forensic examination and accurate documentation of injuries should be recorded on pre-printed forms with pictograms. The service offers/provides replacement clothing where necessary, and at the victim-survivors' request.

Additional best practice standards possible in non-disaster zones include that sexual forensic examiners should meet national training and practice standards, where these exist. Sexual forensic examiners should be supported to undertake continuing professional development to maintain and develop practice skills. SARC budgets should take account of replacement and new technology procurements. SARC service users should have the option to have a forensic examination with collection and storage of samples without reporting to the police, and have anonymised samples passed on to the police for intelligence purposes.

Community and social support

The IASC (2007) identifies family and community and social networks as the second tier of mental health support systems. Women often experience social stigma associated with rape and sexual violence, and may be ostracised by their family and community (Wang and Rowley, 2007). Community-wide awareness-raising about available rape and sexual violence services and how to access them can aid in reducing stigma that may be associated with rape and sexual violence (Holmes and Bhuvanendra, 2014). In some regions, standalone health services and support groups designated as specifically for sexual violence may be stigmatising for women (IASC, 2007), in addition to potentially increasing the risk of targeted re-victimisation (WHO, 2007). Non-sexual violence-specific women's networks and groups in safe spaces (for example, activity centres and wellness centres) can provide longer-term assistance and emotional and integrative social support for victim-survivors of rape (WHO, 2012b). Poor social networks are associated with greater adverse mental health outcomes (Wang and Rowley, 2007). Access to women-only spaces of group-based therapeutic activities may reduce isolation (WHO, 2012c) and contribute to health and wellbeing. Women who are disadvantaged or detained in residential institutions are less likely to have access to rape and sexual violence services (Kelly et al, 2006).

Non-threatening community programmes that mobilise community-wide awareness of and challenge the underlying cause (gender inequality) of rape and sexual violence, such as the Rethinking Power Programme (Haiti), were found to be successful in changing men's attitudes to normalised gender-based violence against women and reducing perpetration (Holmes and Bhuvanendra, 2014). A systematic review of initiatives to reduce sexual violence in conflict and post-conflict zones in lower and middle income countries found community engagement in service design and delivery to be effective (Spangaro et al, 2013). However, better research is needed to evaluate these programmes (Rowley et al, 2012).

Best practice standards for community and social support intervention

In humanitarian emergencies, health services for victim-survivors of rape and sexual violence should collaborate with existing women's networks and groups to establish existing functioning services, referral mechanisms, safety of access, and offer to host if required. Health services should collaborate with existing local services to host and/or facilitate community-based general, culturally appropriate support activities for women that are staffed by trained sexual violence counsellors and social workers. Health services should be active in community-wide programmes that challenge sociocultural norms and practices of gender-based sexual violence.

Additional best practice standards possible in non-disaster zones include that SARCs, in collaboration with other sector service providers, should develop support groups for underserved populations and women in residential institutions such as prisons, detention centres and mental health hospitals.

Specialist referral and follow-up care

Situations of humanitarian emergencies

Victim-survivors with healthcare needs beyond the scope of the sexual violence healthcare facility should be referred and safely transported to an appropriate facility with the necessary resources to provide care (IAWG, 2010). If a victim-survivor has no safe place to go, the health service should arrange necessary shelter, protection and social service support (IAWG, 2010). Legal support should be provided if requested (The Sphere Project, 2011).

Victim-survivors should receive counselling about ongoing care for any injuries and information regarding how to take prescribed treatments (WHO, 2004b). Follow-up arrangements to provide ongoing physical, mental and sexual and reproductive healthcare should be arranged during the first consultation (WHO, 2004b).

Services for victims of rape in non-disaster zones

Health services responding to sexual violence and rape have developed in multimodal ways in different contexts, and specialist sexual assault services have developed knowledge and expertise and have improved health, social and legal outcomes for women victim-survivors of sexual violence and rape (Lovett et al, 2004; Kim et al, 2007a; Campbell et al, 2008; SVRI, 2011; Ferreira et al, 2013; Holmes and Bhuvanendra, 2014; Toon and Gurusamy, 2014). Specialist one-stop shop services are more likely easier for victim-survivors to navigate, and enable greater access to a range of follow-up service options. Specialist centres, however, often cover large regional areas, which may pose difficulties for those living further away to access ongoing follow-up care. Therefore it is important that health sector sexual violence and rape services are flexible and mutually developed and integrated into existing local health services (Wall and Stathopoulos, 2012; WHO, 2013a), supported by regional specialist centres. Information and support should also be available to victim-survivors outside of office hours, and service users should have access to follow-up counselling, support groups and gender-based violence-sensitive self-defence classes, if requested (Lovett et al, 2004).

Best practice standards for specialist referral and follow-up care

In humanitarian emergencies, formalised 24-hour/seven-days-a-week confidential referral protocols for secondary and tertiary healthcare service referrals for care that is beyond the scope of the facility should be in place. Health services should arrange for protection, shelter and/or social service support if the victim-survivor has no safe place to go. Legal support should be accessible to victim-survivors attending the sexual violence health service. Information for ongoing care and arrangements for follow-up appointments should be clearly communicated during the health consultation.

Additional best practices standards possible in non-disaster zones include that SARCs, in collaboration with other sector service providers, should develop and formalise clear protocols for out-of-office hours support. SARCs, in collaboration with other sector service providers, should develop and formalise clear protocols for follow-up counselling services. Continuing care sexual assault services should be integrated into existing local health services, supported by a specialist SARC. SARCs, in collaboration with other services, should develop referral mechanisms to women-centred and gender-based violence-sensitive self-defence classes.

Quality and monitoring

Situations of humanitarian emergencies

Service providers should have access to clear protocols covering health interventions and referral mechanisms (IAWG, 2010; The Sphere Project, 2011). Information needs for developing a local protocol for rape and sexual violence health services can be found in the WHO's (2004b) *Clinical management of rape survivors*. For the longer term, community recovery phase emergency planners must be mindful that in parallel with social disruption, the increased risk of violence against women may continue for some time after the acute phase, and pre-existing sexual violence services may be disrupted and/or be experiencing demand beyond capacity (IASC, 2005).

Service providers should have access to initial, refresher and further training and supportive supervision to support their practice and service development (IASC, 2007; WHO, 2013a). Once the disaster zone is stabilised, service providers should look to expand rape and sexual violence health services (IASC, 2005). The quality of care provided to victim-survivors of rape should be regularly assessed (IASC, 2005); if standards have not been met, services should explain why this is so, assess the potential harms to the affected population, and where possible, seek solutions to improve the service (The Sphere Project, 2011). However, The Sphere Project (2011) acknowledges the difficulties posed by some emergency zones, and as such recognises that achievement of minimum standards may be outside the control of service providers and humanitarian effort.

The already low reporting of sexual violence and rape is likely to decrease further in disaster contexts, even though the incidence of sexual violence is likely to increase. Reporting sexual violence in emergency zones may pose increased physical, psychological and social risks to a victim-survivor's wellbeing. The WHO (2007) has produced ethical and safety recommendations for monitoring and recording sexual violence in emergencies, which should be taken into account by service providers. Information-gathering should be legitimate, such as for human rights documentation, for needs assessments, or for informing the provision of sexual violence and rape services. If it is safe and ethical to do so, anonymous aggregated data of incidents of rape and sexual violence should be collated to inform prevention and response services (WHO, 2007; The Sphere Project, 2011). Agencies/organisations can obtain support for best practice gender-based violence data management in humanitarian settings from the interagency Gender-Based Violence Information Management System (GBVIMS Global Team, 2013). The IASC (IASC Reference Group for Mental Health and Psychosocial Support in Emergency Settings, 2012) has produced guidance for humanitarian actors to map mental health and psychological support provided using the '4Ws' approach: 'Who is where, when, doing what?'

Services for victims of rape in non-disaster zones

There is a dilemma as to the extent to which services should be specialised. While many NAPs recognise the links between multiple forms of violence against women, specialised services for particular types of violence may obscure the links between them (UN Women, 2012a). Models of specific services for sexual violence have an advantage of providing expert and focused sexual violence services (UN Women, 2012a) yet may, inadvertently, discourage potential victim-survivors of sexual violence within intimate partner relations from accessing sexual violence services. There is added complexity for victim-survivors naming sexual violence and rape in intimate partner relations (Kelly, 1988). Patterson (2009) points out that victim-survivors of rape in intimate partner relations may fall between sexual assault services, where sexual violence is prioritised, and domestic violence services, where non-sexual intimate partner violence is prioritised, and therefore advocates cross-training of service providers. Some SARCs, for example, in Malaysia, Canada and Central America, and SANE projects in North America, are increasing the scope of rape and sexual violence services to incorporate domestic violence services (Lovett et al, 2004), and in the UK, some advocates are dual independent domestic and sexual violence advocates (Cox et al, 2013).

In their review of sexual assault services, Lovett et al (2004) found that black and minority ethnic (BME) women attending sexual violence services were under-represented, and that adolescents and women with non-recent experiences of rape may fall between services. While clearly breaking new ground in advancing health-led sexual violence services, it is likely that some populations (young women, women from minority ethnic groups, women with historic experiences of rape, and women experiencing rape in intimate relations) are marginalised by current SARC/SART configurations.

Monitoring the proportion of women accessing services provided with emergency contraception, prophylaxis treatments, and first-line psychological support have been proposed by the WHO (2013a) as potential evaluation measures of health sector-led sexual violence and rape services. Systems-wide monitoring could involve surveys to establish the proportion of health services that had completed a review of systems (policies, protocols, training, resources and practices) for responding to sexual violence and rape, and the number of health practitioner higher education programmes that had embedded training and education on sexual violence in undergraduate and postgraduate curricula (WHO, 2013a).

Best practice standards for quality and monitoring

In humanitarian emergencies, sexual violence and rape services should provide clear intervention, treatment and referral protocols. Service providers should receive ongoing training and supervision to support the expansion and improvement of the service, including protocols for establishing forensic examination and evidence collection. Service managers should engage in a process of continuous and collaborative multisectoral service improvement. Health services for victim-survivors of rape should undertake regular audits to monitor the attainment of standards and agree a multisectoral developmental action plan. Health services should collate anonymous aggregated data of reported incidents of sexual violence and rape to inform a prevention and service response, if safe and ethical to do so.

Additional best practices standards possible in non-disaster zones include that SARCs should have clear intervention, treatment and referral protocols developed in collaboration with other sectors. They should use social media to communicate information about the service to under-represented communities including why, when and how to access the service. They should be clear about the scope of their services, and have in place clear and formalised referral mechanisms to service providers for other forms of gender-based violence outside of their remit. They should collaborate with other sector service providers to extend and improve services for rape and sexual violence victim-survivors.

Health-led rape and sexual violence services should monitor the demographic of service users, and collaborate with minority women's groups to develop culturally competent and accessible services. They should reflect the interrelation between multiple forms of gender-based violence, monitor the prevalence of intimate partner sexual violence and rape in their caseload, and support cross-training of sexual violence advocates in domestic violence advocacy. They should provide services for victim-survivors of intimate partner sexual violence, and communicate this service to communities and to providers of other forms of gender-based violence services. Victim-survivors of intimate partner sexual violence and rape attending health-led rape and sexual violence services should have access to dual-trained (sexual and domestic violence) advocates. Service users should be able to inform and participate in audit and evaluation strategies. SARCs should anonymously monitor the number of victim-survivors who were offered and/or received emergency contraception, prophylaxis treatments and first-line psychological support. Health services and regional health authorities should undertake a cyclical audit and review of health service-wide systems (policies, protocols, training, resources and practices) for responding to sexual violence and rape. Integration of education and training on first-line support for sexual violence and rape into health professions' undergraduate curricula should be monitored by health professions' regulatory bodies (or another agency, in contexts where these do not exist).

Public health and the prevention of violence

There has been significant development of a public health model of violence prevention, including the prevention of rape (WHO, 2012a, 2014b), as discussed earlier in Chapter 1. This goes beyond the traditional focus of health services to minimise harms from having been subjected to sexual violence or rape, extending to forensic services and primary prevention (Kilonzo et al, 2013; Loots et al, 2011). The enhanced provision of forensic evidence for the criminal justice system by health services contributes to prevention through the deterrent effect of the increased likelihood of successful prosecution. The health sector can contribute to rape prevention by interventions against associated forms of violence, such as child abuse or intimate partner violence (Kilonzo et al, 2013).

The health sector can contribute to prevention by assisting the development of strategy and NAPs, by more adequately recording incidence and prevalence of forms of gender-based violence against women in health data systems, and documenting and communicating its health burden, but this requires investment in gender-based violence data collection and research (García-Moreno et al, 2014b).

There is increasing interest in the contribution of public health programmes to the development of educational and awareness-raising programmes that may change attitudes conducive to rape (WHO, 2013d; DeGue et al, 2014; Holmes and Bhuvanendra, 2014; Walden and Wall, 2014). For sexual assault awareness month in 2014, the US National Sexual Violence Resource Center (NSVRC, 2014) provided a brief that explicated health professionals and health services' role in prevention as raising awareness by displaying information (posters and brochures) about sexual violence and local resources; developing mutually collaborative relationships and referral pathways with local specialist sexual violence services and rape crisis centres; working with others to improve the quality and profile of healthcare following sexual violence and rape; and sponsoring and participating in community awareness and prevention initiatives. (Interventions in culture, media and education are more fully discussed later, in Chapter 5.)

The health sector could facilitate interventions in collaboration and coordination with other sectors (García-Moreno et al, 2014a), even though the complexity of multisectoral prevention strategies poses challenges for measures of effectiveness (Ellsberg et al, 2014). This is because successful violence against women prevention programmes are multisectoral and community-wide, since they need to engage with the wider transformation of gender power imbalances and gender inequality that is central to the prevention of violence against women and girls (Michau et al, 2014).

Conclusion

The health impacts of sexual violence and rape are myriad, and are known to include sexual and reproductive health problems, including unwanted pregnancy, HIV and sexually transmitted diseases; mental health problems and health risk coping strategies; physical injuries and longer-term disability; and social ostracisation. Further research is needed to better explicate the causal relationship between sexual violence and rape, and later onset, long-term conditions.

Health-led services for victim-survivors of rape and sexual violence in humanitarian emergencies are well served by international policy documents. Despite limited research establishing the effectiveness of integrated rape services in disaster contexts, there are many effective health-led rape and sexual violence service initiatives worldwide.

The overarching definition of best practice for services for victim-survivors of rape is a health-led, multisectoral 'one-stop shop' unit, housed in a hospital or primary healthcare facility with a separate entrance, offering and providing health interventions, forensic evidence collection, advocacy and counselling, and which is effectively integrated with mainstream health services. Practice standards for this health-led intervention are differentiated into six domains: capable and care conducive environment; health and medical care; forensic examination and evidence collection; community and social support; specialist referral and follow-up care; and quality and monitoring. These standards are relevant to both non-disaster zones and humanitarian emergencies.

Best practices for victim-survivors of rape in disaster and non-disaster settings are broadly the same – there are few 'non-essential' best practices for rape. This chapter has presented the best practice standards for health-led rape and sexual violence services in disaster and non-disaster zones, and these are collated in Table 3.1 at the end of this chapter.

The best practice standards identified for disaster zones formulate core minimum standards for non-disaster zones. Services for victim-survivors of rape and sexual violence are likely to be disrupted in disaster zones at the same time as sexual violence increases. All health-led rape services, irrespective of location, should work to implement the best practice standards for health-led rape and sexual violence services in disaster zones as a minimum.

Non-disaster zone health-led rape and sexual violence services should facilitate critical service evaluation and develop multisectoral action plans to work towards and develop, refine, monitor and evaluate the best practice standards for non-disaster zones. As a priority, non-disaster zones must integrate health-led sexual violence services into routine emergency preparedness plans.

PFA (IASC, 2007) for mental health and psychosocial support in emergency settings is a succinct yet comprehensive framework to guide all providers of services for people in acute distress after a traumatic event, such as rape and sexual violence. As a non-medical mental health intervention, PFA is a useful concept to guide practice in both disaster and non-disaster zones. PFA training would be advantageous for all service providers in disaster and non-disaster zones who encounter both current and historic victim-survivors of rape and sexual violence in their caseload, and it is recommended that PFA or its equivalent should be incorporated into service provider training in all zones. There is currently a lack of identifiable comprehensive and formalised systems of territory-wide mental health service provision specifically for victim-survivors of rape and sexual violence experiencing severe and/or enduring mental health problems.

The development of nurses' roles to deliver health and medical interventions including forensic examination has been successful in terms of improving access, capacity and service outcomes, and in other areas, nurse-led CBT services have had similar results. In developing services, the potential of nurses to deliver further health interventions and mental health support services should be explored.

Remaining challenges for health services include the better development and resourcing of the mental healthcare of victim-survivors of rape during the medium and long term; ensuring that the needs of victim-survivors of rape from intimate partners are appropriately addressed; the improvement of data collection so as to be able to robustly identify the mental as well as physical health consequences of rape and sexual violence, in a sufficiently quantified form to be analysed in the global burden of disease project (www.who.int/topics/global_burden_of_disease/en/); and effective cooperation with other services and interventions in the building of a comprehensive strategy.

While the primary importance of health services in relation to rape is to assist the healing of the victim-survivor, they can also contribute to the prevention of rape in several ways. By assisting the recovery of the victim-survivor, they can contribute to the prosecution of the rapist and to the ability of the victim-survivor to speak out and educate the public and policy-makers. Prevention initiatives involve mobilising accessible, care-conducive and flexible sexual violence health services integrated with specialist, third, social and criminal justice service sectors; delivering excellence in forensic evidence collection; addressing sexual violence services in emergency plans; and implementing robust quality monitoring, evaluation and development strategies.

Two examples of promising practices in the health field are a health-based centre in a non-conflict zone – the SARC at St Mary's, UK, discussed below – and health-based services in a conflict zone – the IRC, discussed later, in Chapter 6.

Health-based centre in a non-conflict zone: Sexual Assault Referral Centre, St Mary's, UK

The provision of services to support victim-survivors of rape takes different forms and is centred in varied organisational settings. There are challenges common to all service provision, which are addressed in various ways. This example of best practice is a health-based centre. SARCs were initially principally concerned with improving the medico-legal response to rape (Lovett et al, 2004), and as such, the focus was on achieving good practice standards for immediate health interventions and forensic evidence collection (if desired). Today, these core services have expanded to also include sexual and reproductive health interventions (unbiased counselling, emergency contraception, prevention of unwanted pregnancy, abortion support and screening for sexually transmitted diseases), crisis support, mental health examinations, counselling and advocacy.

In the UK, a SARC provides sexual violence and rape services to a geographically defined area; it should be easily and safely accessible, available 24 hours a day, seven days a week. Ideally they should be standalone units in established health service facilities.

St Mary's SARC, in the UK, delivers an integrated, comprehensive service to victim-survivors of rape and sexual violence under one roof; it is centrally located, and has its own private entrance that is security-monitored. It is housed in a bright, refurbished standalone unit within a hospital complex. Victim-survivors have access to a crisis worker and advocate from the time they first access the SARC until the time they 'self-discharge'.

Furthermore, SARCs provide unbiased information and counselling, partner violence screening, risk of harm assessment, risk of homicide assessment, vulnerability assessment, legal support, independent sexual violence advocacy, proactive follow-up, practical advice, social support, counselling, follow-up services, a 24-hour telephone helpline and outreach services that are also provided for situations where it would not be possible or safe for the person to attend the SARC. Research at St Mary's SARC indicates greater completion of post-exposure prophylaxis and follow-up at genitourinary medicine appointments for service users, with proactive support from ISVAs.

The interdisciplinary and multisectoral integrated service of St Mary's SARC is reflected in the centre's steering group, and the embedded collaborative working relationships with local, regional and national NGO, health, legal and social services. An international audience attend St Mary's SARC annual conference. St Mary's, as an internationally recognised site of excellence and innovation, offers a suite of education and training programmes for forensic examiners, the police and counsellors, and the clinical director has written a clinician's guide to forensic practice. St Mary's SARC has supported the development of an integrated health-led rape and sexual violence service worldwide. Staff from St Mary's SARC share and exchange good practices and innovations with specialist sexual violence centres from around the world. Health-led, multisectoral SARCs are transferable (with adequate resources) to other settings.

SARCs are made up of multisectoral, multidisciplinary teams. Configurations of SARC teams may vary, but this best practice site team is comprised of a clinical director, a service manager, sexual violence advocates, crisis workers, counsellors, forensic physician (or nurse) examiners, a consultant paediatrician and police liaison officers. This frontline service team is supported by a public relations (PR) and communications officer, administration officers, a training and development officer and a research officer. The SARC's research officer supports an ongoing programme of research.

The SARC monitors diversity and group representation among service users. In order to widen service access, St Mary's SARC has worked with social care, the police, children's services, the education sector, BME services and the voluntary sector. St Mary's has recently secured funding for a young people's advocate for early intervention and engagement with children at risk of sexual exploitation. St Mary's SARC has a Facebook page and Twitter account that distribute news and events information. Its website has service introductory information available in six languages. The SARC provides services for historic as well as recent rape and sexual violence. In recognition of the intersections of multiple forms of violence, St Mary's now routinely enquires about intimate partner violence. Sexual violence in the domestic setting was also the theme for the 2013 St Mary's SARC annual conference.

SARCs were developed to provide a 'one-stop shop' for victim-survivors of rape and sexual violence. This approach precludes victim-survivors from having to navigate multiple services, and also ensures that all victim-survivors have equitable access to good quality services. SARCs work by providing victim-survivors with access to the full range of specialist and expert providers of medical, health, social and legal services for rape and sexual violence under one roof at the time of first attendance. The goals of SARCs are to limit the physical and mental health consequences of rape and sexual violence; provide a quality forensic service; support victim-survivors through the criminal justice system if they choose to report; and to prevent any form of secondary victimisation.

Above and beyond the core of best practice at St Mary's SARC is the routine availability of service options for service users (what, where and when) for the development of a personalised programme of service interventions. All services are available irrespective of whether the victim-survivor chooses to report to the police or not. St Mary's SARC offers the full range of medical and forensic examination and evidence collection and storage options. Service users can choose whether to have a forensic examination and evidence collection or not, and any forensic evidence can be stored for up to seven years, if desired, anonymously. Furthermore, they can choose to have their anonymous forensic evidence sent to the police for police intelligence purposes. In this way, victim-survivors are in full control of their engagement with the criminal justice system. If a victim-survivor chooses to report to the police, the police interview can also be undertaken at St Mary's, if that is what the victim-survivor chooses. All service users have access to an ISVA service, irrespective of whether the victim-survivor has chosen to report or not. The same scale of option choices applies to St Mary's other service interventions – for example, service users can choose to have follow-up services at the SARC, or can choose to be referred to other service providers of sexual and reproductive healthcare, mental healthcare and counselling.

Service users have access to an interpreter service that has a core of interpreters with experience in sexual violence and rape. In developing interpreter services, St Mary's has also worked with the organisation, Freedom from Torture. All of the services are free to all at the point of delivery, and transport arrangements for services are made under NHS normal operating arrangements.

Outcomes of SARC services are challenging to evaluate, often being a mix of many different interventions and services provided simultaneously to victim-survivors of rape and sexual violence, each with individual experiences and service requirements. St Mary's SARC measures its success on reported service user experience, and on a comprehensive programme of audit and service monitoring from which directions for service improvements and future research are developed, which is in line with best practice benchmarks.

In developing services for rape and sexual violence that reflect the range of service user experiences, SARCs should consider how best to respond to service users who experience sexual violence and/or rape from an intimate partner. This may involve greater integrated working with domestic violence services and/or cross-training in domestic violence advocacy for SARC ISVAs. Cross-training could be in the form of a dual sexual violence/domestic violence advocacy qualification, or in the form of primary and secondary advocacy training based on the practitioner's principal role. SARCs should monitor their service user demographic, and develop strategies to increase under-represented service user groups' access to sexual violence and rape services. In areas where there is low service uptake, regional centres of excellence, with hub and spoke (centre and satellites) service support models, could be used to ensure consistent delivery of and equitable access to quality SARC services. SARCs should have formalised referral pathways to and from mental health services, specialist violence and abuse trauma therapeutic services and general health services.

Table 3.1: Best practice standards for health-led services for victim-survivors of rape and sexual violence in disaster and non-disaster zones

Domain	Best practice standards
Capable and care conducive environment	The service is delivered with respect to the core principles of The Sphere Project (2011) *Humanitarian charter* and is women-centred.
	The service is established and developed through a multisectoral approach that strengthens established services in collaboration with local populations rather than developing new ones, where possible.
	The service provides and distributes information (once the service is established) for women and communities about the service and why, when and where to access it, via multimedia platforms and mobile technologies.
	The service is accessible and available at a healthcare facility that is safe for women to access, to travel to and free from user fees.
	The service offers a private consultation area, is confidential, and ensures victim-survivors' safety and dignity.
	The service is delivered by workers skilled and trained in how to ask about and respond to sexual violence, local laws and services, cultural competence and culturally appropriate care for victim-survivors of sexual violence and rape.
	The service has male and female service providers (or chaperones, if not possible) fluent in local languages.
	Service providers should communicate supportively at the victim-survivor's pace, listen actively, and provide accurate information and compassionate, non-judgmental care and options.
	Service providers are able to give psychological first aid (PFA) to victim-survivors of rape and sexual violence as part of their usual care.
	The service has sufficient supplies and equipment.
	Treatment and interventions can be started without a medical examination if the victim-survivor chooses.
	The service has lockable, secure files for records.

Domain	Best practice standards
Health and medical care	The service offers/provides treatment and documentation of physical injuries, wound care and tetanus prevention.
	24-hour/seven-days-a-week referral mechanisms are in place for care that is beyond the scope of the primary facility.
	The medical history and physical examination are conducted with victim-survivor understanding and consent, and pre-printed forms are used to guide the process and thorough documentation. The history should include: time since sexual assault and type of assault, health risks (injury, pregnancy, HIV and sexually transmitted infections), and mental health assessment.
	The service offers/provides sexual and reproductive healthcare that includes: unbiased counselling, emergency contraception and prevention of unwanted pregnancy, safe abortion care (where abortion is legal) and post-exposure prophylaxis and treatment for sexually transmitted diseases including Hepatitis B and HIV.
	Service providers are able to give PFA to victim-survivors of rape and sexual violence as part of their usual care.
	Mental healthcare is integrated into the sexual violence and rape health service.
	Victim-survivors should have access to immediate and follow-up emotional and psychological support and counselling.
	The service should have 24-hour/seven-days-a-week referral systems to specialist mental health services beyond the scope of primary healthcare provision of PFA and basic mental healthcare.
	Training for more complex mental healthcare management should be provided for primary sexual violence healthcare providers if fourth-tier specialised mental health services do not exist.
Forensic examination/ evidence collection	In disaster zones where there are pre-existing forensic examination services, emergency shelters must be prepared to be able to provide sexual violence healthcare services including forensic examination in accordance with local standards and local emergency protocols, and be staffed with a trained sexual assault crisis worker and sexual assault forensic examiner.
	Forensic examination should only be undertaken with the full understanding and consent of the victim-survivor in a private and safe space by a trained sexual assault nurse examiner (SANE) or sexual assault medical examiner (SAME).
	Materials and samples should only be taken if they can be used, stored and processed in accordance with local protocols and legal requirements.
	The forensic examination and accurate documentation of injuries should be recorded on pre-printed forms with pictograms.
	The service offers/provides replacement clothing where necessary, and at the victim-survivors' request.
Community and social support	Health services for victim-survivors of rape and sexual violence should collaborate with existing women's networks and groups to establish existing functioning services, referral mechanisms, safety of access, and offer to host if required.
	Health services should collaborate with existing local service to host and/or facilitate community-based general, culturally appropriate support activities for women that are staffed by trained sexual violence counsellors and social workers.
	Health services should be active in community-wide programmes that challenge sociocultural norms and practices of gender-based sexual violence.

Domain	Best practice standards
Specialist referral and follow-up care	Formalised 24-hour/seven-days-a-week confidential referral protocols should be in place for secondary and tertiary healthcare service referrals for care that is beyond the scope of the facility.
	Health services should arrange for protection, shelter and/or social service support if the victim-survivor has no safe place to go.
	Legal support should be accessible to victim-survivors attending the sexual violence health service.
	Information for ongoing care and arrangements for follow-up appointments should be clearly communicated during the health consultation.
Quality and monitoring	Sexual violence and rape services should provide clear intervention, treatment and referral protocols.
	Service providers should receive ongoing training and supervision to support the expansion and improvement of the service, including protocols for establishing forensic examination and evidence collection.
	Service managers should engage in a process of continuous and collaborative multisectoral service improvement.
	Health services for victim-survivors of rape should undertake regular audits to monitor the attainment of standards and agree a multisectoral developmental action plan.
	Health services should collate anonymous aggregated data of reported incidents of sexual violence and rape to inform prevention and service response if safe and ethical to do so.
Domain	**Additional best practice**
Capable and care conducive environment	All health services (that is, services that are not specifically for rape and sexual violence health) should have a service-relevant policy and protocol to respond to disclosures of rape and sexual violence, and refer victim-survivors to rape and sexual violence services as required.
	Services for rape and sexual violence should be health-led, multisectoral 'one-stop shop' units, housed in health facilities with a separate entrance and offering/providing health interventions, forensic evidence collection, and advocacy and counselling.
	Referral pathways should avoid emergency departments unless fast-track mechanisms for victim-survivors of rape and sexual violence are in place.
	A skilled crisis support worker should greet the victim-survivor on arrival, and stay with the victim-survivor at least until the forensic examiner arrives.
	Medical/forensic examiners should be female unless the victim-survivor specifies otherwise.
	Education and training on first-line support for sexual violence and rape should be integrated into the pre-qualification curricula across all healthcare professions.

Domain	Best practice standards
Health and medical care	During the initial consultation victim-survivors of rape should be assessed for suicidality and responses developed as appropriate.
	An assessment for PTSD should be included in the initial assessment for victim-survivors with a delayed first access.
	Victim-survivors should be supported to understand their experiences as normal. 'Watchful waiting' is advised for the first three months after an assault, unless the person is incapacitated by symptoms.
	Victim-survivors who experience incapacitating, enduring and/or severe mental health consequences should be referred to specialist mental health services for assessment and additional models of psychotherapy such as cognitive behaviour therapies.
	Mental health services should have systems in place so that services are provided by female practitioners if the victim-survivor chooses.
	Service providers should give information so that victim-survivors can take control and make informed decisions.
	Service providers should address victim-survivor expressions of self-blame or guilt.
	Mental health services and practitioners should be sensitive to gender and gender-based violence and offer holistic, comprehensive advocacy services.
	Mental health services and practitioners should be sensitive to gender, and offer women-only specialist group therapies.
	Mental health services providing psychological therapies should have practitioners sub-specialising in rape and sexual violence.
	Mental health services should have formalised referral pathways to and from rape and sexual violence services.
	Mental health services should have formalised referral pathways to specialist violence and abuse trauma therapeutic services.
	Mental health services should have a strategic vision (in addition to policies) for addressing and responding to victim-survivors of rape and sexual violence.
	Mental health services should evaluate thresholds for access and referral pathways to services so that early intervention in terms of low and/or high intensity interventions and onward referral as appropriate becomes formalised and standard for victim-survivors of rape and sexual violence.
Forensic examination/ evidence collection	Sexual forensic examiners should meet national training and practice standards where these exist.
	Sexual forensic examiners should be supported to undertake continuing professional development to maintain and develop practice skills.
	SARC budgets should take account of replacement and new technology procurements.
	SARC service users should have the option to have a forensic examination with collection and storage of samples without reporting to the police.
	SARC service users should have the option to have a forensic examination with collection and storage of samples without reporting to the police, and have anonymised samples passed on to the police for intelligence purposes.
Community and social support	SARCs, in collaboration with other sector service providers, should develop support groups for underserved populations and women in residential institutions such as prisons, detention centres and mental health hospitals.

Domain	Best practice standards
Specialist referral and follow-up care	SARCs, in collaboration with other sector service providers, should develop and formalise clear protocols for out-of-hours support.
	SARCs, in collaboration with other sector service providers, should develop and formalise clear protocols for follow-up counselling services.
	Continuing care sexual assault services should be integrated into existing local health services, supported by a specialist SARC.
	SARCs, in collaboration with other services, should develop referral mechanisms to women-centred and gender-based violence-sensitive self-defence classes.
Quality and monitoring	SARCS should have clear intervention, treatment and referral protocols developed in collaboration with other sectors.
	Health-led rape and sexual violence services should monitor the demographic of service users and collaborate with minority women's groups to develop culturally competent and accessible services.
	SARCs, in collaboration with other sectors, should develop social media to communicate information about the service to underrepresented communities including why, when and how to access.
	SARCs should be clear about scope of their services, and have in place clear and formalised referral mechanisms to service providers for other forms of gender-based violence outside of their remit.
	Health-led rape and sexual violence services should reflect the interrelation between multiple forms of gender-based violence.
	SARCs should collaborate with other sector service providers to extend and improve services for rape and sexual violence victim-survivors.
	Health-led rape and sexual violence services should monitor the prevalence of intimate partner sexual violence and rape in their caseload.
	Health-led rape and sexual violence services should provide services for victim-survivors of intimate partner sexual violence, and communicate this service to communities and to providers for other forms of gender-based violence service.
	Victim-survivors of intimate partner sexual violence and rape attending health-led rape and sexual violence services should have access to dual-trained (sexual and domestic violence) advocates.
	Health-led rape and sexual violence services should support cross-training of sexual violence advocates in domestic violence advocacy.
	Service users should be integrated in audit and evaluation strategies.
	SARCs should anonymously monitor the number of victim-survivors who were offered/and or received emergency contraception, prophylaxis treatments and first-line psychological support.
	Health services and regional health authorities should undertake cyclical audit and review of health service-wide systems (policies, protocols, training, resources and practices) for responding to sexual violence and rape.
	Integration of education and training on first-line support for sexual violence and rape into health professions' undergraduate curricula should be monitored by health professions' regulatory bodies (or another agency, in contexts where these do not exist).

4

Law and the criminal justice system

Introduction

The criminal justice system should provide justice for victims. It is intended to hold perpetrators to account, reducing impunity, and thereby helping to prevent crimes. There have been important developments and promising practices in law and in the criminal justice system concerning rape and other forms of sexual violence, but challenges remain. Three issues are addressed here: the changing approaches to rape in law; the reform of practices in criminal justice systems; and the new forms of treatment of convicted rapists. The legal and criminal justice practices in conflict zones are further addressed next, in Chapter 5.

The principles underpinning the law on rape have been developing, drawing on concepts of human rights and gender equality, although not uniformly so. The definition of rape in law has been developing, albeit unevenly, removing marital exceptions and moving towards a consent-based definition. The care with which victim-survivors are treated in the criminal justice system has implications for its effectiveness because of its consequences on the attrition of cases through the Criminal Justice processes. There are promising practices within the criminal justice system that treat victim-survivors with more respect and better prevent secondary victimisation, but there is still considerable 'attrition', which means that many cases of rape reported to the police do not lead to a conviction. New forms of treatment of convicted sex offenders, including rapists, are emerging, however, that attempt to reform and rehabilitate them.

The law

Legal principles

Rape is illegal everywhere. It is a crime in its own right, without reference or justification to any other legal principle or standard, in many national and some international legal regimes. In some other legal regimes, rape is declared illegal as a result of its relation to other major legal principles, including a form of violence against women that is a violation of human rights; a form of torture that violates human rights; a war crime and also a crime against humanity; and a form of violence against women that is a form of gender discrimination contrary to the equality between women and men. Rape has also been conceptualised as a violation of bodily integrity and sexual autonomy. Further legal principles that are occasionally used to underpin the illegality of rape, but which are widely regarded as inappropriate and in contradiction to best practice in international principles, include a violation of a woman's honour and a violation of the property of husbands or fathers.

Violence against women as a violation of women's human rights

The UN Universal Declaration of Human Rights underpins the legal principle that rape is a violation of human rights. It states that 'All human beings are born free and equal in dignity and rights', continuing in Article 2 that everyone 'is entitled to the rights and freedoms set forth in [the Declaration], without distinction of any kind', including sex.

In 1993, the UN General Assembly passed Resolution 48/104, declaring that violence against women, including rape, was a violation of human rights and a manifestation of gender inequality:

> Affirming that violence against women constitutes a violation of the rights and fundamental freedoms of women and impairs or nullifies their enjoyment of those rights and freedoms, and concerned about the

long-standing failure to protect and promote those rights and freedoms in the case of violence against women....

Recognising that violence against women is a manifestation of historically unequal power relations between men and women, which have led to domination over and discrimination against women by men and to the prevention of the full advancement of women, and that violence against women is one of the crucial social mechanisms by which women are forced into a subordinate position compared with men....

It went on to define violence against women in Articles 1 and 2:

Article 1: For the purposes of this Declaration, the term "violence against women" means any act of gender-based violence that results in, or is likely to result in, physical, sexual or psychological harm or suffering to women, including threats of such acts, coercion or arbitrary deprivation of liberty, whether occurring in public or in private life.

Article 2: Violence against women shall be understood to encompass, but not be limited to, the following:

a) Physical, sexual and psychological violence occurring in the family, including battering, sexual abuse of female children in the household, dowry-related violence, marital rape, female genital mutilation and other traditional practices harmful to women, non-spousal violence and violence related to exploitation;

b) Physical, sexual and psychological violence occurring within the general community, including rape, sexual abuse, sexual harassment and intimidation at work, in educational institutions and elsewhere, trafficking in women and forced prostitution;

c) Physical, sexual and psychological violence perpetrated or condoned by the State, wherever it occurs.

The UN General Assembly further developed the concept of the responsibility of the state to exercise 'due diligence' to ensure that women's human rights were protected. This provides the basis under which international courts hold states to account, and not only the individual rapist.

The application of human rights law to women victims seeking asylum has been significant, if complex (Crawley, 2001). In the Inter-American system, the 1994 *Convention on the prevention, punishment and eradication of violence against women*, also known as the Convention of Belem do Para, is aimed at the 'prevention, punishment and eradication of violence against women' under the principles of human rights law (Organization of American States, 1994). This treaty defines violence against women as being 'any act or conduct, based on gender, which causes death or physical, sexual or psychological harm or suffering to women, whether in the public or the private sphere.'

The *European Convention on human rights* (European Court of Human Rights, 2010) embedded many but not all of the rights articulated in the UN Declaration, in a legally binding Convention signed and ratified by many states in Europe. It has a specific Court, the European Court of Human Rights, to which complainants may take allegations to ascertain if states have transgressed the Convention. It is core to the work of the Council of Europe.

The 2011 Istanbul Convention is the Council of Europe's *Convention on preventing and combating violence against women and domestic violence*. In terms of scope, it is the most advanced treaty in the world, creating a comprehensive legal framework to prevent violence, to protect victims, and to end the impunity of perpetrators. It defines and criminalises various forms of violence against women (including forced marriage, female genital mutilation, stalking, physical and psychological violence, and sexual violence). It also established an international group of independent experts to monitor its implementation at national level. It came into force on 1 August 2014, but applies only to those member states of the Council of Europe that have ratified it.

Rape as a form of torture that violates human rights

The requirement under European human rights law, based on the European Convention of Human Rights, that states must perform due diligence in protecting women from rape, is articulated in judgments of the European Court of Human Rights, including in the cases of *Aydin v Turkey* (no 23178/94), 25 September 1997; *Maslova & Nalbandov v Russia* (no 839/02); and *Salmanoglu & Polattas v Turkey* (no 15828/03).

In some legal regimes, rape is deemed illegal because it is torture, which is named as illegal in treaties. This has become the practice of the European Court of Human Rights (2010) in implementing the *European Convention on human rights*. While there are no specifically enumerated human rights violations relating to rape in the *European Convention on human rights*, the European Court has developed jurisprudence under the articles relating to torture, inhuman and degrading treatment. Article 3 of the *European Convention on human rights* states:

> Prohibition of torture: No one shall be subjected to torture or to inhuman or degrading treatment or punishment.

The European Court has used Article 3 (prohibition of torture) in supporting complaints of victims of rape against the inaction of their own state in the cases of *Aydin v Turkey* (no 23178/94) in 1997, and that of *Maslova and Nalbandov v Russia* (no 839/02) in 2008; and Article 3 (prohibition of degrading treatment) in the case of *M.C. v Bulgaria* (no 39272/98) in 2003, and that of *I. G. v Republic of Moldova* (no 53519/07) in 2012 (European Court of Human Rights, 2015).

Rape as a war crime

The prohibition of rape under international humanitarian law was recognised in the Lieber Code of 24 April 1863, also known as Instructions for the Government of Armies of the United States in the Field (Article 44). While Article 3 of the Geneva Conventions does not explicitly mention rape or other forms of sexual violence, it prohibits 'violence to life and person' including cruel treatment and torture and 'outrages upon personal dignity' (common Article 3). The Third Geneva Convention provides that prisoners of war are, in all circumstances, entitled to 'respect for their persons and their honour' (Article 14, first para). The prohibition of 'outrages upon personal dignity' is recognised in Additional Protocols I and II as a fundamental guarantee for civilians and persons *hors de combat* (Additional Protocol I, Article 75(2). Article 75 of Additional Protocol I specifies that this prohibition covers in particular 'humiliating and degrading treatment, enforced prostitution and any form of indecent assault', while Article 4 of Additional Protocol II specifically adds 'rape' to this list (Additional Protocol I, Article 75(2)). The Fourth Geneva Convention and Additional Protocol I require protection for women and children against rape, enforced prostitution or any other form of indecent assault (Article 27, second para). Rape, enforced prostitution and any form of indecent assault are war crimes under the Statutes of the International Criminal Tribunal for Rwanda and of the Special Court for Sierra Leone (ICTR Statute, Article 4(e)). The expressions 'outrages upon personal dignity' and 'any form of indecent assault' refer to any form of sexual violence.

The Rome Statute of the International Criminal Court (2011) recognises rape as a crime under international criminal law. Article 7(1)g classifies as crimes against humanity:

> … rape, sexual slavery, enforced prostitution, forced pregnancy, enforced sterilisation, or any other form of sexual violence of comparable gravity … [committed] … as part of a widespread or systematic attack directed against any civilian population.

And Article 8(2)(b)(xxii) classifies these same acts as war crimes.

The UN Security Council has contributed to the establishment of rape as a violation of international human rights law in conflict zones. In addition to the Statutes of the International Criminal Tribunal for the former Yugoslavia (ICTY/R, created by UN Security Council resolutions), it has issued several resolutions condemning acts of rape and sexual violence. In Resolution 1743 on Haiti, the UN Security Council condemned 'the grave violations against children affected by armed violence, as well as the widespread rape and other sexual abuse of girls.' Resolution 1034, concerning Bosnia, expressed the Council's concern over evidence that demonstrated 'a consistent pattern of rape.' Similar condemnations can be seen in Resolution 1493 which refers to 'acts of violence systematically perpetrated against civilians' in the Democratic Republic of Congo, including 'sexual violence against women and girls'; and in Resolution 1539 on children and armed conflict, the Council condemned 'sexual violence mostly committed against girls.'

Sexual violence against women has been recognised as a human rights violation under customary law, treaty law and also in the jurisprudence of international human rights courts. The international criminal tribunals created by the UN to deal with war crimes that have taken place during conflicts since the 1990s have been important new actors in the development of law. Thus, it has become an increasingly prominent topic in international law since the creation of the ICTY in 1993. The creation of the UN international criminal tribunals, in particular the International Criminal Tribunal for Rwanda (ICTR) established in 1994, has reflected and sustained a greater concern with prosecuting individuals for violence against women.

In addition, the UN Office of the High Commissioner for Human Rights (2013) stated that sexual offences committed by armed forces and uniformed men in conflict areas should be brought under ordinary criminal law.

Violence against women as a form of gender discrimination

The UN *Convention for the elimination of discrimination against women* addresses violence against women, including rape, as a form of discrimination against women following Recommendation 19 in 1992 (UN, 1979, 1992). At Article 1 of the Convention states:

> For the purposes of the present Convention, the term "discrimination against women" shall mean any distinction, exclusion or restriction made on the basis of sex which has the effect or purpose of impairing or nullifying the recognition, enjoyment or exercise by women, irrespective of their marital status, on a basis of equality of men and women, of human rights and fundamental freedoms in the political, economic, social, cultural, civil or any other field.

UN General Recommendation 19 states:

> Gender-based violence is a form of discrimination that seriously inhibits women's ability to enjoy rights and freedoms on a basis of equality with men.... (UN, 1992)

The Convention in Article 1 defines discrimination against women. The definition of discrimination includes gender-based violence, that is, violence that is directed against a woman because she is a woman or that affects women disproportionately. It includes acts that inflict physical, mental or sexual harm or suffering, threats of such acts, coercion and other deprivations of liberty. Gender-based violence may breach specific provisions of the Convention, regardless of whether those provisions expressly mention violence.

Gender-based violence, which impairs or nullifies the enjoyment by women of human rights and fundamental freedoms under general international law or under human rights conventions, is discrimination within the meaning of Article 1 of the Convention.

The application of the concept of gender discrimination to violence against women is perhaps under-utilised, but there are examples where this has been developed, such as in the work of MacKinnon (1979) on sexual harassment in employment, and that of Edwards (2008) on jurisprudence in UN human rights treaty bodies.

Violence against women as gender discrimination and a violation of human rights

The Council of Europe's (2011) *Convention on preventing and combating violence against women and domestic violence* treats violence against women as both a form of discrimination against women and a violation of human rights. Article 3a states:

> ... "violence against women" is understood as a violation of human rights and a form of discrimination against women and shall mean acts of gender-based violence that result in, or are likely to result in, physical, sexual, psychological or economic harm or suffering to women, including threats of such acts, coercion or arbitrary deprivation of liberty, whether occurring in public or private life.

The Convention creates a comprehensive legal framework that places a duty on states to prevent violence, to protect victims, and to end the impunity of perpetrators.

It offers a detailed listing of the policies considered necessary to achieve this goal:

• comprehensive and coordinated policies, including financial resources to implement the policies, support for the work of civil society organisations in the field, establishment of national coordinating bodies, and the collection of data and research;
• measures to ensure prevention, including awareness-raising, education, training of professionals, preventive intervention and treatment programmes, participation of the private sector and the media;
• protection and support of victims, including actions in the legal system, provision of information, general support services, assistance in complaints, specialist support services, shelters, telephone lines, support for victims of sexual violence,

protection and support for child witnesses, encouraging reporting, including by professionals;

- the provision of remedies in civil law, compensation, safety in matters of custody of children, addressing the civil consequences of forced marriages;
- ensuring the criminalisation of psychological violence, stalking, physical violence, sexual violence including rape (defined as lack of consent), forced marriage, female genital mutilation, forced abortion and forced sterilisation, sexual harassment, with effective, proportionate and dissuasive sanctions;
- taking measures that ensure the implementation of these laws through investigation, prosecution, procedural law and protective measures, including immediate response by law enforcement agencies, risk assessment and management, ensuring the availability of emergency barring orders, restraining or protection orders, protecting victims during judicial processes, providing legal aid;
- ensuring that the residence status of victims does not preclude justice, and that gender-based asylum claims can be recognised; states should cooperate with each other in these matters;
- a group of experts should monitor the implementation of the Convention.

The Convention was adopted by the Council of Europe Committee of Ministers on 7 April 2011, and came into force on 1 August 2014 after sufficient, but not all member states, had ratified it.

Legal definitions

In addition to the underpinning legal principles, there are detailed issues as to the definition of rape in law. The development of best practice has seen three major revisions to the definition of rape in law in respect of: lack of consent rather than use of force; extension in the range of body parts; and removal of the marital exception. Further reforms have included making rape a state and criminal, rather than private and civil, offence, and creating specific offences for rape against children, which can be defined as 'strict liability', in which no defence of 'consent' can be entered (Kelly, 2005).

Consent

On consent, the UN *Handbook for legislation on violence against women* (UNDAW, 2010, p 26) recommends that legislation should remove any requirement that sexual assault be committed by force or violence, and any requirement of proof of penetration; and minimise secondary victimisation of the complainant/survivor in proceedings by enacting a definition of sexual assault that either requires the existence of 'unequivocal and voluntary agreement' and requiring proof by the accused of steps taken to ascertain whether the complainant/survivor was consenting, or that requires that the act must take place in 'coercive circumstances' broadly defined.

In non-conflict zones, the European Parliament (2011a), in Resolution 2010/2209(INI), and the Council of Europe recommend a consent-based standard in the legal definition of rape and sexual abuse (EIGE, 2012a), as does the European Court of Human Rights (in the case of *M.C. v Bulgaria* 39272/98) (2015).

Several EU member states do not reach the internationally recommended standard on rape legislation in relation to consent (European Commission, 2010d). In research funded by the European Commission under the Daphne programme (Lovett and Kelly, 2009), several countries, including Austria, Germany and Hungary, were found to require the use of force before sexual coercion is legally defined as rape.

Hence there is a significant gap between the standards of the European Convention of Human Rights and several EU member states in the legal definition of rape. These states may be regarded as failing in their due diligence to prevent human rights abuses, as found in the above-mentioned case of Bulgaria before the European Court of Human Rights. When the EU accedes to the Convention, as is probable given the commitments made in the Treaty of Lisbon, responsibility for due diligence will continue to fall on individual EU member states, but may also include the EU level.

The issue of the nature of consent in relation to rape emerges in a different form in times of war and genocide. There is debate concerning the decision-making by international war crimes tribunals when they address what constitutes rape, in particular, as to whether 'consent' can be used as a defence against an allegation of rape in the context of the generalised coercion that occurs in war and conflict zones. MacKinnon (2006: 237-246) argues that such a context of generalised coercion provides sufficient grounds for holding that unwanted sex legally constitutes rape, without the need to additionally demonstrate that the woman did not individually consent. This is relevant to international criminal tribunals addressing war crimes that may include rape, and when there is provision of humanitarian assistance to victim-survivors of rape.

Body parts

Laws on rape vary in their definition as to which body parts are relevant. In reviewing the laws of a selection of EU member states, Lovett and Kelly (2009) found that Belgium, Germany, Portugal and Sweden employ a wide definition of rape which covers all forms of penetration by body parts and objects, while Hungary employs a narrow definition restricted to penile-vaginal penetration. The range of body parts included within the law affects whether rape is exclusively a crime by men towards women or not. Scotland, in passing the Sexual Offences (Scotland) Act 2010, changed from a narrow definition of rape (Lovett and Kelly, 2009) to a much wider one where rape is defined as 'penetration of the vagina, anus or mouth by the penis without consent' (Rape Crisis Scotland, no date). The Swedish legal definition of rape is even wider, and includes the penetration of the vagina, anus or mouth by the penis, fingers or any other object without consent, or in a situation where the victim was incapable of giving consent (Swedish Penal Code, 6:1). In 2007 South Africa passed the Criminal Law (Sexual Offences and Related Matters) Amendment Act No 32 which repealed the previous common law offence of rape and replaced it with an expanded statutory offence of rape which is applicable to all forms of sexual penetration without consent, irrespective of gender (Justice and Constitutional Department, 2008). International best practice is to include penetration of any orifice by the penis as rape, and to define penetration by other objects as a further form of serious sexual assault.

No marital exception

No marital exception is allowed for rape under international standards. The UN *Handbook for legislation on violence against women* (UNDAW, 2010, p 26) recommends that legislation should specifically criminalise sexual assault within a relationship (that is, 'marital rape'), either by providing that sexual assault provisions apply 'irrespective of the nature of the relationship' between the perpetrator and complainant, or by stating that 'no marriage or other relationship shall constitute a defence to a charge of sexual assault under the legislation.'

There has been a reduction in the marital exception to rape being a crime, but marital rape remains legal in dozens of countries today. It was criminalised in the Nordic European countries in the 1960/70s, but in some other countries, including the UK, the US, Australia and New Zealand, criminalisation only occurred during the 1990s. A number of South Asian and African countries, including Cambodia, Thailand, Rwanda and Ghana, criminalised marital rape after 2000. International women's and human rights movements (Global Voices, 2012) and international organisations (UN General Assembly, 1993; Council of Europe, 2009b, 2009c) have called on states to reform the law on rape and marriage, and to recognise marital rape as a human rights violation.

In some countries, including Afghanistan, Lebanon, Jordan and Morocco, where rape in marriage has not been criminalised, additional legislation exists which means a victim-survivor of rape can face criminal charges for adultery or prostitution. Women convicted of adultery as a consequence of being raped can face severe sanctions including long prison sentences and even the death penalty. In some countries, unmarried rape victims can be pressured to marry the alleged rapist to reduce the sanctions they face if convicted, to prevent their family being shamed and to end the prosecution of the perpetrators. For example, until January 2014 this was the case under Morocco's Article 475 (Maghri, 2012), the second provision of which specified that if the victim marries the perpetrator, he can no longer be prosecuted except by those empowered to annul the marriage, and only then after the annulment has been announced. This effectively prevented prosecutors from independently pursuing rape charges. Following campaigning in Morocco, Article 475 was finally amended by the Moroccan parliament in January 2014 (BBC News, 2014).

Summary of legal definitions

Many countries around the world are not yet reaching the standards of legislation on rape articulated in the UN *Handbook*, although there has been considerable movement towards them in recent years. This includes some EU member states that are not reaching international standards on laws on rape. Some do not use the threshold of consent but rather encode in law the more restrictive threshold of force, despite the use of the standard of 'consent' (rather than force) in judgments of the European Court of Human Rights, which enforces the European Convention on Human Rights, and in the UN *Handbook for legislation on violence against women*.

Legal competence of the EU on rape law and policy

The extent to which the EU has legal competence to develop legislation and policy on rape and other forms of violence against women is complex. The issues include the identification of the legal principles and judgment under which there is capacity to act at EU-level rather than this being a matter for the member state level only under the principle of conferral and subsidiarity.

There are four ways in which rape is conceptualised in international legal regimes (as discussed above): as a violation of women's human rights (1993 UN General Assembly Resolution 48/104, based on the UN Universal Declaration of Human Rights); as a form of torture (practice of the European Court of Human Rights, based on the European Convention on Human Rights); as a war crime (Rome Statute of the International

Criminal Court); and as a form of gender discrimination (UN, 1992, General Recommendation 19).

The EU also upholds these legal principles of human rights, equality between women and men, and non-discrimination against women. They are included at a high level in the Treaty of Lisbon (divided in two parts into the Treaty on the EU and the Treaty on the Functioning of the EU; European Union, 2007). Articles 2 and 3 in the Treaty on the EU state:

> 2. The Union is founded on the values of respect for human dignity, freedom, democracy, equality, the rule of law and respect for human rights, including the rights of persons belonging to minorities. These values are common to the Member States in a society in which pluralism, non-discrimination, tolerance, justice, solidarity and equality between women and men prevail.
>
> 3. The Union's aim is to promote peace, its values and the well-being of its peoples. It shall combat social exclusion and discrimination, and shall promote social justice and protection, equality between women and men, solidarity between generations and protection of the rights of the child.

Further, the EU is discussing and preparing its potential accession to the European Convention on Human Rights, which is already individually ratified by all member states, on the basis of Article 6.2 of the Treaty on the EU.

Article 8 of the Treaty on the Functioning of the EU states:

> In all its activities, the Union shall aim to eliminate inequalities, and to promote equality, between men and women.

Furthermore, Article 10 states the aim to combat discrimination on grounds of sex:

> In defining and implementing its policies and activities, the Union shall aim to combat discrimination based

on sex, racial or ethnic origin, religion or belief, disability, age or sexual orientation.

More concretely, Article 19 allows for a special procedure for the development of directives to combat discrimination based on sex:

> 1. Without prejudice to other provisions of the Treaties and within the limits of the powers conferred by them upon the Union, the Council, acting unanimously in accordance with a special legislative procedure and after obtaining the consent of the European Parliament, may take appropriate action to combat discrimination based on sex, racial or ethnic origin, religion or belief, disability, age, or sexual orientation.
>
> 2. By way of derogation from paragraph 1, the European Parliament and the Council, acting in accordance with the ordinary legislative procedure, may adopt the basic principles of Union incentive measures, excluding any harmonisation of the laws and regulations of the Member States, to support action taken by the Member States in order to contribute to the achievement of the objectives referred to in paragraph 1.

In various places, EU documents note that specific forms of violence against women constitute gender inequality and gender discrimination that the EU should combat. For example, the conclusions of the EU Council (2010) state:

> Declaration 19 on Article 8, whereby, in its general efforts to eliminate inequalities between women and men, the Union will aim in its different policies to combat all kinds of domestic violence, and the Member States should take all necessary measures to prevent and punish these criminal acts and to support and protect victims.

There is a gap between the commitment of the EU to principles of human rights and the equality between men and women in its treaties on the one hand, and the standard of the legislation and policy on rape in some member states on the other. For example, some member states have failed to meet the standard on consent articulated by the European Court of Human Rights implementing the European Convention on Human Rights (European Court of Human Rights, 2015). While the development of legislative and non-legislative policy action in this field on the European level in recent years is recognised, there remains a case for European legislative action to assist member states in closing the gaps between the national and international standards.

In relation to the prevention of rape and assistance to victims of rape, European legislation and other policy action, as mentioned above, might be developed in the areas of freedom, security and justice; economy and social inclusion; public health; external relations; or research and statistics. However, for the prevention and the sanctioning of rape, European legislation in the area of freedom, security and justice, which covers also the promotion of fundamental rights, could be of particular value. To this end, legislative action to sanction rape could be developed on the basis of Article 82 of the Treaty on the Functioning of the EU, which provides legal competence to the EU level to ensure the mutual recognition of legal judgments on criminal matters, including the identification and enforcement of minimum standards so as to ensure that legislation can be harmonised sufficiently to meet this requirement of mutual recognition. Furthermore, Article 83 provides particular powers in the area of serious crimes that explicitly covers the 'sexual exploitation of women and children', which it is reasonable to interpret as including rape. While the competence to act in this field is restrained to issues that are 'serious' and 'cross-border', these conditions are met in the case of rape; there is no doubt that rape is a serious crime, and offenders may well be 'active' across borders or may cross them in attempts to escape justice. Also, female EU citizens moving across the EU might become victims of rape in a member state other than the one in which they live, with quite different judicial and social consequences.

In addition, Article 153 has been proven suitable as a legal basis to prevent and to sanction harassment on grounds of gender and sexuality in the workplace, which could, in the most serious scenario, include rape. Building on these achievements, common approaches to sanctions and the support for victims of rape in the workplace could be the subject of EU legal action.

While the issue of the legal competence to act at EU rather than member state level is subject to ongoing discussions, a very strong case can be made that the request for legal action at the European level cannot be refused on the grounds of there being no legal basis. In the meantime, developing actions in a common effort to prevent rape and to assist victim-survivors of rape should be a priority for all member states.

Criminal justice system

The criminal justice system intervenes to prevent rape by holding perpetrators to account. This process includes detection, arrest, prosecution, conviction and sentencing. An indicator of its effectiveness in relation to rape is the conviction rate of perpetrators, which remains very low. There are developments in policies to prevent recidivism among offenders, including the use of registers to monitor their whereabouts. There have been innovations in the treatment of offenders, ranging from punitive criminal sanctions to rehabilitative health programmes and buddy support. There have also been improvements in the way data is collected so as to monitor which policy developments are the most effective.

Increasing conviction rates and avoiding secondary victimisation

Increasing conviction rates for perpetrators of rape contributes to rape prevention by reducing the impunity of rapists, thereby increasing deterrence, increasing the possibility of their being subject to processes of reform and rehabilitation, and by making a clear statement to wider society that rape is a serious crime that is not condoned by the state or society. There have been important improvements in the quality of criminal justice systems in relation to rape, including training the police and prosecutors, as part of a drive to improve the conviction rate of rape cases. However, there are remaining serious challenges.

One problem that is important to address is the tendency of the criminal justice system process to create secondary trauma (also described as secondary victimisation) of victim-survivors of rape, through ill-informed processes that are insensitive or victim-blaming (Vetten and Bhana, 2001; Koss, 2006). Assisting victims of rape by preventing secondary trauma to victim-survivors has the added benefit that victim-centric interventions are more effective at increasing conviction rates. Thus criminal justice interventions to reduce secondary trauma also enable improved access to justice, contribute to victim-survivor efforts to rebuild dignity and autonomy, and help to prevent rape by increasing the likelihood that perpetrators will be held to account. The best practices therefore avoid the re-victimisation of women by these processes. There are attempts to reduce the attrition of cases of rape as they proceed through the criminal justice system (Kelly et al, 2005), although not all changes are necessarily improvements (Bumiller, 2008).

A common feature of the specialist unit interventions described below is that they operate under a victim-centric principle, that is, the needs of the victim are at the centre of the process. UN Resolution 15/2010 (UN Economic and Social Council, 2010) adopts the guidelines in the updated model strategies and practical measures on the elimination of violence against women in the field of crime prevention and criminal justice, which recognises, among other things, that crime prevention and criminal justice responses to violence against women must be focused on the needs of the victim and empower individual women who are victims of violence. The sense of control, autonomy, safety and support provided by a victim-centric principle governing the operationalisation of specialist unit interventions is significant: in retaining victim-survivor engagement in the criminal justice system process (Skinner and Taylor, 2009); in enabling the collection of more robust evidence (Sadan et al, 2001); and in making victim-survivors more credible witnesses in court (Sadan et al, 2001). All of these increase conviction rates as well as reduce secondary trauma for victim-survivors.

Some victim-survivors are particularly vulnerable by virtue of their ethnicity, language, minority, refugee or indigenous status, their age, their location in remote or underdeveloped areas, or their disability status. For example, Baillot et al (2014) point to the parallels between rape cases and asylum claims in terms of the challenges associated with disclosure and credibility. They argue that these challenges may be replicated and compounded for women asylum-seekers where their narrative of persecution includes rape, which ultimately makes it difficult for these women to find refuge. The best interventions recognise such vulnerability by ensuring that special attention, intervention or protection required by these victim-survivors is met.

Specialist units and mainstreaming

The improvement of criminal justice system practices is often led by the creation of specialist units that develop expertise that can then be mainstreamed into routine practices. Specialist units have been important for the development of expert knowledge, skills, training practices and appropriate forms of interagency cooperation. After the identification and development of best practice in expert specialist units, this expertise can be mainstreamed into routine service provision.

The spreading of expert knowledge and skills in criminal justice personnel through training has been demonstrated to have a positive impact in a number of ways that contribute to increasing conviction rates and reducing secondary trauma for victim-survivors. For example, the International Association of Women Judges (2012) found that after training judges on instruments that protect women's human rights, those instruments were more likely to be cited in the judicial opinions of the trainees than those of judges who had not received the training. By contrast, prosecutors with little awareness of the needs of rape victim-survivors, or the context in which these cases work, have been found to delay processes and hamper victim-survivors' access to justice when not appropriately trained (Cossins, 2007; Robinson, 2009; Thomas et al, 2011).

One outcome of the development of specialist expert units has been the improvement of methods of interagency working. A common feature of these improved interagency practices involves personnel from a range of criminal justice agencies, and staff from relevant agencies outside the criminal justice system being located together within the specialist unit. Interagency working practices are recognised as good practice in a number of reports. For example, in Resolution 2010/15, the UN recognises that effective and integrated criminal justice responses to violence against women require close cooperation among all key stakeholders, including law enforcement officials, prosecutors, judges, victim advocates, health professionals and forensic scientists (UN Economic and Social Council, 2010). The Department for International Development recognises that impact is more likely when all the various aspects of violence against women are dealt with coherently through targeted support (DFID, 2012), and UN Women (2012a) has called for provision in national actions for the development and implementation of shared services or practice standards, guidelines or codes across the sectors that respond to violence against women and the development of information-sharing protocols. It should be noted that the leadership of interagency working must be done from a victim-centric stance with the involvement of gender expertise.

The gender of specialist staff has been debated, with some calling for staff to be female by default (Kelly, 2005), or that examiners should be female 'unless the service user specifies otherwise' (Kelly and Dubois, 2008, p 51), while others (Jordan, 2002) have argued that enabling victim-survivor choice of the gender of key personnel is crucial. The importance of specially trained personnel and the embedding of training on rape and sexual violence is clearly recognised and promoted by a number of national and international bodies in their strategy documents (DFID, 2012; EIGE, 2012a, 2012b; UN Women, 2012a). As with specialist units (which is where most specialist personnel are currently found), the presence of specialist personnel have been found to have a positive impact on conviction rates in rape cases and in decreasing secondary trauma.

Advocates for victim-survivors

Providing advocates for victim-survivors to support them throughout the criminal justice process has been found to be particularly effective in reducing secondary trauma for victim-survivors, especially keeping them well informed about the progress of their case (Jordan, 2002; Skinner and Taylor, 2009). By supporting victim-survivors in this way, attrition is reduced and conviction rates are increased (Sullivan and Bybee, 1999; Lovett et al, 2004; Robinson, 2009). A number of criminal justice systems employ special advocates, including ISVAs in England and Wales (Robinson, 2009), South Africa's victim advocate officers (Sadan et al, 2001), and the automatic entitlement of victim-survivors of sexual violence to free psychosocial and legal support via an advocate in Austria (Lovett and Kelly, 2009). Kelly (2005) cites the use of support workers/advocates as a promising practice whose role should include debriefing the victim-survivor, and where necessary, developing a safety plan with them. This advocacy takes a variety of forms in different countries, from general support to the provision of specialised legal advice.

The use of specialised legal advocates to support victim-survivors through the legal and courtroom aspects of the criminal justice system has been found to reduce secondary victimisation and improve conviction rates. The trial can be a harrowing experience for victims if their testimony and character are subjected to hostile questioning, and a person who is legally entitled to speak for the victim in this specific legal setting has been found to be of assistance in promoting justice (Londono, 2007; Horvath and Brown, 2009). In the courtroom, narrow stereotypes of 'real rape' or the practices as to what constitutes a 'good case' can get in the way of the delivery of justice (Temkin and Krahé, 2008; Smith and Skinner, 2012; McKimmie et al, 2014). Raitt (2010) argues convincingly that the provision of independent legal representatives for rape victims is the most effective way of supporting rape victims during trials, while Smith and Skinner (2012) note that this is a widespread but not universal practice in the EU.

Role of civil society organisations

Best practices for rape prevention and assisting victims of rape in the criminal justice system often develop where civil society movements, usually feminist-led, have articulated requests for recognition by the state of rape as a serious crime; the right of victim-survivors of rape to justice and reparation; and the right of women to be protected against rape through its criminalisation and prevention. Such movements have been found worldwide in developed, transitional and developing nations, as well as in some post-conflict locations. The development of best practice depends on the ability of women to express their views as to their priorities, and to revise policy practices accordingly via democratic political processes.

Challenges in reforming the criminal justice system

Despite the very positive impacts delivered by these innovative interventions in the criminal justice system, there are number of remaining challenges, including inadequate funding, inadequate training, lack of robust data collection and management systems and lack of formal evaluation. In addition, while specialist units and expert staff have been particularly successful interventions, there is not yet evidence that such expert knowledge, skill and working practices is being consistently mainstreamed throughout the criminal justice system.

Inadequate funding for the ongoing running and maintenance costs of interventions threatens their existence over time, and the delivery of the service to the quality and principles set. Sadan et al (2001) found inadequate funding to be a major factor in preventing South African sexual offences courts operating as effectively as they could, and a lack of funding meant resources such as transport and food for victim-survivors were limited, which had an impact on their performance in court. Funding cuts to ISVA services in the UK have been demonstrated by Towers and Walby (2012), and Järvinen et al (2008) have highlighted the problem of funding for specialist domestic violence courts.

There is a lack of robust data collection and management systems within countries and across countries, which severely hampers efforts to build evidence-based interventions. Baños Smith (2011) argues that the key challenge in preventing violence against women is the limited evidence base on the effectiveness of various interventions. This is reflected in the repeated call for better data collection and monitoring systems found in the strategy documents of numerous organisations. For example, EIGE (2012a, 2012b) calls for the development of official statistics and data collection activities and methodology, and multisectoral, interagency coordination of the development, implementation and evaluation of data collection. EIGE (2012a, 2012b) also calls for mechanisms to ensure that up-to-date research in the field of sexual violence is available for study. UN Women (2012a) calls for NAPs to harmonise the police, prosecution, court and service delivery data collection, and to establish systems to measure support, safety and the satisfaction of victim-survivors. Research that has looked at current data and measurement regimes highlights the need to, at a minimum, disaggregate data by gender and relationship between victim and perpetrator (Sadan et al, 2001; Walby et al, 2012).

There is also a lack of comprehensive evaluation research on interventions to prevent rape and to assist women victim-survivors of rape. A small number of evaluations, such as that by Sadan et al (2001), followed a methodology that set clear measurement criteria and compared the results for specialist intervention against a non-specialist intervention within the same context. The evidence obtained from these studies is particularly valuable.

Ways forward

Following the review of the best emerging practices in the criminal justice system found in the international literature on research findings, evaluation studies, expert recommendations and policy documents, the following ways forward are recommended in order to increase the conviction rate of perpetrators of rape while preventing the secondary trauma of victim-survivors. These require a conducive context, that is, they are framed by the rule of law, a functioning and democratic criminal justice system, clearly expressed political will to prevent rape and assist women victims of rape, and a civil society able to hold government and statutory agencies to account. They need to be evidence-based: interventions should be designed and implemented with reference to what has been demonstrated to work and avoid what has been shown to be detrimental to achieving the intervention's aims. They should be subject to comprehensive evaluations from the start, drawing on dedicated data collection systems that enable the aims of evaluation to be comprehensively assessed while adhering to high standards of confidentiality and ensuring ethical principles for working with individuals within the criminal justice system are met. 'Gold-standard' evaluation methodologies compare the target intervention with alternative interventions that have the same/ similar aims. Standardised data collection and quality monitoring tools should be established across the full range of criminal justice interventions. Interventions should make a contribution back into the continued improvement of practices by making available lessons learned and highlighting what works best, thus enabling future developments to be evidence-based. They should treat the victim-survivor with respect and sensitivity so as to avoid secondary re-victimisation, and be victim-centric, placing the health, safety, dignity, privacy and autonomy needs of the victim-survivor at the centre of the practice. They should provide the victim-survivors with their own advocate to support them throughout the criminal justice process, including legal advocates who can speak for the rape victim-survivor during the trial. They should provide specialist units, including courts, that accumulate expertise and good practices; that engage appropriately led interagency working, which should be embedded within practice and include agencies across and beyond the criminal justice system; and be adequately funded, not only for starting new interventions, but for ongoing running and maintenance costs so that they be sustainably delivered at high quality. Initially, they should be specialist, in order that expert skills and knowledge on rape prevention and assisting women victim-survivors of rape in criminal justice-led interventions can be developed through training for all relevant practitioners. In the longer term, they should be mainstreamed throughout the criminal justice system, so that specialist and expert facilities, training, knowledge and skills become embedded, not isolated, within the criminal justice system.

Such practices should be embedded within wider social, political, economic and cultural practices that are guided by principles of gender equality and equal rights for men and women. This was noted by Navanethem Pillay, the UN Office for the High Commissioner of Human Rights, in her response to the Justice J.S. Verma Committee's report and its recommendations for systemic change in India's response to rape: 'The Committee's recommendations are grounded in a framework of rights, equality and non-discrimination, and represent a paradigm shift towards recognition of women as holders of rights, not just objects of protection. The report should serve as a beacon for many other countries struggling to respect the rights of women more comprehensively by addressing sexual violence through legislation, policies and programmes' (UN Office for the High Commissioner of Human Rights, 2013).

Criminal justice-led interventions need to be sensitive to context, that is, their operationalisation in different locations and contexts contain features that make them more successful in increasing the conviction rate of rape, and in preventing secondary trauma to victim-survivors. In this respect, the establishment of specialist units has been demonstrated to be a very successful intervention for increasing conviction rates while reducing secondary trauma for victim-survivors. UN Women (2012a) states that NAPs should call for the creation and strengthening of well-funded specialised units. There are several examples of good practice.

The Sapphire project allows for a team of expert police detectives and connected staff in London, England, to focus on the investigation of rape. Despite problems, an evaluation of the project found a significant increase in the rate of charging suspects compared with non-specialist teams (MPS, 2005).

In Kabul, Afghanistan, a specialist prosecutor unit for dealing with crimes of violence against women prosecuted nearly 300 cases in its first year, with the rate of prosecution doubling between the first month and the last. The success of this specialist unit led to the opening of a second in Herat in 2011 (Thomas et al, 2011).

From 2008, Austria obliged prosecutor offices to set up special units to deal with cases of sexual and domestic violence (Lovett and Kelly, 2009), while the Department for International Development in the UK promotes the establishment of specialised units, courts and/or court time where possible (DFID, 2012).

Specialist court interventions have also been established, for example, specialist domestic violence courts in England and Wales operate with a dedicated courtroom, separate entrances and waiting areas for victim-survivors and expert, trained staff (Cook et al, 2004; Women's Resource Centre, 2008).

Specialist advocates for victim survivors have been established in at least 14 EU countries, including Austria, Belgium, Denmark, France, Germany and Ireland, with activities ranging from legal representation at trials to more generalised support (Raitt, 2010; Smith and Skinner, 2012).

South Africa's sexual offences courts are also specialist courts that deal exclusively with rape and sexual violence prosecutions. They are separate from other court facilities, and are designed to both protect the victim-survivor from secondary trauma through the use of expert, trained staff who work with the victim-survivor to prepare them for what they will face in court, and through the design of the facility itself, such as separate waiting areas for victim-survivors and separate 'camera rooms' with a CCTV link so that vulnerable victim-survivors, especially children, do not have to give their evidence in front of the perpetrator (Sadan et al, 2001). They have been found to have conviction rates of between 70 and 95 per cent (Thomas et al, 2011) compared with an average conviction rate of around 10 per cent (South African Law Commission, 2001).

While specialist units concentrate on one part of the criminal justice process, the best interventions have strong interagency links across the whole process, sometimes to other specialist units in the process. For example, in 2000, Thuthuzela Care Centres were added to the model of South African rape prevention; these are also specialist facilities staffed by expert and trained personnel who work with the victim-survivor in the immediate aftermath of rape to collect evidence and begin initial investigations. They are attached to, or located close by, sexual offences courts, and staff from the courts and centres work in close collaboration across these two stages of the criminal justice system to ensure that the evidence and outcomes from the investigation are as robust as possible for the purposes of the court, to make sure that victim-survivors are prepared for the court process, including having been referred to counselling before the court hearing, and so that information-sharing about a case can be efficient and effective while maintaining confidentiality (UNICEF, 2009; Johnson, 2012). A study of the factors that are significant in getting a rape case to court found that where there was no medical history for the victim-survivor, and no forensic evidence, the odds of these cases getting to court were 90 per cent lower and 80 per cent lower respectively than those cases with a medical history or forensic evidence (Feist et al, 2007). Further, EIGE calls for specialist interventions to recognise and apply minimum standards for sexual violence-specific services (2012a, 2012b). The need for intervention across the whole criminal justice system is suggested by the implementation of special measures in giving evidence (for example, use of a live television link) that are designed to reduce secondary victimisation. Unless complemented by educational guidance relating to jury decision-making, such reforms may risk compromising the credibility of the complainant by reducing the visibility of their distress, which is (erroneously) perceived by jurors as an indicator of veracity (Callander, 2014).

One of the most robust evaluations of interventions in the criminal justice system is that of Boba and Lilley (2009) concerning the consequences of the Violence Against Women Act 1994 funding (DeGue et al, 2014). This showed that the US$1.6 billion federal funding had a demonstrable effect in reducing the rate of rape, largely due to improved law enforcement. Their methodology depended on the availability of information as to the extent of funding and occurrence of rape by geographic areas over time. They found that a '1% increase in VAWA [Violence Against Women Act] funding was associated with a 0.066% reduction in rape' (Boba and Lilley, 2009, p 180).

Treatment of convicted rapists

While prison is the standard sentence by courts for convicted rapists, there are several treatment programmes that are specific to sex offenders. These include surgical and chemical castration; the use of cognitive and other therapeutic psychological interventions; and the registration of sex offenders with police authorities. These are intended to prevent rape by reducing recidivism, that is, the repetition of the offence by the same perpetrator. The outcomes of these programmes are rarely promising, however.

Surgical castration of sex offenders

One of the most controversial treatments for sexual offending, surgical castration for sexual offenders, is currently practised only in Germany and in the Czech Republic within the EU, but in the past has been used more widely across Europe, particularly in Denmark and Norway. The South Korea National Assembly, however, is considering the introduction of surgical castration to replace chemical castration, which is seen there as ineffective (Ji-hoon, 2012). In the US, both Texas and California mandate castration for repeat offenders before release for civil commitment. In other states, offenders may opt for surgical castration to reduce their sentence.

The procedure in the US is that the most serious sexual offenders, who are civilly committed to state sex offender institutions after serving their criminal sentence, can opt for surgical removal of the testes (bilateral orchiectomy). The procedure is voluntary, and options for chemical castration are also available in some jurisdictions. However, the civil commitment means that offenders are unlikely to be released without undergoing one such procedure.

The intervention has the intention of reducing interest in sex and removing motivation for sexual attack. Proponents identify the treatment as alleviating the suffering tied to an abnormal sex drive. Studies of cancer patients having had such a procedure for medical reasons show a reduction in sex drive and sexual interest.

Evaluations of these practices have typically used rather weak methodologies. Schmucker and Lösel (2008) identify eight studies on surgical castration that have an average odds ratio of 15.03 on subsequent recidivism – ($p<0.01$), meaning that those not castrated have odds of sexual recidivism 15 times higher, providing evidence for reduction in recidivism (re-offending). However, they also identify the eight studies as flawed in that there are no suitably equivalent control groups. A widely quoted German study followed 104 offenders who were surgically castrated, and found only 3 per cent offended, compared with a 46 per cent re-offending rate for sexual offenders who desired the treatment but who were not castrated (Wille and Beier, 1989). Scientific evidence is based on a small number of studies, and many studies on which research has been based are historical. While effect sizes are large, human rights issues will undoubtedly play a large role in the future adoption of surgical castration as a treatment. The issue of whether offenders really consent to such a treatment will become critical to this debate.

There are serious legal and ethical issues with surgical castration as a treatment. The American Civil Liberties Union considers it be a cruel and unusual punishment. The Council of Europe's Committee for the Prevention of Torture has recently criticised both the Czech Republic (2009) and Germany (2012a), noting that offenders may feel coerced into agreeing to such treatment; it is irreversible and affects the offender's ability to procreate; and that the presumed reduction in re-offending is not scientifically proven. Both the Czech and German governments have responded, saying that appropriate safeguards on consent means that the treatment is not degrading, and instead aids the reintegration of offenders into society.

The European Committee for the Prevention of Torture (2010, 2012) and Weinberger et al (2005) have identified neurobiological and psychological factors that may also be associated with sexual drive, and offenders can obtain exogenous testosterone treatment to compensate for the loss of endogenously generated testosterone. The primary issue, however, is whether sexual crimes against women are primarily motivated by biological drivers such as testosterone, or by psychological factors such as lack of empathy, or by sociological and cultural drivers encompassing power, habituation and religious views in society. Since there is considerable evidence that sex crimes against women are not biologically driven, the intervention may be considered misplaced.

Hormonal medication of sex offenders

Hormonal medication, also referred to as androgen deprivation therapy (or ADT) and popularly referred to as 'chemical castration', covers a range of anti-androgenic drug treatments (or anti-androgens) designed to reduce male sexual desire and sexual performance to pre-puberty levels. Effectiveness in terms of recidivism is contested; while a range of studies have found a reduction in odds of recidivism of over three times, the quality of the studies is poor, and results could be explained by offenders self-selecting into treatment. There are medical side effects, and some have identified legal and ethical issues.

Grubin and Beech (2010) report that the main drugs used are cyproterone acetate, or CPA (in the UK, Europe and Canada), and medroxyprogesterone, or MPA (in the US). They also report the increasing use of leuprolide, goserelin and tryptorelin. Such treatment is used in a wide range of countries for high-risk offenders. In Europe, offenders mostly opt in to receive treatment with informed consent. Thus in the UK, Curtis (2012) reports that 100 sex offenders have recently volunteered for such treatment. It is used in many states in the EU, particularly in Scandinavia, Germany, Poland and the Czech Republic. In some states in the US, participation is often a condition of release for high-risk offenders, and selection of participants becomes a legal rather than a medical matter (Harrison, 2007).

Anti-androgenic drugs work by blocking androgen receptors, and thus suppressing the effect of androgens in the male human body. Androgens are hormones that control the activity and development of male sexual development and performance. The most well-known androgen is testosterone. Grubin and Beech (2010) state that the reason that such drugs work is thought to be due to reduced pressure caused by sexual arousal, notwithstanding the 'strong psychological factors that contribute to sexual offending.'

A recent systematic review (Schmucker and Lösel, 2008) of sex offender treatments identified hormonal medication as the most effective treatment out of all non-surgical interventions. Six studies were examined, and a combined efficacy odds-ratio of 3.11 ($p<0.01$) was found when examining the risk of recidivism, meaning that those treated were three times less likely to re-offend. However, Schmucker and Lösel (2008) point out that the results are based on methodologically weak studies. This point is reinforced by more recent research by Rice and Harris (2011), who take a more sceptical approach, arguing that there have been no placebo studies, and that sample selection effects (those choosing to have treatment may be those less likely to re-offend) may account for much of the difference.

Harrison (2007) suggests a number of proposals for best practice. First, the drug used should be CPA rather than MPA, as there are far fewer side effects. The hormonal treatment should be combined with psychological treatment or counselling to improve efficacy. Finally, informed consent must be a priority, with offenders being informed of the effects and side effects of the drug therapy, and being able to withdraw such consent at all times. Rice and Harris (2011) make a strong case for a randomised control trial of hormonal medication, with sex offender volunteers being randomly assigned either to a treatment group with early release, or to a non-treatment group with standard release, with long-term follow-up of both groups.

Cognitive behavioural treatment of sex offenders

A different approach to treatment of sex offenders from that of modifying their bodies is that of behavioural modification, which attempts to reform their minds. There are several models of sex offender treatment that attempt to change the behaviour of convicted sex offenders to reduce the likelihood that they will rape again. These include cognitive behavioural treatment, classical behavioural treatment, insight oriented treatment and therapeutic community treatments.

Schmucker and Lösel (2008) state that, out of these, only cognitive behavioural therapy (CBT) consistently demonstrated a positive impact. Their review of 35 studies showed a significant increase of 46 per cent in the odds of not re-offending when CBT is used. They explain that 'the usually less clearly structured insight-oriented and milieu-therapeutic approaches seem to be of little benefit while highly structured cognitive-behavioural treatment shows good effects' (Schmucker and Lösel, 2008, p 16). Recent authors have come to view specific variants of CBT as particularly effective. The Risk-Need-Responsivity Model used in Canada is one example (Andrews et al, 2011), and the Good Lives Model is another (Ward et al, 2012). They work by assessing risks, identifying needs and developing a programme to change the behaviour of the convicted offender. We discuss the second example in more detail.

Good Lives Model

The Good Lives Model is a community-based programme aimed at sex offenders who are in the community but who are still being managed by offender management services. It was proposed by Tony Ward in a series of publications (Ward, 2002; Ward and Stewart, 2003; Ward and Maruna, 2007), and has been implemented in Australia, the UK, the US and Canada.

The Good Lives Model treatment programme has been given in the form of a module as part of a sex offender group work programme. It aims to develop positive acquisition of goals and skills, namely, a healthy life, knowledge acquisition, achievements, excellence in agency, inner peace, friendship, community spirituality, happiness and creativity. Its aim is to instil knowledge, skills and competence to allow the offender to live a better life and so avoid re-offending. It is not intended to be a complete programme, and other modules on the programme address additional issues such as victim empathy and problem-solving.

The theoretical basis for the programme is that sex offending arises because offenders try to obtain the same goals as other individuals (states of mind, personal experiences and personal characteristics), but in an inappropriate way. The inappropriateness may arise either from an imbalance in goals, where some goals are inappropriately prioritised over others (sexual gratification over intimacy), or through frustration at being unable to achieve such goals. Treatment is carried out in the community on sex offenders who have either received a community sentence, or who are serving part of their sentence on licence in the community.

A small-scale trial was carried out in Northumbria in the UK (Harkins et al, 2012) in which 76 male offenders received the 'Better Lives' module (derived from the Good Lives Model), and 701 received the standard risk prevention module. Attrition rates on the programme were the same in the two groups. From interview data, there was evidence of a more positive outlook towards future life among offenders in the Good Lives Model.

There is currently dispute about the added value that the Good Lives Model provides over the Risk-Needs-Responsivity Model. Andrews et al (2011) question the added value of the Good Lives Model, and point out that the programme needs more systematic scientific evaluation (Andrews et al, 2011). Ward et al (2012) have responded by defending the underlying rehabilitation theories.

While there is promise, there is no current evidence of treatment effectiveness over the current regime of the Risk-Needs-Responsivity model, which is used in many jurisdictions. Consequently, a study of what works in re-offending assesses the Good Lives Model as 'perhaps promising' but with 'no replicated empirical evidence in evaluations' (Lösel, 2010, p 22).

Sex offender registration and notification schemes

Sex offender registration and notification (SORN) is now common in Western countries to keep track of recently released or sentenced sex offenders, and to allow communities to be aware of sex offenders living in their neighbourhood.

There are two forms of registration scheme. The first form (registration only) requires police registration for a fixed period of time depending on the severity of the sexual offence; the second form has an additional community notification component. This can vary from the police supplying information about a named individual on request from a parent, to publicly available web registers of sex offenders with mapped locations.

SORN laws cover most sexual offences including rape, and are common in many Western countries. They are intended to serve four purposes: first, to allow local law enforcement knowledge of the sex offenders who may reside in a specific area; second, to act as a disincentive for existing sex offenders to re-offend; third, to act as a disincentive for potential new offenders to start offending; and finally, to improve public knowledge about potentially dangerous individuals living in a community, and thus to improve safety.

The legislation is applied to convicted sex offenders from release from prison after conviction or after a non-custodial sentence is imposed. Registration is also sometimes required of sex offenders who accept a police caution and therefore accept guilt. Registration periods depend on the seriousness of the offence, with lifetime registration required for serious offences in some countries. Depending on the jurisdiction, juveniles might receive a shorter period of registration compared with adult offenders. There is usually a requirement on the offender to notify all changes of address, and sometimes to reconfirm their current address each year. Non-compliance attracts a criminal sanction.

In the US, registration legislation was first introduced in California in 1947, with federal legislation in 1994 (the Jacob Wetterling Act) being introduced to require all states to introduce SORN registries, following the kidnap of an 11-year-old boy in 1989 in Minnesota. An extra requirement of community notification introduced in New Jersey in the 1990s was consolidated into the Adam Walsh Child Protection and Safety Act 2007. This requires states to maintain a public and free-to-access register of the location of sex offenders anywhere in the US. Registration periods depend on the seriousness of the offence; the most serious (tier 3) require lifetime registration, tier 2 offences require 25 years of notification from release, and tier 1 offences 15 years. The legislation allows a reduction of five years for tier 1 offences if the offender has not been convicted for 10 years, with registration effectively stopping at 10 years. A tier 3 juvenile sexual offender can also have the registration term reduced to 25 years if they have no convictions in that time.

Canada's National Sex Offender Registry came into force at the end of 2004, with the passing of the Sex Offender Information Registration Act. The registration period varies from 10 years to life according to the length of the sentence awarded, and there are no discounted periods for juveniles. There is no public access to the registry.

In Australia, the responsibility for sex offender registers lies with individual states. More states have introduced closed sex offender registration. The Australian National Child Offender Register also provides national information on child sex offenders, and is used to coordinate state registration systems. Registration times of eight years, fifteen years and life again depend on the severity of offence. Juvenile offenders receive a 50 per cent time reduction. The state of Western Australia has recently introduced an open register, and there are also private registers maintained by individuals.

Turning to England and Wales, a closed sex offender register was introduced in 1997, with its operation subsequently modified by the Sexual Offences Act 2003 – it now forms part of the Violent and Sexual Offender Register. Enquiry about a named person can be made if there is just cause (the child sex offender disclosure scheme). The length of time to which such individuals are to be registered is determined by the length of sentence received, and ranges from two years for a caution, seven years for a sentence of six months or less, ten years for a sentence between six months and 30 months, and indefinite for longer prison sentences. Those under 18 at the time of conviction are required to register for only half the registration time.

In France, the Fichier judiciaire automatisé des auteurs d'infractions sexuelles provides for automatic registration for serious child and adult sexual offences receiving a sentence of five years or more.

In Ireland, there is a requirement for convicted sex offenders to notify the police of their current address. This notification requirement can be indefinite for offences that have been sentenced to two years or more in custody.

South Korea is an exception in that the jurisdiction posts names and details of convicted sex offenders on the internet for anyone to download. There is no requirement for the offender to register, and the procedure is more concerned with public shaming than with aiding law enforcement and detection.

Assessment of the effectiveness of such registration and notification is fraught with difficulty, as the majority of such assessments tend to be historical comparisons between offenders convicted before and after the legislation was put in place. These are often known as before-after studies. They have the risk that a beneficial effect of the legislation is balanced out by an increase in the number or nature of the sexual offending over time. An additional problem is that registration may or may not have been accompanied by community notification, and that other legislation to address sexual recidivism, such as civil commitment, or the abolition of discretionary parole has also been introduced in a similar timeframe and might blur the result. Some studies look at aggregate sexual offending rates and assess the disincentive for both new offenders and existing offenders; other studies have looked solely at recidivism rates.

Nearly all evaluation studies have been carried out in the US. A group of studies have looked at the potential decrease in recidivism and timing of re-offending following SORN. One of the earliest studies (Schram and Milloy, 1995) assessed community notification, comparing, on the one hand, 90 sex offenders released from prison between 1990 and 1993 in Washington State and subject to registration in Washington State and the highest level of community notification with, on the other hand, a matched sample of 90 sex offenders released after 1986 and not subject to notification. There was no difference in the rate of sexual recidivism measured by arrests in the two groups after three years, but there was some evidence that recidivists in the notification group were arrested faster.

Later work by staff at the same institute (Washington State Institute for Public Policy, 2005) looked at over 8,000 sex offenders released between 1986 and 1999 and covering the introduction of two pieces of registration and notification legislation, the first in 1990, and an amended form in 1997. Once adjustment for offender characteristics had been made, there was a significant difference in sexual recidivism following the 1990 legislation, and a further decline after 1997. However, as stated in the report, this may have been caused by a general state-wide decrease in re-offending. Similarly, a study in Minnesota (Duwe and Donnay, 2008) showed a significant reduction in sexual re-arrest and re-conviction compared with a pre-notification group. However, other studies have come to different conclusions. A New Jersey study showed that community notification had no effect on sexual recidivism (Zgoba et al, 2008), a South Carolina study reached similar conclusions (Letourneau et al, 2009), and a study in Arkansas (Maddan et al, 2011) also showed no effect of registration and notification on recidivism.

Other studies have focused on comparing rates of sexual crime in different states within the US. The earliest study was that of Vasquez, Maddan and Walker (2007), who used a time series approach to examine the effect of the notification component of SORN schemes on rape. They found mixed results, with three states (Hawaii, Idaho and Nebraska) showing significant reductions in rape rates, but with California showing a significant increase. Some studies have focused on only one state. Thus, Sandler, Freeman and Socia (2008) examined before-after rates for rape and for other sexual offences in the state of New York, and found no legislative effect; and Letourneau et al (2010) looked at the effect of notification on juvenile sexual offending rates in North Carolina, and found no effect once other criminal justice changes were taken into account. Agan (2011) focused on the effect of registration rather than notification, and examined state-level data for rape and sexual offending. She found no evidence that the legislation had an effect overall. Ackerman, Sacks and Greenberg (2012) have recently re-examined US state-level data and focused specifically on rape, using a panel data approach and controlling for other legislative changes across all states. They conclude that the notification component of SORN schemes have not brought about dramatic reductions in the rates at which rape occurs.

A second smaller strand of work has examined the re-offending trajectories of sex offenders released before notification and after notification. In a study in Iowa, Tewksbury and Jennings (2010) examined the three distinct post-release trajectories of reconviction for a pre-SORN and a post-SORN group, and found them to be of similar shape with similar proportions of offenders; there was no statistical evidence of any effect of the SORN legislation. Similarly, a study in New Jersey (Tewksbury et al, 2012) found no differences in either the shape or proportions of offenders in the two trajectory groups.

The negative effects of SORN policies on offenders also need to be considered. Letourneau et al (2010) summarise these effects in numerous studies that include impeding employment and housing; disruption of supportive relationships; and subjection of the offender to harassment and rejection. These all deter the reintegration of the offender back into society, and may increase the risk of recidivism. Another criticism of registers is that they are too broad in scope, often capturing minor juvenile sexual offending rather than only the more dangerous adult forms.

Thus, although some studies have shown decreases in recidivism and changes in sexual offending rates, the consensus appears to be that in most states, registration and notification laws have had little effect. Is there any evidence that public safety is increased and fear of crime is decreased? A study by Anderson and Sample (2008) provides some evidence. In a survey of Nebraska residents, they found that nearly 90 per cent of respondents knew of the existence of a register, and around 35 per cent had accessed it. Of the third of respondents who answered questions on safety, over 89 per cent said they felt safer knowing of the existence of a register, and 35 per cent had taken action, such as talking to neighbours or their children. However, action in providing enhanced security provisions was unusual. Bandy (2011) found that there was no evidence that individuals took increased self-protective measures against sexual offending, but community members did increase protection for children.

Since evidential efficacy is weak, it is hard to identify best practice. If such a policy is considered, it seems to act best both as a law enforcement policy, and as a way of decreasing fear of crime. Human rights issues for the offender have been considered in Europe, but are considered less relevant in the US. Policies tend to be driven by well-publicised extreme events, and the rationale for their introduction requires consideration, together with the human rights issues and the potential effect on offenders who are attempting to desist.

SORN is not a best practice, but a practice that is common among many jurisdictions. While there is little evidence of prevention of re-offending by sex offenders (and more specifically, rapists), and of deterrence of new sexual offending, there is some evidence that the communities in which offenders live feel more secure, although preventative action is not likely to take place. Implementation of such a system would need an integrated and comprehensive criminal records system across the whole of the country to which a registration scheme can be added. In countries with strong regional autonomy with their own records, this may be hard to achieve. Procedures for secure access by professionals need to be designed, and data security issues need to be considered. Given these prerequisites, transfer of this methodology to other countries would be feasible.

Future evaluation studies need to focus on a variety of outcome measures, including the views of the community, changes in reported and convicted sex offender rates, changes in recidivism rates, and negative effects of vigilantism on the offender. Research also needs to take place in other jurisdictions outside the US, as its high gun ownership may be influencing issues related to public safety and protection.

Conclusion

Rape is a crime everywhere, but the definition and legal principle varies between countries, and not everywhere is yet reaching the best practice standards developed by international bodies such as the UN and Council of Europe. Best practice, as defined by in the UN *Handbook for legislation* and the Council of Europe's Istanbul Convention, includes a definition of rape as a violation of bodily integrity and sexual autonomy; specifies that it includes penetration of all orifices, not only the vagina; identifies lack of consent as a sufficient threshold not requiring the additional use of physical force; and refuses marital exemption. However, not all member states of the EU are reaching this standard, as shown in the cases before the European Court of Human Rights. The underpinning legal principles have been developed by the UN in Resolution 48/104 of the General Assembly in 1993, and in Recommendation 19 of the *Convention on the elimination of discrimination against women* (UN, 1992). Based on these documents, rape is seen both as a violation of human rights and also as a form of discrimination against women. Some further international jurisdictions, including the European Convention on Human Rights, criminalise rape through its conceptualisation as a form of torture, which is a violation of human rights.

The EU could improve the laws on rape in member states by setting minimum standards that meet those of international bodies including the UN, the European Court of Human Rights and the Council of Europe's Istanbul Convention, to support mutual recognition by member state judiciaries of the criminalisation of rape. This could be realised through a directive on all forms of violence against women, or specifically on rape, if there were sufficient interest. There is potential scope for a directive to introduce minimum standards for the definition of rape using Article 82 or 83 of the Treaty on the Functioning of the EU, and for a directive on all forms of violence against women, since these constitute gender discrimination in the same way as harassment, under Articles 19 or 157 of the Treaty on the Functioning of the EU (see Walby, 2013b).

An example of a promising development in legal principles for the criminalisation of rape can be found in Mexico, where this is specified as gender-based and systemic; however, its implementation is not complete, so this remains as an example of principles rather than practice. This is described in the case study below.

There are high rates of attrition in cases of rape as they progress through the criminal justice system in many countries. However, there are examples of promising practices to increase the proportion of rapes reported to the police that end with the conviction of the rapist.

One of the most effective practices has been the development of specialist courts, which use expertise existing in the field to implement procedures that are sensitive to the needs of victim-survivors, thereby simultaneously addressing the goals of assisting victims and preventing rape by reducing the impunity experienced by rapists. An example of such best practice is provided in a case study below: 'Specialised courts: sexual offences courts in South Africa'.

We are unable to recommend any promising practices in the treatment of perpetrators of rape, despite our review of the extensive investment there has been in such programmes. However, we identify an alternative intervention in relation to perpetrators, which is to identify them during their preparations to commit rape, and before they commit the act itself. This example involves the use of innovative technologies to identify would-be perpetrators engaged in grooming children in online chatrooms. Our promising practice in relation to perpetrators is: 'Identifying potential perpetrators in cyberspace'.

Integrating a better understanding of rape within law, Mexico

The law is an important instrument in preventing rape in challenging the impunity of rapists. It is central to the working of the criminal system, and is also significant in its effects at the symbolic and cultural level in defining what is wrong. The example here, of developments in Mexican law, concerns its integration of a better understanding of rape into law.

The general law to guarantee women access to a life free from violence was adopted in Mexico in 2007: *ley general de acceso de las mujeres a una vida libre de violencia*. Preceding this law, a 2004 initiative of a general law on feminicide proposed the introduction of 'gender crimes' in the Penal Code (Borzacchiello, 2012). There was a later amendment in 2012 (Congreso de Estados Unidos Mexicanos, 2012).

The law is in compliance with international obligations to promote women's human rights (UN, 1992; Organization of American States, 1994; see also ONU Mujeres et al, 2011). In particular, the Inter-American Belem do Para Convention, characterised by a feminist understanding of violence, a legally binding status and the establishment of monitoring procedures, has been influential in national legislation on violence against women in the whole Latin American region, including Mexico (Friedman, 2009; Roggeband, 2014). The process of making the law included the creation of a team of 60 researchers, experts in violence against women, who, under the guide of Marcela Lagarde, feminist academic and Member of the Congress, elaborated a diagnosis of feminicide violence in Mexico (Lagarde, 2008). Feminist organisations participated in the elaboration of the law, and contributed to its concept of violence (Borzacchiello, 2012).

The concept of 'feminicide', articulated by Lagarde (2005, 2006a, 2006b, 2008), suggests the systemic character of violence against women, rooted in structural inequalities between women and men, the violation of women's human rights in the public and private spheres, and state responsibility in breaking the rule of law and favouring impunity, which moves Lagarde (2005, p 155) to claim that 'feminicide is a State crime.' Article 21 of the law states:

> Feminicide violence is the extreme form of gender violence against women, the product of violation of her human rights, in the public and private spheres, that is made of a variety of misogynous [hate against woman that is manifested through violent and cruel acts against her for the mere fact of being a woman (Article 5)] conducts that can imply social and state impunity, and can end up in homicide and other forms of violent death of women.

In cases of feminicide, sanctions foreseen in Article 325 of the Penal Code will apply. The concept of 'feminicide' is different from 'femicide' in that the killing of women is seen as an intentionally gendered act.

The law embeds an holistic and gender-based approach to sexual violence – including rape – and other types of gender violence. Article 5.4 defines gender-based violence as whatever action or omission, based on gender, causing harm or psychological, physical, patrimonial, economic, sexual damage or death, in either private or public spheres. Sexual violence is defined (Article 6.5) as 'whatever act that degrades or damages the body and/or sexuality of the victim' and that 'affects her freedom, dignity and physical integrity. It is an expression of the abuse of power that implies male supremacy over woman, denigrating and conceiving her as an object.'

The intended beneficiaries of the law are victims of violence who are women of any age who are have been affected by the violence defined in the law (Articles 5-6), including rape (as part of sexual violence), and who thereby are given the right to receive medical, psychological and legal attention, as well as education and training. Perpetrators of violence are defined as 'the person who inflicts any kind of violence against women' (Article 5.7). They incur administrative and/or penal sanctions for breaching the law, which vary according to the administrative civil and penal codes of the different federal entities. 'In cases of feminicide, sanctions foreseen in Article 325 of the Penal Code will apply' (Article 21). Perpetrators are obliged to attend re-education programmes, if competent authorities so establish.

The main mechanisms through which the law is supposed to work are the following: institutional coordination through a national system (Articles 35-37) and a comprehensive programme (Article 38) to prevent,

153

attend, sanction and eradicate violence against women, both of which have been assigned a budget line in federal budgetary law (Article 39); distribution of competencies among the federation, the federal states, the federal district and municipalities (Articles 40-50); attention to victim-survivors of violence, including shelters for raped women (Articles 51-59); and a gender violence alert (Articles 22-26). The national system to prevent, attend, sanction and eradicate violence against women establishes guidelines for coordinating the different governmental entities (Articles 35-50). For the prevention, attention, sanctioning and elimination of violence against women, the comprehensive programme includes education and research measures such as gender education and training of public personnel working in justice, the police and other relevant areas, as well as statistical diagnosis on the causes, frequency and consequences of violence to assess implemented measures. There is a biannual publication of general and statistical information on cases of violence and their incorporation into the national database on cases of violence, established in response to the *Convention on the elimination of all forms of discrimination against women* (ratified by Mexico in 1981) and to the Belem do Para Inter-American Convention to prevent, sanction and eradicate violence against women (ratified by Mexico in 1998). The authorities are to provide legal, budgetary and administrative measures to guarantee women's right to a life free from violence (Article 2). They have the obligation to create mechanisms to psychologically and legally support victim-survivors, and avoid secondary victimisation (Articles 13, 14 and 15). Institutional actors that fail to comply with the law incur administrative sanctions (Article 60). Civil society organisations concerned with women's rights are involved in the implementation of the law. Federal entities are asked to promote the participation of women's organisations in the implementation of state programmes, and to receive from these organisations proposals and recommendations to improve measures against violence (Article 49). The introduction of gender education into schools and universities has begun, while gender training of the police is awaiting implementation (Corte Interamericana de Derechos Humanos, 2009; Borzacchiello, 2012).

The Mexican state is responsible for repairing the damage caused by feminicide violence by providing, within the framework of international human rights, an investigation of violations of women's human rights and sanctioning of perpetrators; specialised and free legal, medical and psychological attention to victims; measures to prevent the violation of women's human rights; acceptance by the state of its responsibility in the caused damage and commitment to repair it; investigation and sanction of omitted or negligent actions by public authorities that led to impunity of the violation of victims' human rights; design of public policies that avoid committing crimes against women; and verification of the facts and information on the truth (Article 26).

The creation in 2006 of a special public prosecutor to investigate crimes on violence against women is a step towards a gender expert treatment of feminicide cases. Since 2008, the prosecutor is also responsible for trafficking, and since 2012, the office joined with the prosecutor on human rights, attention to victims and community service. However, the special public prosecutor's capacity for effectively investigating and sanctioning institutional violence depends both on the harmonisation of penal codes of the federal entities incorporating the law, and on adequate funding (Borzacchiello, 2012; Equis: Justicia para las Mujeres, 2012; for the prosecutor's budget information, see México Infórmate and Special Prosecutor on violence's budget at http://es.scribd.com/doc/108649493/Presupuesto-Fiscalias; for the monitoring of judicial sentences, see Articulación Regional Feminista por los Derechos Humanos y la Justicia de Género at www.articulacionfeminista.org/a2/index.cfm?aplicacion=app003&cnl=41&opc=9). The difficulties in implementing the Mexican law show that the formulation and implementation of anti-rape measures need to be carefully connected if the law is to be effective.

The 2007 Mexican law on violence against women aims at establishing coordination between the federation, the 31 federal states, the federal district and 2,465 municipalities to prevent, sanction and eradicate violence, and to support women victim-survivors, including victims of rape (Articles 1-3). These institutional actors are obliged to organise the governmental machinery in order to reach the objectives, including by investigating, sanctioning and repairing the damage that this inflicts on women (Articles 19-20). Assistance to victims of rape and prevention of rape are included within the broad conceptualisation of 'feminicide violence', which includes sexual violence. For the first time, the general law has given visibility to violence against women, women-murders and rape-murders; it has confronted public authorities with the problem; and has created instruments for making a diagnosis of violence, enabling reports, such as those jointly elaborated with UN Women, InMujeres (Federal District Women's Institute) and the Mexican Congress, which followed the increase in women-murders between 1985 and 2009 (ONU Mujeres et al, 2011). The law has created a framework for implementing actions to eliminate violence against women in the federation, federal entities and municipalities, and to combat impunity. Its status of general law creates pressure on federal states to implement it at the local level.

The law addresses institutional violence, conceived as institutional acts or omissions that limit women's access to protection from violence, thereby providing a legal basis to investigate and combat cases of impunity and institutional legitimisation of violence, including rape. 'Institutional violence' is defined as the 'acts or omissions of civil servants of whatever government level that discriminate, or have the aim to delay, hinder, or impede the enjoyment and exercise of human rights of women and their access to public policies to prevent, attend, investigate, sanction, and eradicate different types of violence, including rape' (Article 18).

The Mexican law pioneers a form of emergency intervention in specific areas known as the 'gender violence alert', which national or federal human rights organisations, civil society or international organisations can request, and the federal government, through the governance secretary (Article 25), can declare when crimes against life, freedom, integrity and the security of women trouble social peace in a given territory and society claims it; when an unfair disadvantage hinders full exercise of women's human rights; and when human rights organisations at the national or federal levels, civil society or international organisations demand it (Article 24). It requires emergency government actions to tackle feminicide violence in a given territory (Article 22). The aim of the alert is to guarantee the security of women, the end of violence against them, and the elimination of inequalities. It requires the establishment of an interinstitutional and multidisciplinary gender expert group that monitors the alert, the implementation of preventive justice and security measures to combat feminicide violence, the elaboration of reports on the affected area on the basis of indicators of violence against women, the necessary economic resources to face the situation (Article 23), as well as informing the population about the reasons for declaring the alert. Competent public authorities must assist victim-survivors of violence – including rape – through protection actions and programmes, provision of free, fast and specialised medical, psychological and legal attention to victims, shelters, interpreters to accompany Indigenous women in the process, training programmes and job opportunities for victim-survivors, and compulsory re-education programmes for perpetrators.

However, there has been limited implementation of the law. To date, only 23 federal entities out of 32 have adopted their own law on violence against women, which is the first step to implement the law, and only three federal entities (Aguascalientes, San Luis Potosí and Yucatán) have adopted the regulation that enables the implementation of the law. This shows that, despite the pioneer design of a law that addresses gender-based and institutional components of violence against women, and the progress that the 2007 general law has promoted, its implementation is still problematic (Borzacchiello, 2012). The implementation gap is mainly due to difficulties in the harmonisation of laws on violence, civil and penal codes, equality and of other legislative and institutional measures and policies between the federation and the federal entities that the implementation of the general law requires (ONU Mujeres et al, 2011). Mexican NGOs and international institutions report that implementation works better at the federal level than in the federal states (Borzacchiello, 2012), but even at the federal level, the implementation of the mechanisms that were established on the basis of the law, such as the national system and the national programme on violence against women, needs improvement (ONU Mujeres et al, 2011; Borzacchiello, 2012).

The strengths of the law lie in its conceptualisation of violence as the result of gender inequality, its use of gender-equal language, and its attempts to empower women victim-survivors. The feminist interpretation of violence in the law reflects the participation of feminist institutional, academic and civil society actors in the elaboration of the law. The Mexican law embeds the holistic and systemic nature of 'feminicide violence', which is not only (rape-)murder, but also a broader system of male domination, in legal institutions. The conceptualisation as gender-based promotes the understanding that this violence is rooted in a system of gender inequality, and that promoting gender equality can help to prevent rape and improve assistance to victims. The main strengths of the 2007 Mexican law as a practice to prevent rape and assist victim-survivors of rape are: gender sensitive analysis; comprehensive and systemic understanding of violence; making violence visible; addressing violence in both public and private arenas; addressing state legitimation of violence; addressing the impunity of perpetrators; use of gender expertise in the diagnosis of the problem and its embedding in institutions; institutional coordination and identification of the responsibility of each level of government; specific funding; emergency instruments to address violence in specific contexts; inclusion of gender expert NGOs in policy-making; preventive approach; attention to victim-survivors; and periodical improvements of the law by incorporating feedback.

Its more general aspects appear to be transferable to other settings. These include the holistic, gender-based and systemic conceptualisation of 'feminicide violence', the empowerment of feminist NGOs, the preventive approach, the use of gender expertise, and the creation of specialised structures and mechanisms to coordinate institutions and to assign competencies to the different levels of government. The more specific aspects of the Mexican law require more adaptation before they would be suitable for transfer elsewhere, such as the emphasis on institutional violence by public authorities through omissions and negligence that led to the impunity of feminicide crimes, and the establishment of a mechanism of gender violence alert. The weakness of the law lies in its limited implementation.

Specialised courts: sexual offences courts, South Africa

The holding of perpetrators to account for their actions is a challenge to the criminal justice systems around the world that few successfully address. The rate of conviction of rapists for crimes reported to the police is very low everywhere. There have been many attempts to improve the functioning of the criminal justice system in relation to rape, with the goal of increasing the rate of conviction (reducing the attrition rate) while preventing the secondary traumatisation of the victim in the process. This best practice example of specialised sexual offences courts in South Africa addresses this challenge.

The sexual offences court intervention, as part of this wider strategic vision, should be understood within the context of rape and sexual violence in South Africa: population surveys suggest a prevalence rate of around 134 rapes/attempted rapes per 100,000 of the population, and an estimated prevalence rate of 68-72 per 100,000 of the adult population (Statistics South Africa, 2000). Police statistics find a lower prevalence rate (in South Africa, as elsewhere, not all victim-survivors report to the police: one estimate suggests that eight out of nine cases goes unreported; see South African Law Commission, 2001) of around 114 per 100,000 of the total population, with just over 55,000 rape cases being reported to the police in 2003/04 (South African Law Commission, 2001). An estimated 40 per cent of rapes are of children (Statistics South Africa, 2000); in 2000 over 25,500 sexual offences against children were reported to the police (Sadan et al, 2001).

Findings from population surveys suggest an estimated 35 per cent of rapes involve relatives and intimate partners compared with an estimated 25 per cent involving a stranger, while 55 per cent of rapes reported to the police are committed by strangers. Patterns of reporting in South Africa, then, are similar to those found elsewhere, but rates are among the highest in the world, including those of South Africa's neighbours (Statistics South Africa, 2000). A survey that asked men in South Africa if they had raped found that more than one quarter (27.6 per cent) had raped a woman or a girl, including 4.6 per cent in the last year, and that nearly half (46.3 per cent) of rapists had raped more than one woman or girl (Jewkes et al, 2009).

Against this backdrop, in 2007 the law on rape and sexual violence in South Africa was substantially amended in order to reflect the commitment to criminalisation, reducing the impunity with which perpetrators can act, and to support access to justice for victim-survivors.

The Justice and Constitutional Department highlight the new Act (Criminal Law (Sexual Offences and Related Matters) Amendment Act No 32 of 2007) as a key part of South Africa's efforts to fight sexual crimes (Justice and Constitutional Department, 2008). Among other measures, it repeals the previous common law offence of rape, and replaces it with an expanded statutory offence of rape that is applicable to all forms of sexual penetration without consent, irrespective of gender. The Act also makes provisions for the sanctioning of perpetrators, including a National Register of Sex Offenders (Justice and Constitutional Department, 2008).

The government of South Africa recognises that its 'anti-rape strategy' must address the wider social acceptance of rape and sexual violence against women and children in order to make real impact. Strengthening the criminal justice response to rape and sexual violence is one strand in this strategy, and is designed to demonstrate that rape and sexual violence against women are serious criminal offences, and to support victim-survivors to obtain justice. Violence against women and children is clearly identified as a key priority in the strategic visions of criminal justice agencies, and has been designated a priority crime area (Sadan et al, 2001).

The idea of specialist courts is not new: the first sexual offences court in South Africa was established in 1993 in Wynberg by the attorney-general of the Western Cape in response to a public outcry over the way two rape cases were dealt with by the Cape Town magistrates' court (Rasool, 2000). Evaluation of early courts found these to be an effective way of dealing with cases of rape and sexual violence, particularly those involving children. Since their establishment in 1999, the sexual offences courts come under the authority of the Sexual Offences and Community Affairs Department in the office of the national director of public prosecutions. The role of the department is to establish best practices and policies that seek to eradicate victimisation of women and children, while improving prosecution, particularly in the areas of sexual offences, maintenance, child justice and domestic violence (UNICEF, 2009).

Sexual offences courts are specialised courts hearing only sexual offence cases. They are staffed by specially trained individuals from a number of agencies in the criminal justice system and beyond. Evaluation studies have found significantly higher conviction rates for cases of rape and sexual violence compared with those delivered by non-specialist courts as well as other benefits

They are separate from regular courts and are staffed by specialist personnel from numerous criminal justice system agencies and other relevant staff. A typical sexual offences court would comprise: a separate courtroom devoted to sexual violence crimes; a separate waiting room for victim-survivors and witnesses for the prosecution; a camera room with closed circuit television (CCTV) so vulnerable victim-survivors do not have to testify face-to-face in court; two specialist prosecutors (one who deals with the in-court procedures and the other who works with and prepares the victim-survivor for appearing in court); a victim adviser officer; and a social worker (Sadan et al, 2001).

There were 59 courts in operation by 2007 around the country, with plans for additional ones to be set up (Thomas et al, 2011). In addition, there were 25 Thuthuzela Care Centres in operation in 2010/11, with plans to expand the number to 55 by 2016/17, which offer a wide range of specialised services to victim-survivors (NPA, 2012).

Despite the positive findings, a number of limitations and weaknesses with the courts have been highlighted. One major concern is the high caseload in the courts, and the backlog of cases; Sadan et al (2001) found that the backlog was clearing over time, but nevertheless, the caseload remains exceedingly high. The other is the under-resourcing of the courts; this prevents some from meeting the best practice standards under which they are supposed to operate. For example, Sadan et al (2001) found that Cape Town sexual offences court, which deals exclusively with cases involving children, relied on the police to transport both victims and the accused to court – this sometimes involved children having to travel long distances in the same bus as the person who had raped or abused them. A lack of resources also meant that Cape Town sexual offences court could not provide lunch or refreshments for victim-survivors during the course of a very long day: this had an impact on the quality of evidence the children were able to give in court, and thus on court outcomes.

While the training programmes for staff were initially comprehensive (375 individuals being trained to coincide with the development of the sexual offences court programme) (Vetten, 2001), little intersectoral training occurs, and ongoing training is problematic, not for the lack of availability, but because staff are too busy to attend (Sadan et al, 2001). A further consequence of the very high workload placed on staff in sexual offences courts, many of whom are on 24-hour call, as well as dealing with very distressing and stressful cases without adequate counselling and supervision support, has been concomitantly high rates of sickness and staff leaving: training regimes are finding it difficult to keep up with the rate of staff replacement, and so new staff are not always fully trained (Sadan et al, 2001).

The infrastructure of some sexual offences courts is not ideal: they should include at least one dedicated courtroom for cases of rape and sexual violence, and a separate waiting room for victim-survivors: while most provide this, the waiting rooms have found to be of insufficient size to accommodate the number of people waiting for court hearings that day, and access to the court and/or waiting room and other facilities is not usually adequately separated (Vetten, 2001). For example, the four courts at Wynberg are on the fifth floor of the magistrates' court building, but there is only one entrance and one lift; and in the Cape Town sexual offences court, the toilets are located at the opposite end of the building to the court waiting room (Sadan et al, 2001).

Sexual offences courts are specialist courts designed to improve and streamline the handling and prosecuting cases of rape, sexual abuse and sexual violence (Quast, 2008). Some specialise in child victim-survivors, who are under 18 (Sadan et al, 2001). They contribute to South Africa's anti-rape strategy by addressing three aims: reducing secondary trauma through ill-informed, insensitive, blaming treatment of rape victim-survivors by member of the criminal justice system and wider society (Vetten, 2001); improving conviction rates; and reducing the lead time for finalising cases (UNICEF, 2009). This strategic vision seeks to achieve the 'holistic' management of sexual offence matters by all role-players, and to re-orient the investigative process from being police-driven to being prosecutor-driven. This is reflected in their design (Vetten, 2001).

Sexual offences courts are designed to improve and streamline the process of handling and prosecuting cases of sexual abuse (Quast, 2008). Staff are specifically trained in dealing with victim-survivors of rape and sexual violence in order to progress cases through the criminal justice system. Special prosecutors are the lynchpin of the system and are on 24-hour call, so that a victim-survivor can meet with a prosecutor as soon as possible after reporting a rape, and can begin preparing for court. That special prosecutor should then remain with the case through to its conclusion, providing consistency for the victim-survivor, and strengthening communication and information-sharing (Vetten, 2001). The sexual offences court process is designed to ensure the most robust case is presented at court. The use of specially trained staff has been found to help keep victim-survivors within the system, to extract better quality evidence (forensic, physical and witness), and to prepare victim-survivors to be robust witnesses in court, all of which contribute to increasing the conviction rate (Sadan et al, 2001; Cook et al, 2004; UNICEF, 2009). The use of specially trained staff also reduces secondary trauma to victim-survivors as they travel through the criminal justice process (Sadan et al, 2001; UNICEF, 2009), and the expert handling of cases in dedicated facilities shortens the time it takes for cases to travel from report to court outcome (Quast, 2008; UNICEF, 2009). All three are clearly interconnected and support each other.

Sexual offences courts are designed to be interagency, that is, personnel from different agencies within the criminal justice system, and other sectors, work in close collaboration. They include actors from across a number of government agencies, and some welfare and voluntary sector agencies, including special prosecutors, the police, victim adviser officers, social workers and staff from health. In 2000, one-stop centres for the immediate aftermath of a rape and the initial evidence-gathering and investigation stages were added to the model with the aim of improving the investigation and prosecution of rape cases (UNICEF, 2009). Thuthuzela Care Centres are attached to, or located close by, sexual offences courts, open 24 hours, and staffed by personnel trained to deal with victim-survivors of rape and sexual violence – medical professionals, social workers, police officers, victim assistant officers, a prosecutor and a dedicated case monitor who liaises between the victim-survivor and the court system (Johnson, 2012).

The Thuthuzela Care Centres have significantly contributed to the success of the model in increasing conviction rates and reducing secondary trauma for victims through efficient and effective evidence collection practices, and good communication with the police and prosecutors (Johnson, 2012). When victim-survivors report to police stations, they are transferred to the nearest centre, where a forensic examination takes place and physical evidence is gathered; an interview with a specialist officer is conducted and the victim-survivor's statement is recorded. Consultation with a specialist prosecutor from the sexual offences court is arranged as soon as possible after the initial report is made, and the victim-survivor works with a victim assistance officer to prepare for the court process.

The South African sexual offences courts can be considered good practice for several reasons: specialist courts are a policy intervention to prevent rape, which proved that rapists will be convicted and held to account, and to assist victims of rape by reducing their trauma. Sexual offences courts in South Africa are part of a comprehensive national 'anti-rape' strategy that identifies rape prevention and assisting women victim-survivors of rape as policy priorities across the criminal justice system.

They are designed to be victim-centric through the specialist training of staff to work with women and children who have experienced rape, and through the design of the court infrastructure, which enables victim-survivors to avoid unnecessary interaction with the perpetrator as far as possible. They operate under a principle of interagency cooperation and are staffed by personnel from all the criminal justice agencies, as well as those relevant agencies from outside the criminal justice system.

Average conviction rates of between 70 and 95 per cent have been reported for sexual offences courts (Thomas et al, 2011). Sadan et al's study (2001) found an average conviction rate for the Wynberg sexual offences court (1995-2000 inclusive) of 68.5 per cent, ranging from 65 to 76 per cent over the course of the six years. In the same study, Cape Town sexual offences court was found to have an average conviction rate of 55.5 per cent over four years (1996-99 inclusive), ranging from 41 to 66 per cent. By contrast, the South African Law Commission (2001) reports an average conviction rate for rape (all ages) countrywide of 8.9 per cent in 1998.

Case resolution, prior to the establishment of the sexual offences courts and Thuthuzela Care Centres took an average of 18 months to two years; within the sexual offences court/ Thuthuzela Care Centre system the typical case is resolved within six months from the date of the first report. This reduction in case time has positive knock-on effects for conviction rates (Quast, 2008).

There may also be some early signs of changing culture in South Africa, in part as a consequence of the work of the sexual offences courts: the National Prosecuting Authority's strategic plan 2012-17 reports that in 2012, sexual offences decreased by 3.1 per cent compared with 2009/10. This was due to a recorded decrease in all crimes against women and children, except the murder of adult females (which rose by 5.6 per cent) and sexual offences against children under the age of 18 (which rose by 2.6 per cent).

Sexual offences courts contribute back into the continued development of specialist court interventions by making available lessons learned and highlighting what works best, thus adding to the evidence base; embedded in a comprehensive national 'anti-rape' commitment by the authorities through strategy, law and policy priority status; and holistic management of sexual offences through the criminal justice process (linking back to evidence-gathering and investigation and forward to sanction and rehabilitation). Evaluative data from expert studies and other sources, including government reviews, is publicly available for use in the continual development of specialist court interventions in both South Africa and elsewhere – such data has been widely reported in international reviews of criminal justice interventions for rape prevention and assisting women victim-survivors of rape (see, for example, Quast, 2008; Mossman et al, 2009; Thomas et al, 2011).

Specialist court interventions are easily transferable to other settings: in fact, a number of other countries have or are in the process of developing specialist courts for rape and sexual violence cases, or for domestic violence hearings, many of which include an element of sexual abuse. For example, England and Wales have a system of specialist domestic violence courts that operate in a similar manner to sexual offences courts. A comprehensive evaluation of the specialist domestic violence court intervention found they enhanced both the effectiveness of court and support systems for victim-survivors; made advocacy and information-sharing easier to accomplish; and increased victim-survivor participation and satisfaction, which led to improved public confidence in the criminal justice system (Cook et al, 2004). Mossman et al (2009), Vetten (2001) and Rasool (2000) argue that the South African experience with specialised courts provides lessons learned about continual improvements that can help increase the efficiency of such specialised courts in other locations and contexts, although Johnson (2012) provides a note of caution, warning that the replication of the South African model in other contexts and/or locations requires a number of key criteria to be met, including a fundamental respect by all for the rule of law; a functioning and democratic police service; clear political will to stem the tide of sexual violence; and a civil society that is vibrant and supports accountability in all relevant sectors. Sexual offences courts are also being championed as potential interventions in other contexts that are similarly dealing with what appears to be an endemic 'rape culture'. For example, in an opinion piece in *The Hindu* on 14 January 2013, Gopalan Balagopal positions South Africa's anti-rape strategy with its sexual offences courts and connected Thuthuzela Care Centres as an exemplar of dealing with rape culture, and calls for the model to be transplanted to India.

Based on this case study and the international literature, a number of recommendations are made for future development and implementation of specialist courts. They should be: victim-centric, and specialist courts should place the health, safety, dignity, privacy and autonomy needs of the victim-survivor at the centre of the practice. Interagency working should be embedded within the practice, and should include agencies across and beyond the criminal justice system. They should be adequately funded. It is not enough to fund the establishment of specialist courts – ongoing running and maintenance costs must be adequate to ensure that the other best practice criteria can be sustainably delivered, and that the intervention can continue to evolve in ways that ensure their contribution to rape prevention and assisting women victim-survivors of rape. Comprehensive evaluations should be built in from the start of specialist court programmes; this will require dedicated data collection systems that enable the aims of evaluation to be comprehensively assessed while adhering to high standards of confidentiality and ensuring ethical principles for working with individuals within the criminal justice system are met. 'Gold-standard' evaluation methodologies compare the target intervention (specialist courts) with alternative interventions with the same/similar aims, in order to achieve this standardised data collection, and quality monitoring tools should be established across the full range of criminal justice interventions designed to prevent rape and to assist women victim-survivors of rape in order to enable robust comparison. They should be embedded in a comprehensive national 'anti-rape' commitment by the authorities through strategy, law and policy priority status. There should be holistic management of sexual offences through the criminal justice process (linking back to evidence-gathering and investigation, and forward to sanction and rehabilitation). Interventions in other parts of the process should adhere to the same best practice criteria as specialist courts in order that the full impact of such intervention for the prevention of rape and assistance to women victim-survivors of rape can be realised. They should be specialist: this is an intermediate-term recommendation in order that expert skills and knowledge on rape prevention and assisting women victim-survivors of rape in the criminal justice system through interventions such as specialist courts can be developed. The long-term recommendation is that best practices for rape prevention and assisting women victim-survivors of rape are mainstreamed throughout the criminal justice system.

Identifying potential perpetrators of rape in cyberspace: the ISIS and ICOP toolkits, European Union

The prevention of rape ideally requires action before a rape is perpetrated. One way to attempt this is to identify those who are intending to rape, and to stop them before they actually rape. This best practice example concerns the identification of men who intend to rape as they engage with their intended or potential victims online, attempting to deceive a child or a young person into entering a vulnerable situation. It seeks to identify these men in online chatrooms. It is an intervention that seeks to prevent rape by identifying would-be rapists as they attempt to recruit victims online.

Potential perpetrators of rape, particularly of children and young people, can hide behind multiple identities online. Unravelling these multiple digital personas is a non-trivial problem owing to the large amounts of text communicated in online social media, and the large numbers of digital personas involved. The cognitive load for cybercrime investigators is immense – existing tools lack the sophisticated capabilities required to analyse digital personas in order to provide investigators with clues as to the identity of the individual or group hiding behind one or more of them.

There are three main ways in which computer-mediated interaction connects with rape. The first and perhaps most frequently referred to is that of cyber-rape itself, where invented online characters engage in virtual rape in cyberspace (Dibbell, 1998; Powers, 2003; Nunes, 2006). Second, the internet and social networks can be an important source of education, information and awareness, both for the public and for victims (Burnett and Buerkle, 2004). A third connection is where rape may be a consequence of interaction online, such as where people meet on dating sites and go on to meet offline, grooming, cyberstalking and cyber-gender harassment, where threats are made to rape offline (Halder and Jaishankar, 2009; Citron, 2011; Rambaree, no date).

Identifying potential perpetrators of rape in cyberspace is directed at this third level of preventing rape as a consequence of online interaction. The intervention involves developing and applying software to identify potential perpetrators of rape in order to prevent future attacks, and also to help identify victims who may need support. The intervention has two pillars: the UK-funded ISIS project is focused on detecting age and gender deception specifically for the purpose of identifying adults masquerading in social networking sites grooming children and young people (ISIS, 2013). A follow-on project, funded by the EU Safer Internet programme, extends development to image analysis in order to assist law enforcement in the identification of new child abuse media circulating in peer-to-peer networks (Peersman et al, 2014).

The software is new and constantly in development and is currently focused on child protection. The two toolkits are currently being trialled by law enforcement in several European countries. They can be applied in any country to aid the identification of potential perpetrators of rape if accompanied by the right training and resources. An increasing number of rape cases may be both prevented and facilitated by acknowledging the role that this digital world plays for people across the world. Further research and improved awareness and legislation could extend this approach to rape prevention.

The text analysis toolkit has been tested in trials involving a masquerading adult and over 250 children in England. Across over 700 identifications, the ISIS toolkit had an accuracy rating of 93 per cent for assessing age in contrast to the children who were correct in 15.6 per cent of guesses (accuracy varied across year groups and ranged between 10.3 per cent in Year 7 and 21.6 per cent in Year 11). The accuracy ratings using the toolkit were thus significantly more accurate than those of the children themselves. For the purpose of personal protection rather than law enforcement, a free-to-download application, 'Child Defence', has been developed that enables children themselves to scan webchat through their mobile phones and to quickly detect whether the person they are chatting to is trying to deceive them (ISIS Forensics, 2013).

The primary purpose of this development intervention is to assist law enforcement and civic organisations (such as schools, health and social care services) to identify potential perpetrators of rape and sexual exploitation that originate in or are facilitated by computer-mediated interaction. The ISIS toolkit supports identification of patterns typical to a person's online presence and its interaction with other participants. This is achieved through structural analysis of the text (natural language analysis techniques), which extracts details such as the user names of those who are participating in the chat, or date and time information that can be used to model the conversation flow to identify patterns and trends over time.

The toolkit can quickly analyse and present intelligence about a particular participant including, for example, stylistic characteristics such as keywords, names, topics, etc that are frequently used or identifying patterns of online/offline times. Use of semantic categorisation allows parts of a conversation to be classified based on their meaning (for example, whether sexual or aggressive in nature) (Rashid et al, 2013). By applying these techniques to the model of a participant's conversation, it is possible to view any trends that may occur over the duration of the conversation, for example, to help determine if a conversation is becoming increasingly sexualised. The iCOP toolkit applies similar matching and profiling methods and new techniques of image analysis to detect child abuse media.

Trials with law enforcement are in the early stages, but early results are promising. At this level, however, there are a number of challenges. First, the extent of technical expertise and priority given within different law enforcement agencies to cybercrime is variable across different countries. While the time needed to track through many false negatives will be considerably reduced, in most countries, the rules concerning evidence demand that data obtained through the toolkit is still verified by law enforcement representatives. Furthermore, the protection of privacy rights and the ethics of routine monitoring have been an underlying concern for the project. To what extent does the potential detection and prevention of rape and abuse authorise the routine monitoring of individual activity in cyberspace? Careful application using country-specific policing methods therefore currently ensures that the toolkits aid law enforcement and do not transgress jurisdictional boundaries. This current practice restricts the potential of the toolkit, but observes human rights. It also has the effect of limiting access by potential perpetrators who might subvert the toolkit by hacking into the design. Furthermore, divisions of on/offline law enforcement and civic interventions may serve to weaken the prevention and response to rape. Practitioners may consider they do not possess sufficient technical expertise when mediated environments are introduced, and also because victims may consider that behaviours in mediated environments are different from offline behaviours – for example, viewing a screen rather than a face-to-face relationship. This may be exacerbated in conflict zones and developing countries where offline lives can be devastated by the proximity of war, poverty and disease. For example, Cassim (2011, p 123) notes that 'The increase in broadband access has resulted in an increase in internet users. Thus, Africa has become a "safe haven" for online fraudsters. African countries are preoccupied with pressing issues such as poverty, the AIDS crisis, the fuel crisis, political instability, ethnic instability and traditional crimes, such as murder, rape and theft. As a result, the fight against cybercrime is lagging behind.'

The toolkit is an example of good practice since it is focused on the prevention of rape. The intervention is transferrable and could be adopted by law enforcement in many other countries with appropriate training and resources. There are two key recommendations arising from this project. First, cyberspace should be included as one of the arenas in which actions contributing to rape occur. In order to make better use of existing resources, a key recommendation would be to begin to mobilise the competencies in civic actions to be alert to the role of cyberspace in rape and abuse. Offline responses such as shelters, rape crisis centres and health services focus support in the offline environment of victims, and rarely become involved in online prevention, other than through education. The intervention providing the app to children accepts the victim's positioning in the ontology of cyberspace and offline space as part of one digital world (May-Chahal et al, 2014). Second, the developing recognition of cybercrimes should extend to the recruitment of women for the purposes of rape and for other forms of sexual exploitation. Some cybercrimes are clearly recognised under EU Conventions, international law and national jurisdictions, but the emphasis in the area of rape has been primarily on children, with clear legislation around child abuse images and grooming online existing in many countries. However, this has not applied to the prosecution of cybercrimes against adult women to the same extent, that continue to be less defined in law and less researched (Halder and Jaishankar, 2009).

5

Conflict zones

Introduction

Rape is more common in conflict zones. This is linked to the greater use of violence during wartime, the absence of a consistent criminal justice infrastructure, the disruption of informal protections from households and the community, the greater gender imbalance in decision-making in militarised zones, and the specific use of rape as a weapon of war.

There is sometimes a division in analysis and policy between concern with the higher rate of rape and sexual violence by a range of men in conflict zones, and the specific use of rape as a weapon of war by soldiers. However, for some issues, such as services to support victim-survivors, there are shared features between conflict zones and other locations of humanitarian crises.

A range of responses to attempt to prevent rape and to care more effectively for victim-survivors has been tailored to meet the circumstances found in conflict zones and humanitarian crises. Some were introduced earlier, as special instances in the development of policies in Chapter 3 on victim services and healthcare systems and Chapter 4 on law and justice. But it is appropriate to pull them together in this chapter, not least because there is a distinctive policy field with its own priorities, logics for action and set of key decision-makers involved. It is a field that is constructed around the logics of 'security' and 'crisis', albeit that the content of the concept of 'security' is deeply contested. In the UN, it involves the UN Security Council. In the EU, it involves the High Commissioner for External Relations. In the UK, it involves the Foreign Office, Ministry of Defence and Department for International Development.

Following a review of the nature of international concern for rape in war, this chapter addresses services for victim-survivors; legal principles, definitions and their implementation in justice systems; and the attempt to address the gender imbalance in decision-making. Throughout, there is concern to address rape in a context that is more saturated than usual with other forms of violence. Perhaps the most striking difference between the policy field of 'conflict zones' and other policy fields lies in the determination to change the gender imbalance in decision-making that has been at the heart of the UN Security Council resolutions to prevent gender and sexual violence in conflict zones. While reducing the gender imbalance in conflict zones is a feature of many feminist interventions, it has received a strikingly high profile in this context.

International concern about links between rape in war

Sometimes there is a clear boundary between sexual exploitation in prostitution/sex work that is nonetheless ostensibly consensual, and rape where there is no consent, although sometimes the boundary is blurred as the consequence of the coercive environment found in conflict zones. The arrival of armies has often been associated with a rise in prostitution and sexual exploitation (Enloe, 1990). A UNIFEM report noted an association 'between the arrival of peacekeeping personnel and increased prostitution, sexual exploitation and HIV/ AIDS infection' (Rehn and Johnson Sirleaf, 2002, p 61). For example, there was a high level of allegations concerning sexual exploitation, and abuse was levelled against the UN Department of Peacekeeping Operations 2008-09, in particular, the UN Organisation Mission in the Democratic Republic of Congo (UN, 2010b).

The majority of sexual violence is conducted by the fighting forces during conflict, but perpetrators in post-conflict zones can also include peacekeeping troops, and community and family members (UN, 2010b; Willett, 2010; Simić, 2012).

The use of rape as a weapon of war was long ago noted by Brownmiller (1976). The UNHCR (2003, p 7) reported on evidence gathered about rape and sexual violence used against women in times of war. From Sierra Leone to Rwanda, from Bosnia-Herzegovina to Afghanistan, rape has been used as a tactic of war. Sexual violence and rape as a warfare tactic has been documented in Bosnia, Cambodia, Liberia, Peru, Somalia and Uganda. The UNHCR report estimates over 500,000 women in Rwanda were raped in 1994, 60,000 in Croatia and Bosnia-Herzegovina between 1991 and 2001, 64,000 in Sierra Leone, and 32,000 in South Kivu province in the Democratic Republic of Congo in 2005.

There have been many condemnations of rape in times of war, including from international bodies, and multiple resolutions from the UN, including UN Security Council Resolution 1743 (concerning Haiti), 1034 (concerning Bosnia), 1493 (concerning the Democratic Republic of the Congo) and 1539 (concerning children). In 2013, the G8 (Canada, France, Germany, Italy, Japan, Russia, the UK and US) made a *Declaration on preventing sexual violence in conflict*, which declared that rape and other serious violence amount to war crimes and grave breaches of the Geneva Conventions, so states ought to investigate and prosecute such acts, wherever they occur (G8, 2013). The Council of Europe (2009a) issued a resolution in 2009 condemning the use of rape as a weapon. The European Parliament passed resolutions in 2008, 2009 and 2011 calling for action to support women who were victims of rape in war, especially in the Democratic Republic of Congo (European Parliament, 2011b).

Services for victim-survivors

The services needed by victim-survivors of rape are very similar in both conflict and non-conflict zones, but the resources available to provide the services are likely to be substantially less in conflict zones. A set of recommendations for services in conflict zones has been constructed by international agencies. These were detailed in Chapter 3 earlier, and are not repeated here. The case study of good practice for this chapter is that of the work of the International Rescue Committee (IRC) in the provision of health-based services for victim-survivors of rape in conflict zones, discussed below.

International law and justice

Rape is illegal, whether it is a weapon of war or not. However, much of the interest in legal aspects of rape in conflict zones has concerned the use of rape as a weapon of war.

There are several legal regimes relevant to rape in conflict zones (see Chapter 4 earlier). Rape was illegal under international humanitarian law articulated in the Lieber Code of 24 April 1863, also known as Instructions for the Armies of the US in the Field (Article 44). The early versions of the Geneva Convention did not contain protections to civilians (although there were incremental additions to the Convention), but in the 1949 (Fourth) Geneva Convention, under the auspices of the UN, there was a requirement to protect women and children from rape and other forms of sexual violence. Rape is recognised as a crime under international law in the Rome Statute of the International Criminal Court (2011). It is considered not only as a war crime, but additionally, if it is committed as 'part of a widespread or systematic attack against any civilian population' (Article 7(1)g), it is classified as a crime against humanity.

Several of the various international criminal courts established by the UN Security Council to implement international law have included prosecutions for rape. However, the achievement of convictions for rape in war has been very rare.

In non-conflict zones, the definition of rape hinges on the absence of consent. In conflict zones, the issue of consent is different because of the generalised context of coercion. Indeed, MacKinnon (2006) argues that this generalised coercion means that there should be no requirement on victim-survivors to additionally prove that they did not consent when making complaints of rape.

Challenging the gender imbalance in decision-making

Challenges to the gender imbalance in decision-making have been part of the major interventions to prevent rape in conflict zones. With a shift of the meaning of security to include the social and human dimension, there has been an increased focus on civilians and women in peacekeeping operations. Civilians stopped just being victims, and became 'actors' in the peacekeeping process.

The aim has been to attempt to change the gender composition of decision-makers in conflict zones, and to narrow the gender gap in the composition of peacekeepers and negotiators to assist in the vocalisation of women's perspectives in the development of policies and programmes to decrease sexual violence (Hudson, 2000; Carey, 2001; Bridges and Horsfall, 2009). A more sustainable and long-term peace with fewer incidents of rape is associated with (post)-conflict zones where local women, local women's NGOs and other civilians have been actively involved in the peacekeeping process, and as political and legal advisers, as election and human rights monitors, and as information specialists or administrators. Thus, increasing women's participation in decision-making in peacekeeping forces and other (post)-conflict institutions is intended to prevent rape and other sexual and gendered violence.

The inclusion of women in decision-making aids the sustainability of the peace process, not merely constituting an abstract norm (Tryggestad, 2010). It offers an alternative to elite brokered and dominated negotiations that can result in a situation in which many countries fall back into conflict five or six years after a peace agreement (Collier, 2007). The process of increasing women's participation in decision-making processes is sometimes conceptualised as 'women's empowerment', which can be understood to be 'a process of awareness and capacity building leading to greater participation, to greater decision-making power and control, and to transformative action' (Karl, 1995, p 14), although not all commentators find this conceptualisation useful, since the location of 'power' is curiously opaque, and it is not clear who or what is doing the empowerment.

UN Security Council resolutions

The inclusion of women in decision-making has been mandated by a series of UN Security Council resolutions starting with Resolution 1325 (Jacobs et al, 2000; UN Security Council 2000, 2008; Shepherd, 2006; Farr et al, 2009).

UN Security Council Resolution 1325 on women, peace and security calls on governments to increase the representation of women in all institutions that deal with the prevention, management and resolution of conflict. It includes women as military observers, civilian police and humanitarian personnel. The implementation of Resolution 1325 requires gender equality at all levels of peacekeeping, peacemaking, peacebuilding and post-conflict reconstruction. It aims not only to ensure equality in representation, but calls for interventions that address gender-based violence against women during conflict, to train local security forces in gender awareness, to provide funding to protect women during conflict, to rebuild institutions that provide services that are essential to women, and to support women's organisations working in peacekeeping and peacemaking (UN Security Council, 2000).

UN Security Council Resolution 1820 (2008) on women, war and peace confronts sexual violence in conflict and post-conflict situations. The key provisions recognise a direct relationship between the systematic use of sexual violence as an instrument of conflict, and the maintenance of international peace and security. It requires the Security Council to consider appropriate steps to end the violence, and interventions to penalise perpetrators. Specifically, UN Resolution 1820 recognises that mass rape used in war, genocide and ethnic cleansing was a 'weapon'. It recognises that women and children can be targeted for rape, and calls for the immediate cessation of the use of sexual violence against civilians in armed conflict; the exclusion of sexual violence crimes from amnesty provisions in the context of conflict resolution processes; and an international acknowledgement of the importance of ending impunity for such acts.

A series of further Security Council resolutions have incrementally developed this agenda. Security Council Resolution 1889 (2009) contains measures to protect women and children from sexual violence in conflict situations by (1) asking the Secretary-General to appoint a special representative to lead and coordinate the UN's work on the issue; (2) to send a team of experts to situations of particular concern; and (3) to mandate peacekeepers to protect women and children (UN Security Council, 2009). UN Security Council Resolution 1889 (2009) reaffirms Resolution 1325 from 2000 (see above) by condemning sexual violence against women in conflict situations. It urges UN member states and civil society organisations to consider the need for protection and empowerment of women and girls, including those associated with armed groups, in post-conflict programming (UN Security Council, 2009). UN Security Council Resolution 1960 (2010) asks the UN Secretary-General to list those parties credibly suspected of committing or being responsible for patterns of sexual violence in situations on the Council's agenda. It also calls for the establishment of monitoring, analysis and reporting arrangements specific to conflict-related sexual violence (UN Security Council, 2010). UN Security Council Resolution 2106 (2013a) aims at strengthening the monitoring and prevention of sexual violence in conflict. UN Security Council Resolution 2122 (2013b) reiterates the importance of women's involvement in conflict prevention, resolution and peacebuilding.

Implementation of UN Security Council resolutions

In line with the UN Security Council resolutions, UN interventions in post-conflict zones have been concentrated on increasing the number of women in peace operations; appointing gender experts within peace operations; and gender training. The Secretary General's strategic framework to guide the UN's implementation of Resolution 1325 focuses on prevention of conflict and all forms of violence against women and girls in conflict and post-conflict situations; women participate equally with men, and gender equality is promoted in peace and security decision-making processes at national, local, regional and international levels; women's and girls' rights are protected and promoted in conflict-affected situations; and women and girls' specific relief needs are met, and women's capacities to act as agents in relief and recovery are reinforced in conflict and post-conflict situations (UN, 2011).

The UN maintains the responsibility for gender mainstreaming and gender balance in decision-making in peacekeeping missions (WRC, 2007; UN, 2000, 2006a; UN Secretary-General, 2004; UN Security Council, 2001), but ultimately, it is member states that are accountable for the number of women military peacekeepers. The UN has very little influence over the recruitment of peacekeeping troops at a national level (Hudson, 2000). This suggests that interventions must be directed towards the recruitment process at the national level, since countries vary significantly in the proportion of women in their military forces and diplomatic agencies.

Scandinavian peacekeeping missions have traditionally had a higher representation of women peacekeepers than any other region. Helland and Kristensen (1999) find that although the high percentage of women is partly a reflection of the economic, political and social climate, with generally high levels of gender equality, it is also a result of direct and practical interventions in the recruitment process. Sweden does not require military training as a pre-requisite for entry into peacekeeping missions, and life skills and education are taken into consideration. Women and men who lack military training receive basic military training prior to any mission (Helland and Kristensen, 1999; Olsson, 1999). Hudson's (2000) research found that in Norway, there is a 'holistic understanding' of women's contributions during missions, not only to peacekeeping, but to long-term reconstruction and post-conflict developments.

Peace missions with high percentages of women, such as Namibia (40 per cent) and South Africa (50 per cent), have been successful (Carey, 2001). A higher proportion of women among the international peacekeeping missions tends to have positive effects on local-level representation and democracy: when a 30 per cent critical mass of mission personnel are female, local women more quickly join peace committees (Carey, 2001). Further, local women confide more in female than in male peacekeepers, and find it easier to report sexual violence to other women. There are examples from Somalia where women experienced body searches by men as extremely humiliating, and reports from the peace missions in Bosnia and Rwanda, where women provided valuable assistance to victim-survivors of sexual violence (Carey, 2001). The presence of women in the case of peacekeeping and negotiations in post-conflict zones is crucial for the development and implementation of successful programmes and for women's empowerment, and is linked to the elimination of violence against women (Carey, 2001).

Involving women in the peacekeeping process is expected to reduce the risk of sexual violence and rape, and increases the likelihood of women accessing help. Moreover, women's presence assists in engendering trust, improving the reputation of peacekeepers and in facilitating the peace process (Stiehm, 1997; Hudson, 2000; Carey, 2001; Karamé, 2001; Skjelsbaek, 2001; DeGroot, 2002; International Alert, 2002; Allred, 2006; Hagen, 2006; Bridges and Horsfall, 2009). It is also likely that the increased presence of women explains how and why sexual misconduct by military peacekeeping troops was placed on the agenda in the first place (the Namibia mission) (Hudson, 2000).

However, despite the UN resolutions and the many calls for change, women are still under-represented at all levels of peacekeeping processes (UN, 2007; UN Women, 2012a). Tickner (1992) argues that masculine values underpin international politics and limit possible interventions by policy-makers; the state is not a neutral 'provider of security', but rather sustains and delivers policy primarily in the interests of men. Shepherd (2006), by contrast, is sceptical of strategies that she sees as 'essentialising' gendered categories.

Although there are some existing gender experts and gender training within the UN system (Rehn and Johnson Sirleaf, 2002; Willet, 2010), the representation of women in peacekeeping missions is as low as 2-2.7 per cent (UN, 2007, 2012).

In a review of 14 out of 35 major peace negotiations since the adoption of Resolution 1325, UNIFEM found that only 1.2 per cent of the signatories of peace agreements were women; women accounted for 9.6 per cent of negotiating delegations; and not a single woman served as a negotiator, mediator, signatory or witness in the peace negotiations in Indonesia, Nepal, Somalia, Cote d'Ivoire, the Philippines or the Central African Republic (Goetz, 2008). Women are not only missing from the formal peace processes, but negotiations and programmes are also too often externally imposed on local populations and lack strong local roots (Dharmapuri, 2013). Consequently, the voices of local women are excluded, both by peacekeeping troops and local decision-makers.

Positive examples, however, do exist. UNIFEM in Burundi worked on capacity-building with local groups of women to enable them to participate in the peace talks. This intervention also showed the importance of using the 'time between the end of a conflict and the beginning of the reconstruction process in order to promote the participation of women in peace efforts' (UNDP, 2001, p 11). The challenge here lies in developing participatory processes of implementation to overcome the idea of the 'natural bond' between the protector and the protected in security situations (Enloe, 2007). Willett (2010) applied this reasoning to peacekeeping forces, and concludes that the peacekeeper/protector can claim to speak on behalf of the protected, and therefore lacks incentive to include women as well as local women's groups in decision-making. Willett (2010, p 147) writes, 'gender mainstreaming in peacekeeping means changing the relationships between masculinised protectors and feminised protected.' This would mean challenging the notion that the military is the most expert source of understanding the nature of security. Peace negotiations should include a variety of different views of the character of a society.

The UN 10-year impact study of Resolution 1325 shows that although there has been success in supporting the adoption of laws to combat sexual violence and in training the judiciary and the police, violence remains widespread. The security of women has only been improved by missions that supported active protection measures, such as joint protection teams involving both international peacekeepers and local groups. The impact study concludes that a 'more concerted and robust response from national and international actors is required to fight against SGBV [sexual and gender-based violence] as it remains highly prevalent' (UN, 2010b, p 10).

Other UN interventions

The UN special representative of the Secretary-General on sexual violence in conflict, who chairs the network UN Action, underlines the importance of empowering women and awareness-raising for the prevention of rape and the protection of victims. The special representative is mandated with five priorities to address rape in conflict and post-conflict zones: (1) to end impunity for conflict-related sexual violence; (2) to empower women to seek redress; (3) to mobilise political ownership; (4) to increase recognition of rape; and (5) to harmonise the UN's response to rape in conflict and post-conflict zones.

The UNHCR (2003) has issued guidelines for prevention and response in order to address sexual and gender-based violence against refugees, returnees and internally displaced people. These include involving and respecting the refugees themselves; ensuring a coordinated multisectoral approach; ensuring the safety and confidentiality of the victim; identifying points of particular vulnerability; transforming sociocultural norms, with an emphasis on empowering women and girls; rebuilding family and community structures and support systems; designing effective services and facilities; working with formal and traditional legal systems to ensure that their practices conform to international human rights standards; and monitoring and documenting incidents of sexual and gender-based violence.

Conclusion

In addition to formal compliance with UN Security Council Resolution 1325, and following the guidelines of UNHCR (2003), further recommendations can be made:

- ensure that the intervention is victim-centric and gender sensitive;
- establish joint protection teams and implement codes of conduct for peacekeeping forces;
- ensure coordinated multisectoral action by all actors (community services, health, protection, security);

- establish formal ways of holding actors accountable, including those involved in programmes targeting sexual exploitation and violence;
- prosecute people responsible for serious violations of international humanitarian law, including rape, sexual slavery, forced prostitution or any other form of sexual violence, by special courts;
- offer tailored training for senior managers, gender advisers and programme staff on how to integrate and mainstream a gender perspective in programmes;
- engage local security forces in gender awareness;
- peace consolidation, female leadership and gender mainstreaming in peacekeeping missions;
- practice local community participation as important for all stages of programming for prevention and responses to sexual and gender-based violence, including the planning stage;
- provide specialist gender expertise and also mainstream actions to prevent and respond to sexual and gender-based violence in already existing programmes, as special programmes to prevent sexual abuse and rape are less likely to be sustainable over the long term.

Women's participation in peace negotiations and peace agreements should include: raising awareness on Resolution 1325 provisions through workshops and its translation into local languages; coaching and technical assistance to women's groups and delegates to mainstream gender in peace agreements; training women's organisations and potential representatives in negotiation skills, advocacy and in-depth understanding of Resolution 1325 provisions; and establishing gender units in peacekeeping operations to ensure that women are not only represented in peace negotiations, but are also informed and able to articulate their concerns.

An example of a good practice in conflict zones is: 'Health-based services in a conflict zone: the International Rescue Committee (IRC)'.

Health-based services in a conflict zone: the International Rescue Committee (IRC)

Conflict zones (zones of newly emerging or re-emerging conflict, ongoing conflict and post-conflict) pose special problems for the provision of specialised services to support victim-survivors. Mobilising comprehensive services to respond locally in conflict zones is logistically complex, with many programmes and international organisations reporting multisector, multi-agency working to prevent and respond to rape and sexual violence against women in conflict zones (UN Action Against Sexual Violence in Conflict, 2015). Health-based services are potentially sites of good practices in such a context of humanitarian emergencies. This example of best practice is drawn from the work of the IRC, an organisation delivering tailored suites of practices and responding to the multifaceted contexts of conflict zones.

The IRC is an established organisation responding to humanitarian crises. In particular, its focus is to offer aid to refugees. One of the cornerstones of its work is to develop and implement programmes to prevent and respond to rape and sexual violence against women, during and following humanitarian crises. Working with local partners where possible, it shapes programmes of intervention for rape and sexual violence in relation to the community's priorities and existing infrastructure. The IRC has systems to support three distinct phases in conflict zones:

• it provides emergency crisis response teams and first responder services to victim-survivors of rape and sexual violence;
• it supports local establishment (or re-establishment) of long-term, integrated and women-centred health, mental health and legal services for victim-survivors of rape and sexual violence; and
• it supports long-term projects in post-conflict societies that continue to support rape and sexual violence services, and works to promote gender equality through the prevention of gender-based violence against women, and the promotion of women's economic independence and full democratic participation in social life.

The annual report on the impact of IRC programmes of intervention indicates that in 2012, IRC programmes provided care and counselling for over 22,000 survivors of sexual violence, and provided education about sexual violence to over 982,000 men, women and children to enable them to lead sexual violence prevention initiatives in their communities. In their Syrian report (IRC, 2013), the IRC documents the accounts of Syrian women and girls who cite rape as the primary reason for their displacement, and also documents the lack of health and psychosocial services available to victim-survivors.

However, the IRC (2013) clearly articulates difficulties in the delivery of services for victim-survivors of rape and sexual violence in conflict zones. Healthcare workers are often targets of violence themselves, and international aid organisations may not be able to gain access to the conflict zone directly, limiting service provision in conflict zones. In addition, many refugees are hard to reach, living not in refugee camps, but dispersed in very poor conditions across urban and rural areas, and are generally underserved. In their Syrian field report, the IRC (2013) found few services for sexual violence and rape in place for Syrian refugees displaced in Jordan, Lebanon and Iraq. To provide effective sexual violence and rape prevention and response services directly in conflict zones and in refugee camps in neighbouring non-conflict zones, organisations such as the IRC and countries hosting refugees are dependent on financial aid, and donors must respond to humanitarian aid funding appeals.

The IRC's programmes of intervention are developed in collaboration with local partners where possible, and their aims are to respond to the immediate needs of victim-survivors of rape and sexual violence in conflict zones and to prevent further violence; establish local infrastructure of integrated health, mental health and legal services for both the immediate and long-term needs of victim-survivors of rape and sexual violence in conflict zones; and build long-term capacity in rape and sexual violence services and community responses to end violence against women, to promote women's economic independence and full democratic participation in social life.

The IRC emergency response teams are made up of a range of specialist practitioners that assess and coordinate an appropriate response in acute and/or ongoing humanitarian crises. An expert in the prevention and provision of services for victim-survivors of rape and sexual violence forms part of this response team to establish a programme of intervention for victim-survivors of rape and sexual violence, in collaboration with local and international partners.

Programmes of intervention for rape and sexual violence prevention and assistance are supported by the IRC's Gender-Based Violence Technical Unit. The IRC maintains an emergency response team and pre-positioned emergency supplies that can be mobilised to anywhere in the world within 72 hours. It is currently running programmes to prevent and respond to sexual violence and rape in many different conflict zones and post-conflict zones around the world.

The IRC's programmes of intervention are comprehensive and holistic in respect of providing immediate responses for the prevention of rape and sexual violence against women and services for victim-survivors of rape and sexual violence in newly emerging humanitarian crises; establishing long-term community prevention initiatives and victim-survivor support and services in conflict and post-conflict zones; promoting women's reintegration and full democratic participation in social life in conflict and post-conflict zones; providing programmes that address logistic complexity; and providing reports on the status of crises and on the humanitarian aid needed to respond.

As a first responder to humanitarian crises in conflict zones, IRC programmes have a history of providing comprehensive and confidential health and psychosocial support services to victim-survivors within health facilities, and presently IRC teams are responding to recently increasing reports of sexual violence and rape in North Kivu, Democratic Republic of Congo. Once a service has been established, awareness-raising information about the rape and sexual violence services available to victim-survivors is distributed to communities, often by IRC community workers.

In developing long-term services, the IRC works with local partners to build long-term capacity and to develop a community collective of a comprehensive range of health, mental health and legal services for the immediate and long-term needs of victim-survivors of rape and sexual violence. It recognises the criticality of local women's networks, and works collaboratively with local partners to develop services, community referral pathways for victim-survivors and women's support systems. Central to IRC programmes of aid are the creation of local, safe spaces for women. These local women's centres provide access to sexual violence-specific resources, support and referrals for victim-survivors. In addition, they offer emotional support and social interaction, and house literacy and skills-building classes and information about health.

Presently the IRC has opened women's centres for Syrian refuges in the Lebanon. The centres have trained caseworkers and counsellors, offer support groups, and provide confidential, specialised sexual violence and rape and referrals to other services.

In Iraq the IRC has provided workshops and awareness-raising activities for Syrian refugees to address violence against women and girls, and trained the Iraqi police in how to respond to sexual violence.

In Jordan, the IRC is providing primary healthcare, free medicine and essential items to Syrian refugees, and for women refugees in particular it is providing emotional support, reproductive healthcare and hygiene materials. Recognising women and girls as a refugee group at high risk, the IRC, in collaboration with other agencies, prioritises the protection of women and girls at refugee camps.

In promoting gender equality and women's democratic participation, the IRC's long-term intervention programmes focus on women's access to violence response services; promoting community responses to end violence against women; increasing women's economic independence; increasing women's democratic participation in social life; and women's advocacy at national level. The IRC's women's centres' skills-building classes are linked with other income-generation activities to promote women's economic independence. IRC teams work with local leaders to promote women's rights. Reflecting the interconnections of multiple forms of gender-based sexual violence, the IRC has recently launched a campaign to address domestic violence in post-conflict zones.

The International Campaign to Stop Rape and Gender Violence in Conflict (www.stoprapeinconflict.org) has three pillars: prevention, protection and prosecution. These call on political leadership to prevent rape in conflict, to protect victim-survivors of rape, and to prosecute those responsible. Indeed, a high-level panel convened during the 67th UN General Assembly (UN Women, 2012b) called 'on world leaders for stronger actions to secure justice for survivors of conflict-related sexual violence and gender-based crimes' (UN Women, 2012b). Evident here is the political will to move beyond prevention and protection to encompass justice; justice is interpreted as including not only prosecution of those responsible, but also justice for survivors.

Justice for survivors involves care and services for survivors, the means for survivors to recover losses, and to fully participate as equal members in society (Bachelet and Bangura, cited in UN Women, 2012b).

In terms of quality monitoring, the IRC programmes for rape and sexual violence interventions are supported by the IRC's Gender-Based Violence Technical Unit. This is concerned with programme quality, and is responsible for developing policy and practice, programmes of staff learning and development, research, and for providing technical support. The IRC monitors its programmes' activities, and collects data on rape and sexual violence to produce reports and to target responses and programme interventions appropriately.

While the interventions identified in this best practice case study are clearly aimed at women's recovery and protection from rape and sexual violence, difficulties in service provision, and access in conflict zones and refugee camps and for displaced populations remains widespread (IRC, 2013). In addition, justice in terms of holding those responsible to account is also limited. It can therefore can be concluded that although developments have been forged in responding to rape and sexual violence in conflict and post-conflict zones, inadequacies remain, and services may take many years to become established.

Pressing and difficult issues for global communities in responding to rape and sexual violence in conflict zones are access to conflict zones to provide supplies and services for victim-survivors of rape, and initiatives to promote the collection of evidence of rape and sexual violence so that those responsible can be called to account.

The international community should develop strategic global contingency plans including funding initiatives that place gender-based violence as a priority to provide for an immediate response to rape and sexual violence in the acute phases of emerging humanitarian crises, for long-term rape and sexual violence prevention, and assistance capacity-building for ongoing conflict zones, displaced populations and post-conflict zones.

6

Culture, media and education

Introduction

The propagation of misleading myths about rape is damaging to victim-survivors in general, and especially when they attempt to seek justice. Rape myths and rape culture take diverse forms in new and old media and cultural industries, while the commercialisation of sex, and the circulation of extreme pornography, produce an environment that is less than ideal. There are innovative interventions in media and education to change public understandings of the nature of rape. Such initiatives include the development of projects to get bystanders positively involved, the use of new media to engage counter-hegemonic meanings and the development of educational programmes on healthy relationships in schools.

The concept of culture can be defined in contrasting ways: broadly, as overarching and all-encompassing of all social activities imbued with meaning; and narrowly, as a collection of social institutions that are significant in shaping meaningful practices in society, including the media and education, and which jointly, with other social institutions such as the economy, state and violence, constitute society as a whole. In this chapter, we take the narrower definition and focus on specific practices in defined institutions. We avoid the conflation of the two definitions, which can lead to over-estimating the effects of changes in one 'cultural institution' for society as a whole. To challenge and address the causes of sexual violence, the necessary strategy needs to address the full range of relevant institutions in society, not only those concerned with culture.

Civil society is multidimensional and contradictory on gendered issues. It is at one and the same time a location where new projects to contest and confront rape are imagined and constructed, and also where misogynist representations of women that are demeaning and glorify sexual violence exist. Masculinity is itself varied and contested, taking different forms in different places (Connell, 1995; Hearn, 2012, 2013).

Media

While most democracies uphold the freedom of the press as a value, some forms of regulatory practice have developed where excess has a detrimental effect on rape victim-survivors or in promoting sexual violence. Media regulation has been developed to try to offer anonymity to rape victims in court cases and to restrict the circulation of some images, for example, pornography involving children.

Some research suggests that the media perpetuates a 'rape culture', a concept that describes a culture where rape and sexualised violence are normalised and sometimes condoned (Burt, 1980). Norms prevalent in rape cultures blame and sexually objectify the victim rather than the perpetrator (Suarez and Gadalla, 2010). Analysis of reports concerning rape in a South African newspaper suggested the articles contributed to the reproduction of such 'rape myths' that blame the victim while reducing the perpetrator's culpability, and perpetuated racial as well as gender stereotypes (Bonnes, 2013). Dominant cultural attitudes may facilitate a 'continued tolerance of aggression toward women and thus the occurrence of sexual violence' (Iconis, 2008, p 47). Rape myths typically shift blame for rape from the rapist to the victim, and present it as a rare event. These include the myths that rapists are usually solitary strangers, that women cannot be raped if they did not want it, that women dressing in a culturally unacceptable way are 'asking for it', and that 'date rape' is not rape. The myths can be held by both men and women, and may be associated with the denial of rape victims that they have been raped, as well as denial by the offenders that they are rapists. Some studies have shown a correlation between rape myth acceptance and willingness to consider rape (Check and Malamuth, 1983; Bohner et al, 1998, 2005).

The myths about rape can have a detrimental impact on the access to justice of rape victim-survivors. They may contribute to the unwillingness of many victims to report rape to the police (Cohn et al, 2013), and have implications for how court cases are conducted and on the likelihood of conviction (Temkin and Krahé, 2008).

Feminist research and advocacy have long been concerned with the media's role and responsibility in reproducing gender stereotypes (Gill, 2007), and the way in which the popular press seeks the sensational in reporting sex crimes to keep or increase its readership (Soothill and Walby, 1991). There is concern about the growth of violent pornography and of the sexualisation of culture. Dines (2010) argues that culture is influenced by pornography, writing of the ways in which popular culture has become permeated by the images and ideas of pornography. Coy (2009) and Coy and Garner (2010) describe how processes of objectification develop, and how the sexualisation of popular culture limits girls' horizons. Debates on preventing sexual violence through interventions in the media (Buiten and Salo, 2007; EVAW et al, 2012; Ferguson, 2012; Machisa and van Dorp, 2012) have focused around the role of the media in sexual objectification; its normalisation of misogyny and violence against women by pathologising individual male perpetrators or by obscuring the role of perpetrators (Buiten and Salo, 2007); its sensationalistic reporting which trivialises the experiences of women victim-survivors of violence (Machisa and van Dorp, 2012); and the role of pornography in men's attitudes towards violence against women (Hald et al, 2009). The reality of sexual violence in society is often hidden, emerging only as occasional scandals. Although rapes of women by gangs of men are committed in countries as diverse as South Africa, Papua New Guinea and in parts of the US (Watts and Zimmerman, 2002), publicity concerning such reports of rape is less common. However, recent high-profile cases of sexual violence, such as the gang rape and subsequent death of a 23-year-old woman in India, increased the visibility of violence against women, and provided an opportunity to explore how best to challenge violence against women (Karzi, 2013). The normalisation of the objectification of women and violence against women indicate that the media sector is unlikely to adopt a gender-sensitive approach without huge political or public intervention (Larasi, 2012).

Media regulation

Media regulation has been suggested as one way to address these issues (EVAW Coalition, 2012; EVAW et al, 2012). Of several examples, three are particularly important – first, to make illegal the circulation of extreme pornography, such as that including children; second, to hide the identity of victim-survivors of rape who go to court, to reduce stigma; and third, to regulate the press more broadly, as proposed during the Leveson Inquiry (2012).

The most extreme forms of pornography are illegal in most countries, although the setting of the boundary as to what counts as 'extreme' is subject to ongoing contestation. The growth of the internet and new media makes the policing of pornography difficult. Nevertheless, there are interventions against more extreme forms of pornography.

The experience of rape victims during trials of alleged perpetrators is affected by the images and information presented in the press. In order to reduce the impact of the process on the victim, there have been attempts to prevent the victim from being publicly revealed through regulation of the press. However, the issue of anonymity represents a tension between the competing rights of the individual to privacy and the freedom of the press. The regulation of the media to provide anonymity for complainants in rape cases is practised in many countries, either through legislation (for example, Australia, the UK, India, New Zealand and Sweden) or through policy (for example, Canada and most of the US, with the exception of Florida and South Carolina) (Elliot, 2012), and research shows that there is strong public support for non-disclosure of victims' names (Denno, 1993). Once a complaint has been made, the claimant is often automatically entitled to lifelong anonymity. The purpose of the intervention is to avoid re-victimisation; to remove the distress rape victims suffered when their names and the personal details of their lives were revealed in the press; and to increase reporting rates, since publicity is often understood to be a deterrent to women reporting rapes. Further, reporting rates increase with interventions that shift the focus away from the victim-survivor towards the behaviour of the defendant (Clay-Warner and Harbin Burt, 2005).

In the UK, the Leveson Inquiry fuelled recent debates around sexism in the media (a judicial public inquiry into the culture and practices of British media, set up by the government after the *News of the World* phone hacking scandals in 2011; see www.levesoninquiry.org.uk/). During this Inquiry, women's organisations argued that newspapers glamorise, sexualise, and occasionally eroticise violent crimes against women and girls, and that this, in turn, normalises rape. A civil society study found widespread sexual objectification of victim-survivors, 'blame the victim' attitudes, and 'consistent, systematic sexism' throughout British media (EVAW et al, 2012). Media reports on crimes of violence against women were found not only to be directly inaccurate, but that they uphold stereotypes and false attitudes towards violence against women and girls. The study suggests interventions such as a new press code, with clear rules on sexist discrimination, and the setting up of a complaints body that includes experts on equality. The setting up of a new media watchdog is also suggested, a watchdog able to intervene in discriminatory media reporting and which reflects UK equalities legislation. The purpose of such proposed intervention is to prevent normalisation of rape, and the spread of what women's organisations have labelled a 'rape culture'.

Education

'School- and college-based programmes are designed to raise awareness, address gender norms, bystander behaviours, and knowledge and attitudes about rape and sexual assault' (WHO, 2014b, p 77). Interventions to prevent sexual violence include educational programmes for male children and youth. Boys' attitudes towards violence against girls have been identified as part of the problem of rape, and involving boys (and men) in educational programmes to prevent rape has been suggested to be part of the solution (see Flood, 2011).

There are many speculative education programmes, but little evidence that they work. The WHO (2014b, p 77) find that 'few programmes have been rigorously evaluated.' In a systematic review of strategies to prevent sexual violence perpetration, DeGue et al (2014) found that the majority of the interventions noted in the 140 outcome evaluation studies reviewed were brief psycho-educational programmes focused on increasing knowledge or changing attitudes, none of which had been shown to be effective when a rigorous 'public health' method of evaluation was used. The US Centers for Disease Control and Prevention (Breiding et al, 2014) finds that little is known about what works to prevent sexual violence, noting that only one programme had been shown to prevent sexual violence perpetration.

However, other accounts of interventions are more mixed, although they largely show that attitudes have been changed rather than that rape has been prevented. Violence prevention education delivered in schools and universities in particular have been evaluated as having positive effects on boys' attitudes towards violence against women (Whitaker et al, 2006), although there is a call for more evaluations (Lonsway et al, 2009). Male pupils and students who have attended rape education sessions are less likely to uphold rape myths than those who have not (Morrison et al, 2004). There is some evidence to suggest that various educational programmes have reduced men's (self-reported) likelihood to commit rape (Lonsway et al, 2009). Oddly, few educational rape prevention programmes are explicitly directed towards boys or men – only 8 per cent in the US (Morrison et al, 2004). Only one programme, 'Safe Dates', was considered to have met evidential standards needed to demonstrate that it had reduced men's actual sexual violence as well as changed their attitudes (Foshee et al, 2004).

Despite the lack of favourable rigorous evaluation, there have been many innovative and experimental developments in educational programmes to prevent rape. The purpose of the intervention is to reduce rape acceptance among young people (in secondary and tertiary education), with the intention of reducing real rape events. Programmes are generally didactic, that is, in the form of video and lecture presentations, although workshops and interactive theatre are sometimes used. Efficacy has been assessed by psychological attitude measures, such as the Illinois Rape Myth Acceptance scale (Payne, 1999), the General Attitudes Towards Rape (GATR) scale (Larsen and Long, 1988), and the RAPE scale (Bumby, 1996). However, the effects of the programmes are debated. Based on the US experience, it can be said that school-based programmes need more careful design, with measurement on attitudes akin to the college-based work. There is evidence that single-sex programmes work better than mixed-sex programmes in a college setting. Education programmes can be effective in some circumstances in reaching their specific goals.

Flores and Hautlaub (1998) examined numerous previous studies on programmes to reduce rape myth acceptance among males. The results showed that a variety of interventions, including human sexuality courses, workshops and video interventions, all appear to be successful in reducing rape myth acceptance, but benefits are sometimes short term. Brecklin and Forde (2001) carried out a meta-analysis of the characteristics of college rape education programmes most likely to increase effectiveness. They found that men in mixed-gender groups had less behavioural change than men in single-sex groups. Anderson and Whiston (2005) carried out the most comprehensive meta-analysis of North American college education programmes. Their analysis of 69 US studies found that rape attitudes, rape-related attitudes, rape knowledge, behavioural intent and incidence of sexual assault all had significant effects. The largest effects were found for increases in rape knowledge and rape attitudes. No significant changes were found for rape empathy and awareness behaviour. Longer interventions were found to be more effective than shorter interventions. Cornelius and Resseguie (2007) reviewed the literature on education programmes for the prevention of dating violence, which encompassed programmes delivered mainly at high school, and included both primary programmes (stopping violence before it occurs) and secondary programmes (stopping/exiting violence). They found that although numerous programmes had been introduced, in general they failed to assess participants on attitudinal scales, and many studies instead 'are simply assuming that changes are occurring' (Cornelius and Resseguie, 2007, p 372). Fay and Medway (2006), however, found that rape myth acceptance decreased in their study of students transitioning to high school with the use of a specific activity programme. More recently, Malo-juvera (2012) found that use of a young adult fiction book, *Speak* (Anderson, 1999), reduced rape myth acceptance in a high school group compared with a control group. In Scotland, sexual health and health promotion practitioners have been engaged in the development, delivery and evaluation of Rape Crisis Scotland's sexual violence prevention pack, a programme of prevention education delivered to young people in schools and youth groups (DMSS Research, 2014).

Community-level interventions

In addition to interventions in the media and in educational settings, there are interventions at community level. According to the WHO (2014b, p 77): 'Social and cultural norm-change programmes aim to modify norms of male sexual entitlement, and can reduce attitudes and beliefs that are supportive of sexual violence.' However, they note that 'Rigorous evaluations of social and cultural norm-change strategies are still needed to assess their impact.'

There are several types of community intervention, including saturation or community-wide messages, social marketing campaigns and bystander campaigns (Lockett and Bishop, 2012).

In Australia, a 'place-based saturation trial' is underway; this study will be evaluating the impact of simultaneous, trans-sector saturation of a community with messages, programmes and interventions formulated in reference to underlying determinants of sexual violence, to which addressing gender inequality and norms is central (WHO, 2013d; Walden and Wall, 2014). Similarly, in contexts of humanitarian crises, Holmes and Bhuvanendra (2014) report that community-wide awareness-raising programmes have been effective in reducing incidences of sexual violence and raising wider comprehension of its impact.

Projects such as the London-based EMPOWER work to raise awareness about specific forms of sexual violence. EMPOWER is a support programme addressing experiences of sexual violence and the exploitation of young women (aged 11–18) as a consequence of their involvement in gang activity. The young women receive support to address risks, improve their sense of identity, confidence and self-esteem, to develop resilience and the capacity for change. There are interventions that target the family level to ensure family members and peers have the tools to intervene. Projects devised to grow strong communities to prevent domestic violence recognise that this can only happen when people (neighbours, friends, or family members) can deal with real-life situations of sexual violence. Approaches and interventions aimed at individual change are more common than community-based interventions that engage whole communities and aim for social norm change (Krug et al, 2002; Lockett and Bishop, 2012). However, there remains a significant challenge to create a sense of ownership and responsibility for addressing violence at the community level.

'Bystander' projects are an example of a community-level intervention. A successful community mobilisation project to engage 'men as allies' and encourage intervention is The Bell Bajo or Ring the Bell advert campaign developed by Breakthrough in India and the US. It shows how bystanders can make small interventions when they suspect domestic violence. In one advert a man hears his neighbour shouting at his wife so he rings the doorbell to ask for some milk. This intervention works on a number of levels that have been proven to be effective – it provides practical advice on how to intervene in situations that could escalate into sexual violence, and also strengthens the cultural norm of safety and respect. The contribution of 'bystanders' to the prevention of rape and other forms of violence could be significant.

Conclusion

There are many interventions concerning media, education and communities that attempt to prevent rape. The intention of the interventions is to reduce the acceptability of rape found in 'rape myths' and 'rape culture', to encourage bystanders to challenge potential perpetrators, and to reduce the additional harm to victims produced by victim-blaming attitudes. The role of 'bystanders' is emerging as significant; it provides a focus of activity in addition to the focus on perpetrators and victim-survivors.

While there has been some considerable success in changing attitudes towards rape, including the acceptability of rape myths and rape culture, demonstrating any effect of these changes in attitudes on reducing the extent of rape is so far elusive. It may be that effects are mediated through the implications of such changes on other social institutions.

Included here are two examples of attempts at cultural change. The first is 'Sexual relations education: Southampton Talking About Relationships (Star)' in the UK, and the second, '#talkaboutit: talking about consent and coercion' in Sweden.

Sexual relations education: Southampton Talking About Relationships (Star), UK

The confronting of 'rape myths' and 'rape culture' is part of the strategy to prevent rape. Education has been repeatedly identified as a relevant site for interventions to prevent rape and sexual violence against women and girls. A study in the UK found that 72 per cent of sexually abused children did not tell anyone about the abuse at the time they were experiencing it (Cawson et al, 2000), while two separate polls of young people, also in the UK, found 77 per cent felt that they did not have enough information and support to deal with physical or sexual violence (ICM, 2006), and 93 per cent had no information about sexual abuse during their sex education classes in school (Baños Smith, 2011).

Interventions to tackle rape prevention are far fewer than those that focus on domestic violence: Southampton Talking About Relationships (Star) was the only project funded under the UK Home Office Violence Against Women and Girls programme in 2000 that focused on rape prevention; four others covered rape and sexual violence more generally, and the remaining 49 focused on domestic violence (Southampton Rape Crisis, 2011).

Star is a rape prevention intervention run by Southampton Rape Crisis (England) that is a voluntary sector organisation: the project employs specific staff to develop and deliver the project (see www.southamptonrapecrisis.com/star_project.html). The Star project is a set of programmes that develop and deliver interactive workshops to young people (in 2010/11, 54 per cent of recipients were male), aged 10-24, in schools, colleges and other youth locations in the Southampton area. Workshops tackle a range of issues around rape and sexual violence and the development of 'healthy relationships', including sexual exploitation, teenage pregnancy, internet safety, cyberbullying and substance use. Star also enables young people who have/are experiencing rape or sexual violence to access the Southampton Rape Crisis counselling service. Since Star first began in 2000, the project has worked with over 70,000 young people in schools, colleges, housing projects, young offenders groups and BME young women's groups. In 2010/11 521 sessions were delivered to 6,990 young people (Southampton Rape Crisis, 2011).

As part of the intervention, young people explore gender stereotypes and the objectification of bodies in popular culture and the normalisation of violence within media including pornography, so that they can explore how these influence the emerging sexualities of young people of both genders (Baños Smith, 2011). In this way Star works to explore the complexities of sexual violence and how it affects young people directly, with both young women and young men who work together, and so develop an appreciation of the pressures and expectations each other experiences while exploring alternative approaches to building 'healthy relationships' together. Interactive sessions are facilitated by both female and male workers who demonstrate in practice collaborative alternative models of male and female behaviours and sexual identities as part of the delivery mechanism.

Funding is a key limitation for Star as it is not guaranteed for the continuation of the work; the UK is currently experiencing increasing cuts to public sector spending budgets for projects like Star, and to reducing monies being available through private trust and grant funds (Towers and Walby, 2012). This may also be exacerbated in the future when schools in the UK move to hold their own budgets, instead of school budgeting for an area being help centrally in the local education authority (LEA). To date, interventions like Star have been commissioned by the LEA, but once budgets move to individual schools, each will have to be individually convinced that investment in projects like Star are worthwhile for their students by recognising the impact on children's behaviour and attainment caused by sexual violence, and by contributing to the wider objective of rape prevention (Baños Smith, 2011).

Star aims to reduce the incidence of rape and sexual abuse and to raise awareness of relevant support services (Southampton Rape Crisis, 2011). It aims to prevent rape by educating and empowering young women and young men to choose gendered cooperative relationship models that are respect-based and that comply with principles of consent. Star has also enabled schools and youth initiatives to develop their in-house policies and procedures to address rape and sexual violence more effectively. The purpose of Star is to equip young people with the knowledge and skills to recognise rape, sexual violence and abuse; know where to go for help; understand what is and is not acceptable behaviour; and to develop 'healthy relationships'. The programmes do this by raising awareness of the issues surrounding rape and sexual abuse, promoting skills to negotiate respect and consent within relationships, improving knowledge about appropriate services and support, and by talking about the different (and gendered) pressures felt by girls and boys. Participants also explore the meaning of consent, the right to say 'no' and how to recognise whether or not another person has given their consent (Baños Smith, 2011).

Star staff work with the youth providers to develop and implement their in-house policy and procedures on rape and sexual violence, which empowers staff to confidently and effectively deal with disclosures by young people, and ensures those young people are directed to the help and support they need to be safe, to recover their health and to regain their dignity, autonomy and sense of control. The intervention works by increasing awareness of the links between unequal relationships and unwanted sexual experiences, while providing the tools young people need to develop more equal relationships with each other.

The impact of Star is cascading beyond the boundaries of the project: for example, Southampton Rape Crisis, through Star, works in collaboration with other agencies to deliver parts of the sex and relationships education curriculum concerning rape, sexual violence and abuse in local schools. These had previously been neglected areas because teachers did not feel they had the skills or knowledge to deliver them (Baños Smith, 2011).

Teachers in schools have been reluctant to engage with Star for fear that talking about rape and sexual violence would cause a significant increase in disclosures from young people, which teaching and other staff feel unprepared to deal with: linking Star to the Southampton Rape Crisis counselling service, and working with staff to develop safeguarding policies and practices, have been key to engaging staff. This is why Star has been able to support schools to work with their own in-house policies regarding the protection and safeguarding of children, and school awareness of violence against women and girls issues has increased. This has enabled schools to get to know its pupils better, which has helped them to deal with behavioural and attainment issues. In one primary school, collaboration between Star, the local domestic violence forum and the school itself found that across two classes, 47 per cent of pupils had been exposed to domestic violence (Baños Smith, 2011).

There has not been a specific independent evaluation of Star. The most comprehensive assessment to date has been the End Violence Against Women Coalition report on 'promising practices' to end violence against women and girls (Baños Smith, 2011). This report identified Star as one of five education-based interventions for rape prevention, which met the designated criteria for promising practice, from across the UK. Despite the lack of formal evaluative evidence, there are a number of alternative measures that demonstrate to some degree the success of Star. For example, a 2010/11 in-house poll of nearly 4,000 young people who had participated in Star programmes found over 85 per cent had improved their understanding of healthy relationships, sexual assault and sexual exploitation, managing risky situations and knowing where to go for help (Southampton Rape Crisis, 2011). Since the beginnings of Star, referrals of young people to the Southampton Rape Crisis counselling service have increased six-fold: young people are now the largest client group of the service (Baños Smith, 2011). Star is award-winning: the 'PEP Talk' programme (Peer Education Pack) for Year 10 students (launched in 2007) was awarded the 'Actions Speak Louder' national award from the Department for Education and Skills/National Youth Agency for excellence in innovative work with young people (Southampton Rape Crisis, 2011).

Star can be considered a best practice case study for several reasons. Evidence shows that young people are at risk of rape and sexual violence, and that they are poorly equipped with the knowledge and skills to develop and negotiate respectful and consensual relationships: Star addresses this evidenced need. It uses an inclusive gendered approach to explore the complexities of sexual violence and how it affects young people, by working with both young women and young men, who collaboratively develop an appreciation of the pressures and expectations each other experience, while exploring alternative approaches to building 'healthy relationships'. Star is relatively easily transferable to other settings where there are youth-based organisations willing to work collaboratively with external organisations and to back up support for young people (provided by Southampton Rape Crisis) for whom the issues are real and lived.

Based on this case study and related research, a number of recommendations are made for the future development and implementation of education-based rape prevention projects.

- They should be gendered: best practice interventions should work with both young men and young women in order to recognise and explore the gendered pressures facing each concerning emerging sexualities and the realities of rape and sexual violence. They should also demonstrate through delivery mechanisms alternative gendered relationship models based on cooperation, respect and consent.
- They should be expert: best practice education-based interventions should be designed by those with expert knowledge of rape prevention, and should be located in, or have access to, expert support organisations in order to ensure that disclosures raised during prevention work are dealt with effectively so that the health, safety and other needs of the victim-survivor are met.
- They should aim to be systemic: best practice interventions should produce a systemic impact beyond the boundaries (physical and temporal) of the project itself.
- They should be collaborative: best practice interventions should work collaboratively with staff in the locations of programme delivery: this also increases systemic impact, including empowering staff to continue the work beyond the life of the project at that particular location.
- They should have adequate funding: best practice interventions should have sustainable and secure funding to both continue and to develop best practices for rape prevention through education-based work.

Comprehensive evaluations should be built in from the start of education-based rape prevention interventions, which will require dedicated data collection systems that enable the aims of evaluation to be comprehensively assessed while adhering to high standards of confidentiality, and ensuring ethical principles for working with individuals are met. 'Gold-standard' evaluation methodologies compare the target intervention (education-based rape prevention) with alternative interventions with the same/similar aims. In order to achieve this standardised data collection and quality, monitoring tools should be established across a range of similar such interventions designed to prevent rape by increasing awareness of the links between unequal relationships and unwanted sexual experiences, while providing the tools to develop more equal relationships, in order to enable robust comparisons of the success of interventions. They should make a contribution back into the continued development of education-based rape prevention interventions by making available lessons learned, and highlighting what works best, thus adding to the evidence base in order that future development, in the same and in other locations and contexts, can be evidence-based.

#talkaboutit: talking about consent and coercion, Sweden

This intervention makes visible how the understanding of rape in popular and public Swedish discourse is more restricted than the actual legal definition. #talkaboutit makes visible the way that rape takes place in the home, and is committed by someone known to the victim, and it enables women to talk about it: 'The law calls it a rape, but they/the women/don't consider it a rape. Women believe they can't be raped by a boyfriend, friend, or husband, that it must a stranger attacking her outside for it to be considered a rape' (Dahlén, 2010). The intervention enables victims of rape to talk about their experiences and to name it as rape since the act took place without their consent, even though many of the experiences described by victims were not violent (see Walby and Myhill, 2001; Walby and Allen, 2004).

The intervention was connected to the allegations against Julian Assange that constituted a possible tension and dilemma; #talkaboutit was quickly described as a conspiracy against Assange and WikiLeaks, which distorted the initial idea and aims. The network argued that #talkaboutit 'was not a campaign against Julian Assange, even though it could be interpreted as such' (JfA, no year), while one of the two main Swedish morning newspapers, *Svenska Dagbladet*, attributed #prataomdet (the Swedish for #talkaboutit) to Assange's arrest.

#talkaboutit could be understood as a social media phenomenon that started on Twitter on 14 December 2010, with a single Twitter hash tag, in the wake of the allegations of rape, sexual molestation and unlawful coercion against Julian Assange (Almestad and Beijbom, 2012). #talkaboutit is a grassroots collective, network, social movement and public campaign that connects to the prevention of rape by raising awareness, creating public debates about the boundaries between consensual sex and rape, highlighting the difficulties in naming and establishing those boundaries, making visible how rape is often committed by a perpetrator known to the victim (Walby and Allen, 2004) and how rape is a consequence of gender inequality (Brown and Walklate, 2012).

It draws attention to the way that that some issues that might be regarded as private are actually public and political issues, and attempts to alleviate some of the stigma attached to talking about experiences of sexual violence. It shows the existence of many hidden and unreported cases of events that are legally defined as rape, but that women and men find hard to name as rape. This case study is based on email exchange with one of the core members of the original network and campaign, who is the co-editor of the book *#talkbout it* (Almestad and Beijbom, 2012).

#talkaboutit started with one woman's tweet (Koljonen, 2010) which initiated a joint effort by a collective of around 20 (some well-established and well-known) journalists and other writers to enable synchronised publishing of self-lived experiences of sexual violence and the difficulties associated with setting the boundaries between consent and coercion. Originally, the group of journalists wanted to use the combined media space they already had access to through their employment and networks. The idea was to create debate from this joined platform on the basis of synchronised publishing of their stories for a bigger impact (Almestad and Beijbom, 2012). The articles about the boundary-setting dilemma were published in the four major Swedish newspapers (*Dagens Nyheter*, *Svenska Dagbladet*, *Expressen* and *Aftonbladet*), and other well-known and well-established newspapers and magazines and social media in Sweden (including ETC, Bang, City, City Skåne, Dagens Arena).

Television also quickly became involved in the campaign. One of Sweden's two key news programmes, the Morning News on Channel Four (TV4 Nyhetsmorgon), with more than 5 million weekly viewers (Sweden's total population is approximately 9 million), invited representatives from the network each day of the week leading up to Christmas 2010, where the campaign as such was discussed as well as the grey area between consent and coercion of sexual relations. Another well-known Swedish television programme, Debatt (Debate), also invited representatives from the network to discuss sexual violence and rape.

Geographically, #talkaboutit started in Stockholm, Sweden, but rapidly spread across the entire country, and later on to Europe and internationally (Escobedo Shepard, 2010; Gentlemen, 2010; Valenti, 2010; Gray, 2011). The campaign has had widespread international reach, with both the English hash tag and the setting up of websites in English. The actual location of the intervention is new social media and the internet, and is, as such, without geographical borders. After the first wave of publications, tweets, media reporting and television debates, a second wave of theatre plays, articles and more recently a book (Almestad and Beijbom, 2012) has created new spaces.

There are currently about 50 people actively involved in the core campaign group. The main involvement, however, comes from the thousands of individual bloggers and social media users who started 'talking about it' through the spread of the Twitter hash tag.

The purpose of the intervention is to raise awareness of sexual violence and rape, to make sexual violence and rape visible in public discourse, to set a new agenda, and to 'shake the boundaries of shame' surrounding sexual relations and rape (Hadley-Kamptz, 2010). The intervention could be understood as part of the continuing feminist struggle to highlight the links between private and public, and how the private is public. Koljonen's initial tweet was meant to highlight the difficulties involved when consenting adults (fail to) communicate sexual boundaries, and that many cases of rape do not overlap with the way in which rape and sexual assault are described and discussed in contemporary public discourse and media.

In the media, rape is often understood as the assault of an unknown perpetrator away from the home, whereas #talkaboutit tells the stories of how some people, predominantly women, experience sexual violence by a boyfriend, a partner or a husband. #talkaboutit makes visible how rape and sexual assault is inaccurately described in public debate and discourse as something that either is or isn't; it works by highlighting the difficulties many women experience in struggling to accept that sexual coercion in their own home, with a partner or acquaintance, constitutes rape. In this sense, the campaign also works as a reaction against the way in which Assange's solicitors criticised the allegations and claimed that what the women were describing did not constitute 'real rape'. #talkaboutit as an intervention works by showing that women's experiences of rape are in alignment with the legal definition of rape.

The involvement of all major Swedish newspapers and the Channel Four news programme means that the campaign reached quite possibly the majority of the Swedish population and a wide international audience. The intended initial recipients, according to Almestad, are best characterised as the Swedish people, involving them in a public discourse.

The intervention worked well, in that it fulfilled its aims to raise awareness and to make the grey areas of consent and coercion visible and subject to public debate. In 2011, Koljonen, who posted the original tweet, and Sofia Mirjamsdotter, who was involved in the original campaign, were awarded the Swedish Grand Journalism Award – the most prestigious journalist award in Sweden – for 'making the private relevant to the public and for making an entire world talk about it' (Swedish Grand Journalism Award, 2011). Koljonen was awarded several other prizes for #talkaboutit, including: 'Women's Deed of the Year' by the Swedish National Shelter Movement (Roks) in 2012 (Roks, 2012), the Swedish Association for Sexuality Education Award in 2011, the Gyllene Haldan Journalism Award in 2011 and the Stockholm Award in the Media category in 2011. Seen as a media campaign and political strategy, #talkaboutit was a success. Newspapers and media from across the entire world contacted the network and wrote articles about it and its aims and methods. Through the Swedish press, it spread beyond a Stockholm-centred media sphere or elite cultural debate.

The methods and social media used could be replicated elsewhere, but there are country-specific considerations to be made. The intervention uses the realisation that traditional media no longer can control what people talk about; #talkaboutit as a future project to be replicated elsewhere would have to draw on the functions of new social media to create a campaign and conversation that cut across all sectors of the media. Although the intervention requires very little resources on the one hand, in terms of material, labour or money, it requires large resources in terms of a social and political climate where gender equality is already a political priority on the other. Sweden is characterised by its high levels of gender equality, and the journalists who started tweeting and publishing texts in the largest Swedish newspapers were, to some extent, already established as feminist writers, and were backed up by editors who were positive to the intervention as such, and to gender equality in general. However, there is no reason to believe that similar collective, grassroots campaigns using new social media and synchronised publishing methods would not connect to the prevention of rape by raising awareness, creating public debates about the boundaries between consensual sex and rape and by making visible how rape is often committed by a perpetrator known to the victim.

7

Economy

Introduction

Gendered economic inequalities contribute to higher rates of rape and other forms of violence against women. Reducing economic inequalities is linked to the reduction of rape and other forms of gender-based violence, while reducing rape and other forms of gender-based violence is likely to improve economic growth and development (Moser and Shrader, 1999; Walby, 2004, 2009; Bedford, 2009). Strengthening women's economic status delivers decreasing rates of rape and increases the range of options available to assist women to avoid situations in which they are particularly vulnerable to rape, including within intimate and family contexts. The best interventions operate at multiple levels, creating systemic change, and locate the strengthening of women's economic status at the core of policy and practice.

The causal pathways linking rape and gendered economic inequalities flow in both directions. Victim-survivors of rape have economic needs, including for income and housing, as well as needs for healthcare and other specialised services. Improvements to the economic wellbeing of women can increase the resilience of women from rape and from some of the consequences of rape. Rape damages women's capacity for employment, and is thus a detriment to the contribution of women to the economy and to economic growth; rape contributes to the social exclusion of women.

Research findings have suggested both that a high proportion of rapes and sexual assaults are carried out by a perpetrator known to the victim, including intimate partners and family members (Walby and Allen, 2004), and that a high proportion of assaults by intimate partners and family members include a sexual element (Kelly, 2000). Therefore, the evidence base that is centred on intimate partner violence against women, if used carefully, can also contribute to identifying the best rape prevention interventions linked to reducing the economic dependency of women. Similarly, there are examples of successful interventions for rape prevention that have targeted women's economic status, the strengthening of which has been shown to reduce rates of rape and sexual violence.

The impact of economic inequalities on violence against women

The impact of gendered economic inequality on violence against women is well recognised by a number of bodies. For example, the UN (2006b) report on ending violence against women argues that economic inequalities can be a causal factor for violence against women, both at the level of individual acts, and at the level of broad-based economic trends that create or exacerbate such violence; and that policies such as structural adjustment, deregulation of economies and privatisation of the public sector can reinforce women's economic and social inequality. Similarly, the WHO has noted the disruptive effects of globalisation on social structures and consequent increases in overall levels of violence in society, including gendered violence (WHO, 2002; WHO, 2005a).

Cross-national comparative studies support these positions; for example, Asal and Brown (2010) found countries with the greatest levels of economic inequality reported the highest rates of intimate partner violence, while the WHO (2005a) reports that countries scoring high on the gender development index are those with low rates of sexual violence against women.

These observations have led to the development of rape prevention strategies that target the associations between gendered economic inequality and rape (see below).

The recognition of the impact of rape and sexual violence on women's employment, with consequences for economic growth, is a further aspect of the relationship between gendered economic inequality and rape. This has led to rape being recognised as a cost to the economy. For example, Walby (2004) estimated the cost of domestic violence (which included sexual assaults) to the UK economy to be £23 billion per annum, Walby and Olive (2014) to the EU economy of €258 billion, while in the US estimates range from US$15 billion to US$260 billion per annum (WHO, 2004a).

Some forms of assistance for women victim-survivors of rape have been delivered as part of a package of support programmes in order to help them strengthen their economic status through access to education, training and/or employment. Such interventions aim to provide women with a tangible means to resist and to exit relationships, locations or contexts that make them particularly vulnerable to rape. They can provide support for income and for integration into the labour market.

Economic and development interventions designed to prevent rape are relatively infrequent, but are gaining ground. In particular, the potential impact of interventions designed to strengthen the economic status of women, such as microfinance projects working with small groups of women in the developing world, are being increasingly recognised and formally incorporated into the design of such interventions, while also providing an evidence base from which more specialist interventions can be developed.

Rape prevention interventions: the evidence base

The relation between economic status and the risk of being raped

The EIGE notes the lack of available and systematically collected data referring specifically to sexual violence (EIGE, 2012a). Despite this, there is evidence to demonstrate that women in weak economic positions are at increased risk of rape. A weak economic status is relative depending on the context and/or location, but women whose access to economic resources is severely limited are more vulnerable to rape because a lack of economic resources restricts them from being able to avoid situations in which they are more vulnerable to rape (for example, being unable to afford to travel by private car or taxi or living in insecure housing).

There are a number of ways women can access economic resources, the most usual being through earned income from employment or welfare receipts, but also through income from pensions or study grants, or through ownership of material assets such as land or property.

In addition, a number of studies that have looked specifically at women's ability to make choices about exiting violent relationships show economic resources are a key factor in women's ability to leave (Short et al, 2000), whereas a lack of economic resources is a key reason women return to violent relationships (Anderson and Saunders, 2003; Agarwal and Panda, 2007).

The role of different forms of income

In one UK study of rape/attempted rape, Kelly (2007) found that the odds of being raped/having an attempted rape by a stranger both outside and inside the home were significantly lower for employed women compared with those of unemployed women. Walby and Allen (2004) similarly found unemployed women's odds of sexual assault were almost double those of employed women. In the same UK study, Walby and Allen (2004) also found women in the poorest households were more likely to have been sexually assaulted than women in richer households, and the proportion of women with low personal earnings (less than £10,000 per annum) experiencing a sexual assault was double that of women with above average earnings (2.0 and 0.7 per cent respectively). Perhaps most significantly, the study revealed that the odds of women who would find it impossible to find £100 at short notice experiencing a sexual assault were more than double (2.3 times greater) those of women for whom finding £100 at short notice would be no problem.

If a wider evidence base is reviewed, studies that have focused on intimate partner, marital or domestic violence that has included rape and/or sexual assaults support the findings above, that weak economic status correlates to higher risks. For example, Johnson et al (2008) found that women in Denmark with no income reported lifetime rates of intimate partner violence by a current partner to be twice that of women with earned or other sources of income. Tolman and Raphael (2000), in their review of US studies of domestic violence, concluded that the prevalence rate among women on welfare is consistently higher than that for women in the general population. The findings from other studies on the effects of employment are more mixed than those found by Kelly (2007) and Walby and Allen (2004), suggesting that employment per se may not be enough to strengthen a woman's economic status. Rather, the type of employment makes a difference to its potential for increasing a woman's resilience. Agarwal and Panda (2007) argue that in India, 'employment' for women may mean unpaid labour for the family enterprise, or that women may not earn enough to widen their available choices by, for example, setting up an independent household. Similarly, Riger et al (2004) found an inverse relationship between work stability and recent intimate partner violence, reporting that higher levels of violence were associated with fewer months' work, even when other factors, such as human capital, were taken into account. 'Precarious' (part-time, insecure, low-paid, low status, with little or no legal protection for workers) employment is associated differently to rape and sexual violence than employment that is stable, high pay and high status and provides legal protections for workers – that is, the 'quality' of employment, not just employment per se, may be the pertinent factor.

Property

Work by Agarwal and Panda in India on marital violence (Panda and Agarwal, 2005; Agarwal and Panda, 2007), found more consistent results when women owned tangible economic resources (land and/or house). The ownership of land and/or a house by women correlated to both reduced risk of violence in the first instance, and with women's ability to exit and remain free from violent relationships. The implication is that laws that allow women equal rights of inheritance are important in reducing marital violence, including rape. This is especially important in those countries, disproportionately in the global south, where employment does not provide a viable route to economic independence for women.

The role of housing

Poor women are also more likely to live in insecure rented accommodation or to be marginally housed or homeless, all of which have been found to increase their vulnerability to rape. Kelly (2007) found the odds of women in vulnerable housing experiencing rape/attempted rape by a known man were significantly higher than those of women living in non-vulnerable housing. Walby and Allen (2004) found the odds of women in social rented housing being sexually assaulted were 2.5 times higher than those of women in owner-occupier housing. Kushel et al (2003) found significantly higher rates of rape and sexual violence for homeless and marginally housed women compared with women in the general population, with 32 per cent of women living in such conditions reporting either physical or sexual victimisation in the previous year. Women in refugee camps or temporary camps set up in the wake of natural or humanitarian disasters are also vulnerable to rape – canvas is easily penetrable and does not provide a safe space for women (Kofaviv, 2012).

'Survival sex'

A lack of economic resources can force women to engage in 'survival sex' in exchange for food, shelter or other essentials (Jewkes et al, 2002). Survival sex practices have been observed in disaster contexts. For example, following the earthquake in Haiti in 2010, it was found that women were forced to exchange sex for food and medicines in relief camps (Kofaviv, 2012). Survival sex is, however, a routine feature across contexts and locations, disaster and non-disaster and developed, transitional and developing nations, where women, young people and children are found to be routinely forced to exchange sex for food and shelter because they do not have the economic means to gain the essential resources they need to survive in alternative ways (Greco and Dawgert, 2007). 'Survival sex' is a phenomenon very close to rape, with a fine line around consent potentially separating the two concepts.

Effects of rape on the economic status of women

It is not only that a weak economic status places women at greater risk of rape – rape and sexual violence have an adverse impact on the economic status of women. It can be a two-way relationship. For example, Estes and Weiner (2001) found 61 per cent of homeless girls reported sexual abuse as the reason for leaving home. Without access to adequate economic resources, these girls are forced to live on the streets or 'sofa surf' where they are more vulnerable to rape, sexual exploitation and 'survival sex'. In their study, Ellis et al (1981) found 50 per cent of sexual assault victims lost their jobs or were forced to quit after being raped.

Victim-survivors of rape incur significant out-of-pocket expenses they could not have foreseen or planned for. For many, this consequence is unaffordable. According to a report by the National Institute of Justice (Miller et al, 1996), the costs of rape and sexual assault for victims can include out-of-pocket expenses such as medical bills and property losses; reduced productivity at work, home and school; and non-monetary losses such as fear, pain, suffering and lost quality of life. For someone living in poverty, these costs can be devastating. For those on the edge of poverty, these costs can push them over the line. While assistance may be available to victim-survivors of rape to cover some of these costs, if such support or services require money 'up front', even if it is later reimbursed, this is simply unaffordable for many.

Promising interventions

While the evidence for an association between the economic status of women and rape is strong, the nature of the links is complex, multidirectional and multilayered.

The best interventions for rape prevention in the context of economic and security policies include the recognition of the relation between the economic situation of women and their vulnerability to sexual violence; enabling women to access the economic resources required in order to be able to avoid locations, contexts and relationships that place them at higher risk of rape; providing funding for an adequate supply of stable, safe and affordable housing and shelter; providing funding for an adequate supply of safe and affordable transport; ensuring that all necessary services to assist victim-survivors of rape are free at the point of use; and stable, safe employment.

In emergency contexts, accommodation in refugee camps for women must be secure, and access to food, shelter, medicines and healthcare should be guaranteed in accordance with the UNHCR guidelines (2003).

There are a number of examples of interventions that demonstrate these best practice criteria and at the same time often assist women victim-survivors of rape by strengthening their economic status. This enables women victim-survivors to avoid high-risk contexts, locations and relationships, thus decreasing the likelihood of re-victimisation, and contributing to long-term rape prevention.

Microfinance

One of the outcomes of microfinance interventions for women is decreasing rates of marital, family and community violence as women raise their awareness, confidence and status, and contribute material wealth to the household and community (Kristof and WuDunn, 2012). Microfinance interventions provide financial services to micro-entrepreneurs and small businesses that lack access to banking and related services due to the high transaction costs associated with serving these types of clients. There are two main mechanisms for the delivery of such financial services: relationship-based banking for individual entrepreneurs and small businesses, and group-based models, where several entrepreneurs come together to apply for loans and other services as a group.

Microfinance interventions with women, currently predominately located in developing countries, usually take the second form. In addition, a common feature of these interventions has been group-based education and training for the women in literacy and numeracy, business, health and their legal and human rights.

Microfinance interventions

Kim et al (2007b) performed an evaluation of Intervention with Microfinance for Aids and Gender Equity (IMAGE) in rural South Africa. Run by an NGO, the intervention has more than 40,000 active clients. It works with groups of five women who serve as guarantors for each other's loans: all five must repay their loans in order to qualify to borrow more credit. Loan centres of approximately 40 women meet fortnightly to repay loans, apply for additional credit and discuss business plans. The intervention includes a participatory learning programme called 'Sisters-for-Life' which comprises two stages: the first provides 10 hours of training on gender roles, cultural beliefs, relationships, communication, domestic violence and HIV infection, and is aimed at strengthening communication skills, critical thinking and leadership. The second encourages wider community mobilisation to engage both youths and men. In addition, women deemed 'natural leaders' by their peers are elected by loan centres to undertake a further week of training, and subsequently work with their centre to address priority issues including HIV infection and intimate partner violence.

The evaluation study recruited both eligible loan recipients and control participants who were women aged 18 and older living in the poorest households in each village for comparative purposes. The IMAGE intervention was found to reduce the levels of past year physical and/or sexual intimate partner violence by more than half, and levels of intimate partner violence were found to consistently decrease in all four intervention villages at follow-up, whereas levels either stayed the same or increased in the four control villages. After two years, the risk of past year physical and/or sexual intimate partner violence was still reduced by more than half among the intervention group.

Qualitative data gathered as part of the study supports anecdotal findings from other similar interventions. Reductions in violence appear to be the result of women feeling enabled to challenge the acceptability of such violence; expect and receive better treatment from partners; leave violent relationships; give material and moral support to those experiencing abuse; mobilise new and existing community groups; and raise public awareness about the need to address both gender-based violence and HIV infection.

The development of such interventions as part of rape prevention strategies is expanding. A microfinance intervention specifically designed to prevent rape and to support women victim-survivors of sexual violence by improving their economic wellbeing is currently underway in the Democratic Republic of Congo. The Care project (Care International, no date) includes the setting up of savings and loans groups in local communities affected by sexual violence. Sexual violence survivors are especially encouraged to join as a way to start earning a living, to reintegrate into the community and to access internal support. Care is also working in camps in the Democratic Republic of Congo for people who have fled their homes. Here the microfinance initiatives aim to give women a means to make a living, thus helping prevent further exposure to sexual violence by making it less likely that they will be forced to put themselves in positions where they are vulnerable to such violence.

The Johns Hopkins School of Nursing is currently conducting a research study to test the effectiveness of an innovative, village-led microfinance programme on sexual and gender-based violence survivors' health, household economic stability and reintegration to family and village. The aim of the study is to build the evidence base for large-scale implementation of economic programmes to improve the health of women survivors of sexual and gender-based violence (Johns Hopkins School of Nursing, no date).

Economic advocacy

In a report for the Pennsylvania Coalition Against Rape, Greco and Dawgert (2007) identify economic advocacy as a core requirement for rape prevention practices and for assisting women victim-survivors of rape. They argue that it is already a thread that runs through the fabric of rape crisis advocacy, but is rarely explicated as such, and is not yet positioned as centrally in such work as it needs to be.

Economic advocacy is defined as the provision of information, advocacy and support to expand economic resources and to reduce/eliminate economic-related risk factors that contribute to sexual violence in the lives of victim-survivors and communities. In centralising the role of economic advocacy, the focus of research work, lobbying for policy change and the range of partners collaborated with is expanded to deal directly with economic issues, such as legal protection for victim-survivors, including early release from leases and employment protection if a victim-survivor cannot work in the aftermath of a rape; broadening crime compensation to cover rent and bills; prioritising victim-survivors on public housing registers; campaigning for affordable, high quality, accessible childcare; the expansion of safe and affordable housing, shelter and public transport; affordable and comprehensive healthcare; minimum wage standards; training on the impacts of rape and sexual violence for staff working in public and private assistance programmes and personnel staff in businesses and organisations; and designing systems to take into account women's and/or victim-survivors' likely economic status in relation to accessing and affording important support and services.

Education, training and employment programmes

Many services working with victim-survivors of rape, particularly those in the voluntary sector, offer support programmes designed to strengthen women's economic status by increasing their ability to access and retain quality employment, and thus to achieve a level of economic resources that enable them to make choices about the context, location and relationships they operate within. For example, Eaves Housing in the UK runs the Scarlet Centre in London, a 'one-stop centre' for women who have experienced rape and sexual violence. As part of the support and recovery programme delivered by the centre, women can access courses and workshops to build skills for 'independent living', including education and training opportunities and skill-building workshops on curriculum vitae writing, as well as budgeting skills and advice on benefits and housing (Eaves Housing, 2013).

Independent sexual violence advisors

The English and Welsh intervention of ISVAs supports individual women who have experienced rape or sexual violence and offers, among other things, advice and help for women in accessing educational, volunteering and employment opportunities and skill-building workshops to help improve their economic status over the long term (Robinson, 2009). Similarly, in the US, SACTs provide education and training programmes (SACT, 2013).

Wider gender equality policies

Interventions based on micro-finance and economic advocacy address the immediate links between the economic and rape. Further interventions would be reforms to reduce gendered economic inequality that would re-shape other institutions that are conducive to rape. For example, the narrowing of the gender gaps in employment so that women were as likely as men to hold top jobs would have positive implications for the gender balance in decision-making that has been identified as an appropriate intervention elsewhere, for example, by the UN Security Council. Hence, policies that reduce gendered economic inequalities are likely to reduce rape and other forms of gender-based violence.

The provision of specialised services for victim-survivors of rape requires economic resources, although the availability of these resources varies considerably. Even within the UK, there are local gaps in the provision of services (Coy et al, 2009, 2011). Cuts in budgets for local government, as part of wider changes in economic policy linked to 'austerity', have led to to reductions in some of these services (Towers and Walby, 2012). There has been widespread concern that the reduction in public spending consequent on the 'austerity' response to fiscal pressures has disproportionately affected women (Women's Budget Group, 2014; Walby, 2015). The UK government, 2010-15, responded to requests from Rape Crisis England & Wales to provide funds on a national basis for rape crisis centres, in order to mitigate the unevenness of local provision (Rape Crisis England & Wales,

2014). The provision of services for victim-survivors depends on both specifically targeted funding initiatives and on government policies for public spending.

Conclusion

The best interventions for rape prevention are those that strengthen women's economic status so that they have adequate economic resources in order to be able to avoid contexts, locations and relationships in which they are vulnerable to rape and sexual violence. Such practices thus result in decreasing rates of rape. The best interventions are gendered, systemic, multilevel, core/centralised, appropriately funded, comprehensively evaluated and make a contribution back into the continual development of economy and development practices by making available lessons learned and highlighting what works best, thus adding to the evidence base.

- Gendered: best practice interventions should recognise and respond to gendered economic inequality and poverty aiming to improve the economic status of women so that they are better able to avoid relationships, contexts and locations where they are vulnerable to rape. Best practice interventions additionally consider the wider relative economic positions of women and men in communities and societies, and seek to contribute to the overall development of the economic status of a society.
- Systemic: best practice interventions change the wider social, cultural and political landscape to reduce poverty and embed economic equality, thus strengthening individual women's economic status and the status of women as a group within communities and the wider society. The best policies are those developed within a wider development of gender equality policies, so as to attend to the multifaceted economic dimensions of rape.
- Multilevel: best practice interventions recognise that economic status is relative, and that the strengthening of women's economic status must consider the links between individuals, their community and wider society, to ensure that improving

the economic status of women in one sphere is not done in such a way that causes increasing risk to women in different contexts or locations. For example, women's economic status is not uniform, since gender intersects with other factors that are associated with poor access to adequate economic resources, such as race (Crenshaw, 1991) or development context (Radford and Tsutsumi, 2004).

- Core: best practice interventions should make economic advocacy a core function that plays a political role in working with local, national and international public and private service providers and policy-makers to ensure that the links between rape and economy and development are understood, and that rape prevention is embedded within economic and development policy and practices, such as employment and property ownership legislation, funding and provision of housing, transport and childcare.
- Appropriately funded: best practice interventions acknowledge the substantial cost to victim-survivors caused by rape, and recognise that the requirement to pay 'up front' for services and support is not a socially just model; best practice models for essential services and support programmes for victim-survivors of rape should be free at the point of use.
- Evaluation: Best practice interventions should build in comprehensive evaluations from the start, including dedicated data collection systems, while adhering to high standards of confidentiality, and ensuring ethical principles for working with vulnerable individuals are met, in order to address the current dearth of evidence-based practice in rape and sexual violence work. This will enable future interventions to be constructed on a robust evidence base that demonstrates what works and highlights lessons learned.
- Mainstreaming: Recognition of the interconnections between rape and gendered economic inequalities, so that the prevention of violence, in particular, rape, can be mainstreamed into economic policy developments; use of EU structural and social funds to support projects to prevent rape; and inclusion of economic assistance to women victim-survivors of rape in the context of humanitarian aid packages.

8

Conclusions

Introduction

There has been much progress in the development of policies to stop rape, but there are many remaining challenges to address before they become comprehensive.

There is a need for further substantial reform in many areas if the widely shared goal of stopping rape, or even the more modest goal of reducing the amount of rape, is to be achieved. In each of several major policy fields, the interventions identified in this book could significantly reduce rape: strategy, coordination and research; victim services and healthcare systems; law and the criminal justice system; conflict zones; culture, media and education; and the economy.

These changes in specific policy areas are more likely if there are wider changes in the system of gender relations, so as to reduce the gender imbalance in decision-making, and to reduce gender inequalities in the economy and elsewhere. In addition, the systematic reduction in the level of all forms of violence is a necessary part of the process of reducing and stopping rape.

In each policy field, there has been specialised expert development followed by their transfer into the mainstream services and policy domains – mainstreaming requires both the development of specific expertise, and then its wider distribution into generic services through training and funding.

Developing a theoretical model of the causes of rape

There have been three strands in the analysis in this book that offer contributions to the development of the theoretical model of the causal pathways leading to rape, and thus the identification of the interventions that can reduce and stop rape.

One strand concerns interventions that reduce the propensity of individuals to rape, or the vulnerability of individuals to being raped. The reduction in the propensity to commit rape is due to increased deterrence by a more capable criminal justice system; improvement in the treatment regimes of convicted rapists; reduced acceptability of rape as a result of changes in culture, media and education; and reduced gender inequality. Variations in the vulnerability to rape are due to increased service provision that reduces repeated domestic rape; and changes in gendered economic inequalities.

A second strand concerns interventions that mitigate the harms to victim-survivors of rape and that support them. These interventions have increased and improved due to reduced toleration of rape in civil society; political pressure to develop, fund, plan and coordinate relevant services for victim-survivors; and the reduction in the gender imbalance in decision-making that has led to increased priorities in allocating resources relevant to victim-survivors.

A third strand concerns the interconnections between the first two strands. The support to victim-survivors has enabled their more robust engagement with the criminal justice system, to endure its humiliations and unsatisfactory treatment, so as to be part of the challenge that insists it must improve. Victim-survivors have been better able to speak out and educate the public, policy-makers and practitioners when they are better supported, leading to improvements in strategy, planning and coordination. A wider epistemic community has developed to which victim-survivors, providers of specialised services, researchers and others have contributed to the creation of new ways of thinking about rape and how it might be stopped. Thus, better specialised support for victim-survivors has led to a better criminal justice system, and to better planning, coordination and knowledge production.

The contribution of the analysis of the interconnections between the different policy fields has implications for the underlying theoretical model accounting for rape. The simplest theoretical model has been one that focuses on the 'risk factors' that correlate directly with rape. The model developed in this book is different in two respects: instead of 'risk factors', there are institutions (or systems), each with a set of internal relations and processes; and each of these institutions (systems) has an effect on the other institutions (systems) in its environment. This makes for a more complex, but more realistic, understanding of the nature of the causal pathways to rape. Changes in one institution have significant repercussions in other institutions: the fields are interconnected.

This reconfiguration of the underlying theoretical model has implications for 'prevention'. 'Prevention' does not involve just one institution or one part of the model; it involves all its institutions or parts. All the institutions and their interactions are relevant for 'prevention'.

This disrupts the simple view that 'prevention' must occur at a moment in time that precedes the problem under consideration. This is because there is not a simple linear process limited to 'action followed by rape' (or 'intervention followed by not rape'). Rather, the events and processes that occur after an individual rape can 'feed back' into the system that causes rape, preventing further rapes in the future. It is possible for rape to produce actions that lead to changes in institutions that prevent rape in the future. The overall system that causes rape is circular, not linear.

The key example concerns assistance to victim-survivors: if a victim-survivor is well supported after rape, this can increase her capacity for action (for example, increasing convictions in the criminal justice system, and increasing public understanding) to prevent future rapes, either to herself or to others. Good support can thus prevent rape. It does not prevent the original rape, but it can prevent future rapes.

The inclusion of good services to victim-survivors within the category of 'prevention' matters in circumstances where policy-makers prioritise 'prevention'. It is important that the category of 'prevention' includes all the things that contribute to prevention.

Hence we conclude that theories of the causation of rape need to deepen in sophistication in order to better establish the foundations for policy based on 'what works'. It is necessary to go beyond the simple models of rape that identify only the 'risk factors' that affect the vulnerability of victims to rape and the propensity of men to rape. It is important to build a complex systems model that includes each of the institutions that currently contributes to rape, and that could potentially be part of prevention.

Each of the relevant institutions has an effect not only on individuals, but also on the other institutions relevant to rape. The effects of institutions on institutions are important – they should not be neglected, as is often the case in the 'risk factor' model.

One implication is that better provision for victim-survivors of rape can prevent rape, in addition to mitigating its harms. Better provision of services has been focused on mitigating the harms of rape on the victim-survivor. But it has wider effects. A better supported victim-survivor is more able to effect changes on relevant institutions. Stronger victim-survivors are better able to endure the criminal justice system, thereby leading to higher conviction rates; to speak out and educate the public and policy-makers on the reality of rape, thereby challenging rape myths; and thus to contribute to rape prevention.

The institutions relevant to the causation and prevention of rape are themselves shaped by wider societal forms, including the gender regime and the system of violence. Gender regimes vary in gendered economic inequalities, gendered imbalances in decision-making, gendered participation in civil society, and gendered violence. Variations in gender inequality shape the institutions of the system of rape: reducing gendered inequalities reduces rape. Societies vary in the extent to which they are violent: institutions generating violence cluster so that if there is more of one form of violence, there are more of the other forms of violence. Reducing violence overall reduces rape.

The production and prevention of rape can be understood to occur at three levels of analysis: societal-level systems (gender regimes, overall violence); social institutions (planning/political, health, law and criminal justice, conflict/military, civil society, economy); and individual victims and rapists.

Strategy and coordination

Progress

Several international and national bodies have contributed to the development of strategy. Several states, including the UK, have developed national strategies to combat rape, sometimes as part of strategies to reduce gender-based violence against women and girls. For example, the UK has a national strategy and annually refreshed plans to end violence against women and girls (HM Government, 2009, 2010, 2015), and specific plans concerning rape (CPS and Police, 2014).

The Council of Europe's (2011) *Convention on preventing and combating violence against women and domestic violence* is a major development specifying the range of actions required, but needs wider ratification to be effective (Council of Europe, 2014b). The monitoring of developments of countries in Europe by the Council of Europe (2006, 2014a) shows that some progress has been achieved.

Many UN agencies have developed strategic plans, including the UN Secretary-General's (2006) report to the UN General Assembly; UN Women (2011, 2012a) and its predecessors, especially UNIFEM and UNDAW; UN human rights entities including the UN special rapporteur on violence against women; the UNHCR (2003); the UN Security Council (2000); and the WHO (2002, 2014b).

There have been several calls for action within the EU. The European Parliament (2011a) called for a new and strengthened EU policy framework to fight violence against women, and, in a series of resolutions in 2008, 2009 and 2011, it (2011b) called on the EU to provide support to victims of sexual abuse in the Congo, where rape was being used as a weapon of war. The European Commission (2010a) has included 'violence against women' as one of its five priorities in its strategy for gender equality (2010-15), and reiterates this commitment for action in the *Women's charter* (2010b), while the Advisory Equal Opportunities Committee of the European Commission (2010c) offered an opinion in favour of developing an EU strategy on violence against women and girls. The General Affairs Council of the EU issued guidelines on violence against women (EU, 2008) for use in external relations.

Further action

Each state should develop a NAP based on an integrated strategy to reduce and eliminate violence against women, with a particular section tackling the different issues related to rape prevention and assistance to victims of rape. Each state should create a body (commission) that oversees the NAP, which might be similar to that established to oversee equal treatment for the protected equality strands. There should be a consultation platform that includes the women's organisations providing services to victims of rape that provides input into the NAP and commission. There should also be adequate financial support from national budgets to implement the plans, including both specialised and mainstream services, and monitoring through gender-sensitive budgeting techniques.

The EU could play a critical role in boosting prevention of rape and the provision of assistance to victims of rape. Legislation in EU member states does not always meet international standards. In the context of the Istanbul Convention that aims at a harmonised approach to tackle violence against women for the better protection of all women in Europe, the member states might avail themselves of more effective tools to prevent rape, assist victim-survivors and to stop the impunity of offenders. Consequently, a comprehensive package of law and policy is recommended at the EU level. Based on the priority of combating violence against women and the relevant funding under the citizenship programme 2014-20, the respective provisions of the strategy for gender equality should be further developed, and their implementation accompanied by an action plan. The action plan should tackle violence against women as a whole, and rape in particular. Member states should be assisted in identifying the detailed policy measures needed to implement the strategy effectively, and advice should be offered to EU entities engaged in external affairs. This should be subject to regular review, evaluation and improvement. An EU office and coordinator should be established to oversee the EU action plan, which might be similar to that established in the case of trafficking (a coordinator with an office and budget). Member states' NAPs should be aligned to the EU strategy and action plan to ensure synergies. The review process might be similar to that used for the national strategic plans on social protection and social inclusion, involving the Open Method of Coordination. There should be a consultation platform that includes the women's organisations that provide services to victims of rape as well as Women Against Violence Europe and the European Women's Lobby (EWL). The strategy and plan should be subject to regular review, evaluation and improvement of EU-level action.

Data, statistics and research

Progress

There have been many calls for better data to inform the development of policy. Article 11 of the Council of Europe's (2011) Istanbul Convention requires that states ratifying the Convention carry out surveys, collect disaggregated administrative statistics and conduct research. The Crime Survey for England and Wales asks a representative sample of the population whether they have been subject to rape and sexual assault as well as other forms of gender-based violence against women and men in the last year (Walby and Allen, 2004). The WHO and EU FRA have conducted surveys on violence against women that ask about rape and other forms of sexual violence, although it is not possible to identify these categories separately from other forms of domestic violence at country-level, and nor are the surveys repeated over time. EIGE (2012b, 2014) have made proposals for the improvement of the administrative statistics.

Further action

There should be a coordinated programme of research and data collection. This should include a measurement framework that is consistent between surveys, criminal justice systems, healthcare systems and specialised services. This programme of research should be funded by national research councils, governmental agencies at state and EU level and the EU Research Framework Programme.

There should be surveys that gather information on the extent of rape and other forms of sexual assault, including both the number of victims and number of incidents per unit of population, the sex of the victim, and the relationship between victim and perpetrator, repeated at regular intervals.

There should be administrative statistics on the processing of cases of rape and sexual assault by the criminal justice system, healthcare system and specialised services. These should include the number of victim-survivors, the number of incidents, the sex of the victim, and the relationship between victim and perpetrator. Each institution should produce statistics that monitor the progress of cases through each system, including the rate of attrition of cases through the criminal justice system.

There should be a programme of research to investigate the causes of rape, in the context of other forms of violence, and of the effectiveness of interventions to prevent it.

Victim services and healthcare systems

Progress

There has been much progress in the establishment of specialised services to victim-survivors of rape, and a substantial body of knowledge is available as to how these can be best delivered. However, provision is uneven.

Further action

Each country's NAP should ensure the establishment of specialised services providing universally accessible assistance for victims of rape, including advice available by phone, expert advisers, centres and shelters, healthcare and legal advice. As shown by the good practice examples in this study, these services should be victim-centred, and delivered by experts in a gender-sensitive manner. Minimum standards should be established and maintained following the guidelines in the Istanbul Convention and from the WHO as discussed in Chapter 3. The funding of these services should be monitored and adjusted to real needs. There should be coordination of the provision of the comprehensive services, at both national and local levels.

Rape causes injuries to mental health as well as to physical health. States should therefore ensure the availability of specialised services for victims of rape within healthcare systems that address both types of injuries, and which are sensitive to victims' needs. In order to achieve this, training of personnel needs to be increased and improved, including of all those who might come into contact with victims of rape. Specialised programmes need to be developed which include forensics to collect evidence to assist the criminal justice system (if the victims want this) in those countries where these are not yet available. Furthermore, best practice services should be context-specific, including those provided in conflict and disaster zones; they should be coordinated with non-healthcare services for victim-survivors, for example, with the rape crisis centres that tend to address historic rapes more than recent rapes; and new research into the most appropriate pathways of care for victims of rape should be undertaken.

There is scope for greater action by the EU to develop strategic planning at EU level and to assist member states in developing policy that would add value to existing policy. The European Parliament has proposed a directive concerning all forms of violence against women. The EU should assist states in providing assistance to victim-survivors of rape through its actions to develop and share best practice. EIGE could be called on, with the relevant funding, to provide guidance based on best practice, and drawing on the Council of Europe's Istanbul Convention. The EU should monitor the provision of these services, using the indicators developed by EIGE. The Open Method of Coordination should be considered as a possible model to assist the development of best practice. In accordance with Article 14 of the Treaty on the Functioning of the EU, services for victim-survivors of rape should be regarded as services of general economic interest and consequently excluded from EU competition rules, thereby allowing EU member states to support them financially without resort to competitive tendering.

Law and the criminal justice system

Progress

There has been much progress in defining the minimum standards needed for legislation on rape and in the reforms needed to the criminal justice system, for example, the UN (2010a) *Handbook for legislation*, the Council of Europe's Istanbul Convention and the Inter-American Convention of Belem do Para. Most states in Europe, including the UK, have reached or nearly reached the legislative standards. There are, however, substantial remaining challenges for the criminal justice system.

Further action

All European states are recommended to sign and ratify the Council of Europe's Istanbul Convention. In its external relations, EU institutions should work towards third countries either adopting the standards of the Istanbul Convention, or signing and ratifying the most appropriate regional conventions, such as the Inter-American Convention of Belem do Para for states in the Americas.

Legislation on rape in each country should reach the minimum level recommended by the UN (2010a) and the Council of Europe's Istanbul Convention (2011). Legislation on rape should eliminate the 'marital exemption', which means that men can rape the women they are married to with impunity; use the threshold of 'absence of consent' rather than that of physical force (and in conflict zones recognise the context of coercion); and make illegal, either as rape or as an equivalently serious offence, the penetration of the body by objects or other body parts without consent.

The conviction rates should be raised to reduce impunity. There should be monitoring of the conviction rate for cases of rape reported to the justice system, and justice should be easily accessible for all victims of rape. There should be improvement of the treatment of victims of rape so as to avoid secondary victimisation, and to reduce the very high attrition of cases through the criminal justice system, thereby ensuring that perpetrators are held to account, and reducing the impunity of rapists. These actions include training of the police, prosecutors, judges, and other relevant officials; the provision of special courts to pioneer improved standards; and the provision of special advisers and advocates to victims including during criminal proceedings. Innovative methods of catching perpetrators of rape should be developed, including those that are using social media to lure potential victims into vulnerable positions (while mindful of the need to protect human rights and civil liberties).

While some instances of violence against women are already targeted by EU legal action, including trafficking, sexual harassment at the workplace and child pornography, the most serious form of violence against women, rape, has not been explicitly tackled. The severity of the issue justifies a careful examination of the possibility of legislative action at the EU level. In order to facilitate judicial cooperation in cases where alleged rapists cross borders, there is a case for a directive under the authority of Article 82 of the Lisbon Treaty (Treaty on the Functioning of the EU) for a directive to establish minimum rules for the definition of rape that are consistent with international law. Furthermore, Article 83 provides particular powers in the area of serious crimes that explicitly covers the 'sexual exploitation of women and children', which it is reasonable to interpret as including rape. Since many aspects of policy to combat rape are shared with other aspects of gender-based violence against women, and there are significant overlaps with other forms of violence, a comprehensive approach would be desirable. Since violence against women is also a form of gender discrimination, such a legislative action could be based on Article 19 of the Treaty on the Functioning of the EU, while the legislation of harassment could be further developed regarding prevention and sanctioning of rape at the workplace on the basis of Article 157. To ensure the implementation of the legislation, institutions that coordinate and monitor policy development and implementation are necessary as well as the creation of an administrative framework, ensuring that the relevant personnel, including the police, are adequately trained, that courts have adequate expertise and that resources are made available to fund specialised services to support victim-survivors. This is also relevant to EU external relations.

Conflict zones

Progress

There has been progress in identifying the increased rates of rape in zones where there are high rates of conflict and violence by international entities, including the UN Security Council, the UNHCR and the G8. There have been interventions to reduce the link between militarised violence and rape by these entities, especially by applying the principle of gender balance in decision-making to the governance of conflict zones, including among peacekeepers.

Further action

The inclusion of assistance to victims of rape should be a routine part of policies and packages of humanitarian assistance. The EU should assist in the delivery of justice in conflict zones, including through cooperation with international tribunals and courts.

The principle of gender balance in decision-making could be fruitfully extended to other institutions, both inside and outside of conflict zones, for example, criminal justice systems in non-conflict zones, since it has wider relevance and application.

Culture, media and education

Progress

There has been much innovation in the development of programmes to challenge attitudes that are conducive to rape.

Further action

The media should be challenged to avoid reproducing myths about rape. Regulations should ensure the anonymity of rape victims. In addition, as shown by the good practice examples, media, including social media, if used in an innovative way, could promote better public understanding of the issues involved in rape. Educational programmes should promote healthy forms of sexual relationships that avoid violence and are based on consent. Consideration should be given to the further regulation of extreme pornography that includes representations of rape, in both offline and online media.

Economy

Progress

Reductions in economic inequalities can reduce rape through the implications for both potential perpetrators and potential victims. However, the long-run decrease in general economic inequality has ended.

Further action

The effects of widespread violence against women, including rape, on the economic situation of both individual women and the economy as a whole, should be clarified and recognised using the findings of costing and gender budgeting techniques.

States should recognise the detrimental impact of rape on social inclusion, their economies and on economic growth. Economic growth strategies that are inclusive of women can then be regarded as measures to fight violence against women. States should implement measures directed at increasing women's access to a livelihood, by narrowing gender gaps in employment and opportunities for wealth creation, and the social inclusion of victims of rape. The rehabilitation of victims and the reduction of the economic costs of rape will be assisted by interventions that take into account the relation between violence against women and economic growth. Programmes to combat rape and other forms of violence against women should therefore be mainstreamed into state programmes that promote economic growth and social inclusion.

In the EU, within the framework of a fully inclusive EU 2020 strategy, European Structural Fund actions could establish better access of victim-survivors to the labour market and help to prevent (further) incidents of rape. Combating rape and other forms of violence against women should therefore be recognised as essential tools to realise the objectives of the EU 2020 strategy for inclusive growth. At the EU level this should include access to the European Structural Fund and the citizenship programme for projects to prevent rape and assist women victims of rape, in recognition of the damaging consequences of this violence to an individual's capacity for employment and livelihood, and thereby the cost of rape to business and society. Programmes to prevent rape and to assist victims of rape contribute to the social inclusion and integration of vulnerable groups, and so should be funded by programmes that aim to assist social inclusion. The citizenship programme should ensure that the activities formerly deployed under the Daphne I-III programmes, for example, the exchange of expertise and best practice on the wider topic of gender-based violence, developed by NGOs across EU member states, should continue.

In policies concerned with sustainable development, the detrimental effects of violence against women should be further highlighted and, accordingly, rape prevention be acknowledged as an indispensable component of economic development and included in goals for post-2015 sustainable development.

Reducing economic inequalities and poverty is likely to reduce the perpetration of rape, since there is a robust association between rates of economic inequality and poverty and rates of violent crime, of which rape is one.

Gender equality

Progress

Progress towards gender equality is likely to reduce rape; progress is uneven. There has been some deepening of gendered democracy and reduction in the gender imbalance in decision-making. However, responses to the financial crisis have deepened economic inequalities and reduced spending on welfare.

Further action

Further actions include the further deepening of gendered democracy, including reducing the gender imbalance in decision-making in key institutions; reducing gendered economic inequalities; reducing other forms of gender-based violence against women; and reducing gendered inequalities in civil society. The wider system of gender inequality, the gender regime, is a major underlying cause of the systems and practices that generate rape. The achievement of the goal of gender equality is necessary in order to achieve the goal of stopping rape.

Violence

Progress

Reducing overall levels of violence is likely to reduce rape; progress is uneven.

Further action

Reducing overall levels of violence is an important part of reducing rape, since reducing violence in one field reduces it elsewhere. If there were fewer armed conflicts, there would be fewer conflict zones, thereby preventing the high rates of rape associated with conflict. It is unlikely that rape can be stopped if violence is routinely deployed in conflicts. Stopping rape means stopping violence more generally.

Top ten policy reforms

1. *Plan.* Have a plan, a strategy, a gender-sensitive perspective, a policy, a form of coordination, and systematic evaluation. All states should have NAPs; all major policy bodies should have a plan.
2. *Data.* Have data to assess if the plan is working – *surveys* to measure the extent of rape and sexual assault in society; *administrative statistics* to assess if each policy body is achieving

their planned contribution; and *research* to investigate new interventions.

3. *Services for victim-survivors.* Provide expert services and healthcare for victim-survivors – specialised services, including mental health, expert advocates and well-trained personnel in mainstream services.

4. *Law.* Ratify the Istanbul Convention and implement its provisions.

5. *Criminal justice.* Reduce the attrition of cases as they proceed through the criminal justice system, from a police report to conviction, and reduce secondary victimisation.

6. *Conflict zones.* Include women in decision-making in all relevant forums, from peacekeeping troops to peace negotiations to disaster committees; prioritise political negotiations rather than armed conflict.

7. *Culture, media and education.* Challenge the new and old media to reduce the propagation of rape myths and rape culture.

8. *Economy.* Ensure all victims have access to income to mitigate the effects of rape – reduce gendered economic inequalities to reduce vulnerability.

9. *Reduce gender inequality.* Reduce the gender inequalities that contribute to rape and other forms of gender-based violence, such as gender imbalance in decision-making.

10. *Reduce violence.* Prioritise policy options that reduce violence, so as to cease feeding violence with violence.

References

Abraham, M. (1999) 'Sexual abuse in South Asian immigrant marriages', *Violence Against Women*, vol 5, no 6, pp 591-618.

ABS (Australian Bureau of Statistics) (1996) *Women's safety survey*, Canberra, ACT: Commonwealth of Australia.

ABS (2006) *Personal safety survey, Australia 2005*, Canberra, ACT: Commonwealth of Australia (www.abs.gov.au/).

ABS (2013) *Personal safety survey Australia 2012*, Canberra, ACT: Commonwealth of Australia (www.abs.gov.au/).

Ackerman, A.R., Sacks, M. and Greenberg, D.F. (2012) 'Legislation targeting sex offenders: are recent policies effective in reducing rape?', *Justice Quarterly*, vol 29, no 6, pp 858-87.

Advocates for Human Rights (2009) 'Coordinated crisis intervention', Stop Violence Against Women (www.stopvaw.org/Coordinated_Crisis_Intervention.html).

Agan, A.Y. (2011) 'Sex offender registries: fear without function?', *Journal of Law and Economics*, vol 54, no 1, pp 207-39.

Agarwal, B. and Panda, P. (2007) 'Toward freedom from domestic violence: the neglected obvious', *Journal of Human Development*, vol 8, no 3, pp 359-88.

Allen, N.E. (2006) 'An examination of the effectiveness of Domestic Violence Coordinating Councils', *Violence Against Women*, vol 12, no 1, pp 343-60.

Allred, K.J. (2006) 'Peacekeepers and prostitutes: how deployed forces fuel the demand for trafficked women and new hope for stopping it', *Armed Forces & Society*, vol 3, no 1, pp 5-23.

Almestad, G. and Beijbom, A. (2012) *#prataomdet*, Stockholm: Kalla Kulor Förlag.

Anderson, A.L. and Sample, L.L. (2008) 'Public awareness and action resulting from sex offender community notification laws', *Criminal Justice Policy Review*, vol 19, no 4, pp 371-96.

Anderson, D. and Saunders, D. (2003) 'Leaving an abusive partner: an empirical review of predictors, the process of leaving, and psychological well-being', *Trauma, Violence, & Abuse*, vol 4, no 2, pp 163-91.

Anderson, L.A. and Whiston, S. (2005) 'Sexual assault education programs: a meta-analytic examination of their effectiveness', *Psychology of Women Quarterly*, vol 25, pp 374-88.

Anderson, L.H. (1999) *Speak*, New York: Farrar Straus Giroux.

Andrews, D.A., Bonta, J. and Wormith, J.S. (2011) 'The Risk-Need-Responsivity (RNR) model: does adding the Good Lives Model contribute to effective crime prevention?', *Criminal Justice and Behavior*, vol 38, no 7, pp 735-55.

Asal, V. and Brown, M. (2010) 'A cross-national exploration of the conditions that produce interpersonal violence', *Politics & Policy*, vol 38, no 2, pp 175-92.

Ashman, L. and Duggan, L. (2004) *Interventions for learning disabled sex offenders*, Campbell Systematic Reviews 2004: 3 (http://campbellcollaboration.org/lib/download/18/).

Astbury, J. (2006) 'Services for victim/survivors of sexual assault: identifying needs, interventions and provision of services in Australia', *ACSSA Issues No 6*, Canberra, ACT: Australian Centre for the Study of Sexual Assault.

AVA (Academy on Violence and Abuse) (2011) *Competencies needed by health professionals for addressing exposure to violence and abuse in patient care*, Shakopee, MN: AVA (www.nsvrc.org/publications/competencies-needed-health-professionals-addressing-exposure-violence-and-abuse-patient).

Baillot, H., Cowan, S. and Munro, V.E. (2014) 'Reason to disbelieve: evaluating the rape claims of women seeking asylum in the UK', *International Journal of Law in Context*, vol 10, no 1, pp 105-39.

Balagopal, G. (2013) 'Thuthuzela – responding to rape in South Africa', *The Hindu*, 14 January (www.thehindu.com/opinion/op-ed/thuthuzela-responding-to-rape-in-south-africa/article4307018.ece).

Bandy, R. (2011) 'Measuring the impact of sex offender notification on community adoption of protective behaviors', *Criminology & Public Policy*, vol 10, no 2, pp 237-63.

Baños Smith, M. (2011) *A different world is possible: Promising practices to prevent violence against women and girls*, London: End Violence Against Women (www.endviolenceagainstwomen. org.uk/data/files/resources/20/promising_practices_report_. pdf).

BBC News (2014) 'Morocco amends controversial rape marriage law', 23 January (www.bbc.co.uk/news/world-africa-25855025).

Bedford, K. (2009) *Developing partnerships: Gender, sexuality and the reformed World Bank*, Minneapolis, MN: University of Minnesota Press.

Behrendt, L. (1993) 'Aboriginal women and the white lies of the feminist movement: implications for Aboriginal women in rights discourse', *Journal of Australian Studies*, vol 35, pp 27-44.

Bein, K. and Hurt, C. (2011) *Strong foundations for healing: Shelter and sexual violence*, National Sexual Assault Coalition Resource Sharing Project (www.nsvrc.org/sites/default/files/ Publications_RSP_Strong-foundation-for-healing-shelter-and-sexual-violence.pdf).

Black, M.C., Basile, K.C., Breiding, M.J., Smith, S.G., Walters, M.L., Merrick, M.T., Chen, J. and Stevens, M.R. (2011) *The National Intimate Partner and Sexual Violence Survey (NISVS): 2010 summary report*, Atlanta, GA: National Center for Injury Prevention and Control and Centers for Disease Control and Prevention (www.cdc.gov/violenceprevention/pdf/ nisvs_report2010-a.pdf).

Boba, R. and Lilley, D. (2009) 'Violence Against Women Act (VAWA) funding: a nationwide assessment of effects on rape and assault', *Violence Against Women*, vol 15, no 2, pp 168-85 (vaw.sagepub.com/content/15/2/168.full. pdf+html?hwoaspck=true).

Bohner, G., Jarvis, C.I., Eyssel, F. and Siebler, F. (2005) 'The causal impact of rape myth acceptance on men's rape proclivity: comparing sexually coercive and noncoercive men', *European Journal of Social Psychology*, vol 35, pp 819-28.

Bohner, G., Reinhard, M., Rutz, S., Sturm, S., Kerschbaum, B. and Effler, D. (1998) 'Rape myths as neutralizing cognitions: evidence for a causal impact of anti-victim attitudes on men's self-reported likelihood of raping', *European Journal of Social Psychology*, vol 28, pp 257-68.

Bonnes, S. (2013) 'Gender and racial stereotyping in rape coverage: an analysis of rape coverage in a South African newspaper, Grocott's Mail', *Feminist Media Studies*, vol 13, no 2, pp 208-27.

Borzacchiello, E. (2012) 'Una mirada al feminicidio en México a través de la Ley general de acceso de las mujeres a una vida libre de violencia', Note for research team.

Bourke, J. (2014) 'Rape as a weapon of war', *The Lancet*, vol 383, no 9934, e19-e20.

Brecklin, L.R. and Forde, D.R. (2001) 'A meta-analysis of rape education programs', *Violence and Victims*, vol 16, pp 303-21.

Breiding, M.J., Chen, J. and Black, M.C. (2014) *Intimate partner violence in the United States – 2010*, Atlanta, GA: National Center for Injury Prevention and Control, and Centers for Disease Control and Prevention (www.cdc.gov/violenceprevention/pdf/cdc_nisvs_ipv_report_2013_v17_single_a.pdf).

Bridges, D. and Horsfall, D. (2009) 'Increasing operational effectiveness in UN peacekeeping: toward a gender-balanced force', *Armed Forces & Society*, vol 36, no 1, pp 120-30.

Brierley, G., Agnew-Davies, R., Bailey, J., Evans, M., Fackrell, M., Ferrari, G., Hollinghurst, S., Howard, L., Howarth, E., Malpass, A., Metters, C., Peters, T.J., Saeed, F., Sardhina, L., Sharp, D. and Feder, G.S. (2013) 'Psychological advocacy toward healing (PATH): study protocol for a randomized controlled trial', *Trials*, vol 14, p 221.

Bronfenbrenner, U. (1977) 'Toward an experimental ecology of human development', *American Psychologist*, vol 32, no 7, pp 513-31.

Bronfenbrenner, U. (1979) *The ecology of human development: Experiments by nature and design*, Cambridge, MA: Harvard University Press.

Brown, J.M. and Walklate, S.L. (eds) (2012) *Handbook on sexual violence*, London: Routledge.

Brownmiller, S. (1976) *Against our will: Men, women and rape*, London: Penguin.

Buiten, D. and Salo, E. (2007) 'Silences stifling transformation: misogyny and gender-based violence in the media', *Agenda: Empowering Women for Gender Equity*, vol 21, no 1, pp 115-21.

Bumby, K.M. (1996) 'Assessing the cognitive distortions of child molesters and rapists: development and validation of the MOLEST and RAPE scales', *Sexual Abuse: Journal of Research and Treatment*, vol 8, no 1, pp 37-54.

Bumiller, K. (2008) *In an abusive state: How neoliberalism appropriated the feminist movement against sexual violence*, Durham, NC: Duke University Press.

Burnett, G. and Buerkle, H. (2004) 'Information exchange in virtual communities: a comparative study', *Journal of Computer-Mediated Communication*, vol 9, no 2.

Burt, M.R. (1980) 'Cultural myths and supports for rape', *Journal of Personality and Social Psychology*, vol 38, no 2, pp 217-30.

Callander, I. (2014) 'The challenge of best evidence in rape trials: the Victims and Witnesses (Scotland) Act 2014', *Edinburgh Law Review*, vol 18, no 2, pp 279-84.

Campbell, J.C. (2002) 'Health consequences of intimate partner violence', *The Lancet*, vol 359, no 9314, pp 1331-6.

Campbell, R. (2006) 'Rape survivors' experiences with the legal and medical systems: do rape victim advocates make a difference?', *Violence Against Women*, vol 12, no 1, pp 30-45.

Campbell, R. and Ahrens, C.E. (1998) 'Innovative community services for rape victims: an application of multiple case study methodology', *American Journal of Community Psychology*, vol 26, no 4, pp 537-71.

Campbell, R., Bybee, D., Ford, J.K. and Patterson, D. (2008) *Systems change analysis of SANE programs: Identifying the mediating mechanisms of criminal justice system impact*, Washington, DC: US Department of Justice (www.ncjrs.gov/pdffiles1/nij/grants/226498.pdf).

Campbell, R., Wasco, S., Ahrens, C., Sefl, T. and Barnes, H.E. (2001) 'Preventing the "second rape": rape survivors' experiences with community service providers', *Journal of Interpersonal Violence*, vol 16, no 12, pp 1239-59.

Care International (no date) 'Democratic Republic of Congo: rape survivors build a future' (www.careinternational.org.uk/ what-we-do/war-conflict-and-peacebuilding/conflict-related-sexual-violence/drc-rape-survivors-build-a-future).

Carey, H.F. (2001) '"Women and peace and security": the politics of implementing gender sensitivity norms in peacekeeping', *International Peacekeeping*, vol 8, no 2, pp 49-68.

Carmody, M. (1992) 'Uniting all women: a historical look at attitudes to rape', in J. Breckenridge and M. Carmody (eds) *Crimes of violence: Australian responses to rape and child sexual assault*, Sydney, NSW: Allen & Unwin, pp 3-17.

Cassim, F. (2011) 'Addressing the growing spectre of cyber crime in Africa: evaluating measures adopted by South Africa and other regional role players', *Comparative and International Law Journal of Southern Africa*, vol 44, no 1, pp 123-38.

Cawson, P., Wattam, C., Brooker, S. and Kelly, G. (2000) *Child maltreatment in the United Kingdom: A study of the prevalence of child abuse and neglect*, London: NSPCC (www.nspcc.org.uk/inform/ research/findings/childmaltreatmentintheunitedkingdom_ wda48252.html).

CDC (2014b) *Sexual violence prevention strategies*, Atlanta, GA: CDC (www.cdc.gov/violenceprevention/sexualviolence/ prevention.html).

Chappell, L. (2002) *Gendering government: Feminist engagement with the state in Australia and Canada*, Vancouver, BC: University of British Columbia Press.

Check, J.V. and Malamuth, N.M. (1983) 'Sex role stereotyping and reactions to depictions of stranger versus acquaintance rape', *Journal of Personality and Social Psychology*, vol 45, pp 344-56.

Chiricos, T. (1987) 'Rates of crime and unemployment: an analysis of aggregate research evidence', *Social Problems*, vol 34, no 2, pp 187–212.

Chowdhury-Hawkins, R., McLean, I., Winterholler, M. and Welch, J. (2008) 'Preferred choice of gender of staff providing care to victims of sexual assault in Sexual Assault Referral Centres (SARCs)', *Journal of Forensic Legal Medicine*, vol 15, no 6, pp 363-7.

Citron, D.K. (2011) 'Misogynistic cyber hate speech', Baltimore, MD: University of Maryland School of Law (http://digitalcommons.law.umaryland.edu/cgi/viewcontent.cgi?article=2143&context=fac_pubs).

Clay-Warner, J. and Harbin B.C. (2005) 'Rape reporting after reforms: have times really changed?', *Violence Against Women*, vol 11, no 2, pp 150-76.

COAG (Council of Australian Governments) (2010) *National plan to reduce violence against women and their children 2010-2022*, Canberra, ACT: COAG.

Cohn, A.M., Zinzow, H.M., Resnick, H.S. and Kilpatrick, D.G. (2013) 'Correlates of reasons for not reporting rape to police: results from a national telephone household probability sample of women with forcible or drug-or-alcohol facilitated/incapacitated rape', *Journal of Interpersonal Violence*, vol 28, no 3, pp 455-73.

Collier, P. (2007) *Post-conflict recovery: How should policies be distinctive?*, Oxford: Centre for the Study of African Economies, Department of Economics, University of Oxford University (http://users.ox.ac.uk/~econpco/research/pdfs/PostConflict-Recovery.pdf).

Congreso de Estados Unidos Mexicanos [Congress of the United Mexican States] (2012) *Diario Oficial de la Federación* [DOF, *Official Bulletin of the Federation*] 01/02/2007, last reform DOF 14/06/2012, 'Ley general de acceso de las mujeres a una vida libre de violencia' ['General law to guarantee women access to a life free from violence'] (www.diputados.gob.mx/LeyesBiblio/pdf/LGAMVLV.pdf).

Connell, R. (1995) *Masculinities*, Cambridge: Polity.

Contreras, J.M., Bott, S., Guedes, A. and Dartnall, E. (2010) *Sexual violence in Latin America and the Caribbean: A desk review*, Sexual Violence Research Initiative, Pretoria, South Africa: Medical Research Council (www.svri.org/SexualViolenceLACaribbean.pdf).

Cook, B., David, F. and Grant, A. (2001) *Sexual violence in Australia*, Canberra, ACT: Australian Institute of Criminology.

Cook, D., Burton, M., Robinson, A. and Vallely, C. (2004) *Evaluation of specialist domestic violence courts/fast-track systems*, London: Crown Prosecution Service and Department for Constitutional Affairs (wlv.openrepository.com/wlv/bitstream/2436/22612/1/Cook%20et%20al%20%282004%29.pdf).

Cornelius, T.L. and Resseguie, N. (2007) 'Primary and secondary prevention programs for dating violence: a review of the literature', *Aggression and Violent Behavior*, vol 12, pp 364-75.

Corte Interamericana de Derechos Humanos (2009) *Caso González y otras ('campo algodonero') vs México*, Sentencia de 16 de noviembre de 2009 (www.corteidh.or.cr/docs/casos/articulos/seriec_205_esp.pdf).

Cossins, A. (2007) *A best practice model for the prosecution of complaints of sexual assault by the NSW criminal justice system*, Sydney, NSW: New South Wales Rape Crisis Centre.

Council of Europe (2006) *Combating violence against women: Stocktaking study on the measures and actions taken in Council of Europe Member States*. Report prepared by C. Hagemann-White, Strasbourg: Council of Europe.

Council of Europe (2009a) *Resolution 1670: Sexual violence against women in armed conflict*, Strasbourg: Council of Europe (http://assembly.coe.int/Main.asp?link=/Documents/AdoptedText/ta09/ERES1670.htm).

Council of Europe (2009b) *Resolution 1691: Rape of women including marital rape*, Strasbourg: Council of Europe (http://assembly.coe.int/Main.asp?link=/Documents/AdoptedText/ta09/ERES1691.htm).

Council of Europe (2009c) *Recommendation 1887: Rape of women including marital rape*, Strasbourg: Council of Europe (http://assembly.coe.int/main.asp?Link=/documents/adoptedtext/ta09/erec1887.htm).

Council of Europe (2011) *Convention on preventing and combating violence against women and domestic violence*, Strasbourg: Council of Europe (www.conventions.coe.int/Treaty/Commun/QueVoulezVous.asp?CL=ENG&NT=210).

Council of Europe (2014a) *Analytical study of the results of the fourth round of monitoring the implementation of Recommendation Rec(2002)5 on the protection of women against violence in Council of Europe Member States*, Report prepared by C. Hagemann-White, Strasbourg: Council of Europe.

Council of Europe (2014b) *Up-date on Convention on preventing and combating violence against women and domestic violence (Istanbul Convention)*, Strasbourg: Council of Europe (www.coe.int/t/dghl/standardsetting/convention-violence/default_en.asp).

Cox, S., Harvey, S. and Holly, J. (2013) *Two sides of the same coin: Supporting people who have experienced sexual violence and mental ill-health*, London: Against Violence and Abuse, Stella Project (www.avaproject.org.uk/our-projects/stella-project.aspx).

Coy, M. (2009) 'Milkshakes, lady lumps and growing up to want boobies: how the sexualisation of popular culture limits girls' horizons', *Child Abuse Review*, vol 18, no 6, pp 372-83.

Coy, M. and Garner, M. (2010) 'Glamour modelling and the marketing of self-sexualization: critical reflections', *International Journal of Cultural Studies*, vol 13, no 6, pp 657-75.

Coy, M., Lovett, J. and Kelly, L. (2008) *Realising rights, fulfilling obligations: A template for an integrated strategy on violence against women for the UK*, London: End Violence Against Women (www.endviolenceagainstwomen.org.uk/data/files/resources/38/realising_rights-jul-08.pdf).

Coy, M., Kelly, L. and Foord, J. (2009) *Map of gaps 2: The postcode lottery of violence against women support services*, London: Equality and Human Rights Commission.

Coy, M., Kelly, L., Foord, J. and Bowstead J. (2011) 'Roads to nowhere? Mapping violence against women services', *Violence Against Women*, vol 17, no 3, pp 404-25.

CPS and Police (2014) *Joint CPS and police action plan on rape*, January (www.cps.gov.uk/publications/equality/vaw/rape_action_plan.pdf).

Crawley, H. (2001) *Refugees and gender: Law and process*, Bristol: Jordan.

Crenshaw, K.W. (1991) 'Mapping the margins: intersectionality, identity politics and violence against women of colour', *Stanford Law Review*, vol 43, no 6, pp 1241-99.

Critelli, F.M. (2012) 'Voices of resistance: seeking shelter services in Pakistan', *Violence Against Women*, vol 18, no 4, pp 437-58.

Culpitt, I. (1999) *Social policy and risk*, London: Sage.

Curtis, P. (2012) 'Should sex offenders be chemically "castrated"?', *Guardian Online Blog* (www.guardian.co.uk/politics/reality-check-with-polly-curtis/2012/mar/13/prisons-and-probation-criminal-justice).

Cybulska, B., Forster, G., Welch, J., Lacey, H., Rogstad, K. and Lazaro, N. (2012) *UK national guidelines on the management of adult and adolescent complainants of sexual assault 2011*, Macclesfield: British Association for Sexual Health & HIV (BASHH) (www.bashh.org/guidelines).

Dahlén, S. (2010) 'Swedish site urges people to talk about sex', *The Local*, 23 December (www.thelocal.se/20101223/31036).

Daly, K. (2005) 'A tale of two studies: restorative justice from a victim's perspective', in E. Elliott and R. Gordon (eds) *New directions in restorative justice: Issues, practice, evaluation*, Cullompton: Willan Publishing, pp 153-74.

Daly, K. (2011) 'Conventional and innovative responses to sexual violence', *Issues*, no 12, Australian Centre for the Study of Sexual Assault (www.aifs.gov.au/acssa/pubs/issue/i12/).

Daly, K. and Bouhours, B. (2010) 'Rape and attrition in the legal process: a comparative analysis of five countries', *Crime and Justice: A Review of Research*, vol 39, pp 565-650.

Daly, K., Curtis-Fawley, S. and Bouhours, B. (2003) *Sexual Offence Cases Finalised in Court, by Conference, and by Formal Caution in South Australia for Young Offenders, 1995 – 2001: Final Report*, Brisbane: School of Criminology and Criminal Justice, Griffith University.

de Visser, R., Smith, A., Rissel, C., Richters, J. and Grulich, A. (2003) 'Experiences of sexual coercion among a representative sample of adults', *Australian and New Zealand Journal of Public Health*, vol 27, no 2, pp 198-203.

Dean, C., Hardiman, A. and Draper, G. (1998) *National standards of practice manual for services against sexual violence*, Melbourne, VIC: CASA House, National Association of Services Against Sexual Violence.

DeGroot, J.J. (2002) '"Wanted: a few good women": gender stereotypes and their implications for peacekeeping', Paper presented at Women in NATO Forces: Annual Conference, 26-31 May (www.nato.int/ims/2002/cwinf2002/cwinf-01.htm).

DeGue, S., Valle, L.A., Holt, M.K., Massetti, G.M., Matjasko, J.L. and Tharp, A.T. (2014) 'A systematic review of primary prevention strategies for sexual violence perpetration', *Aggression and Violent Behavior*, vol 19, no 4, pp 346-62.

Denno, D.W. (1993) 'Perspectives on disclosing rape victims' names', *Fordham Law Review*, vol 61, no 5, pp 1113-31.

Devries, K.M., Mak, J.Y., Bacchus, L.J., Child, J.C., Falder, G., Petzold, M., Astbury, J. and Watts, C.H. (2013) 'Intimate partner violence and incident depressive symptoms and suicide attempts: a systematic review of longitudinal studies', *PLOS Medicine Open Access*, vol 10, no 5, e1001439 (www. plosmedicine.org/article/info%3Adoi%2F10.1371%2Fjournal. pmed.1001439).

DFID (Department for International Development) (2012) *A theory of change for tackling violence against women*, CHASE Guidance Note Series 1, June, London: Violence Against Women and Girls (www.dfid.gov.uk/Documents/publications1/how-to-note-vawg-1.pdf).

DH (Department of Health) (2009) *A resource for developing sexual assault referral centres* (http://webarchive.nationalarchives.gov. uk/20130107105354/http://www.dh.gov.uk/prod_consum_ dh/groups/dh_digitalassets/@dh/@en/@ps/@sta/@perf/ documents/digitalasset/dh_108350.pdf).

DH (2011) *Talking therapies: A four-year plan of action. A supporting document to No health without mental health: A cross-government mental health outcomes strategy for people of all ages*, London: DH (www.iapt.nhs.uk/silo/files/talking-therapies-a-four-year-plan-of-action.pdf).

DH (2012) *IAPT three-year report: The first million patients*, London: DH (www.iapt.nhs.uk/silo/files/iapt-3-year-report. pdf).

Dharmapuri, S. (2013) 'Not just a numbers game: increasing women's participating in UN peacekeeping', *Providing for Peacekeeping 4*, New York, NY: International Peace Institute.

Dibbell, J. (1998) *My tiny life: Crime and passion in a virtual world*, New York: Henry Holt.

Dines, G. (2010) *Pornland: How porn has hijacked our sexuality*, Boston, MA: Beacon Press.

Diniz, D., Madeiro, A. and Rosas, C. (2014) 'Conscientious objection, barriers, and abortion in the case of rape: a study among physicians in Brazil', *Reproductive Health Matters*, vol 22, no 43, pp 141-8.

DMSS Research (2014) 'An independent evaluation of Rape Crisis Scotland's sexual violence prevention project', August (www.rapecrisisscotland.org.uk/workspace/uploads/files/interim_headlines.pdf).

DNA (Daily News & Analysis) India (2013) 'Justice J.S. Verma Committee's Recommendations: Complete list' (www.dnaindia.com/india/report_justice-js-verma-committee-s-recommendations-complete-list_1792005).

Dobash, R.E. and Dobash, R.P. (1992) *Women, violence and social change*, London and New York: Routledge.

Dunne, M., Humphreys, S. and Leach, F. (2003) *The manifestation of gender-based violence in schools*, UNESCO EFA Global Monitoring Report 2003/4, Background Paper.

Duwe, G. and Donnay, W. (2008) 'The impact of Megan's law on sex offender recidivism: the Minnesota experience', *Criminology*, vol 46, no 2, pp 411-46.

Eaves Housing (2013) Scarlet Centre information leaflet (http://i1.cmsfiles.com/eaves/2012/07/Scarlet-Centre-leaflet-2011-web-422825.pdf).

Edwards, A. (2008) 'Violence against women as sex discrimination: Judging the jurisprudence of the United Nations Human Rights Treaty bodies', *Texas Journal of Women and the Law*, vol 18, no 1, pp 1-60.

EIGE (European Institute for Gender Equality) (2011) *Towards effective gender training: Mainstreaming gender into the policies and the programmes of the Institutions of European Union and Member States*, Good Practices in Gender Mainstreaming, Vilnius: EIGE (www.eige.europa.eu/sites/default/files/Good-Practices-in-Gender-Mainstreaming-towards-effective-gender-training_0.pdf).

EIGE (2012a) *The study to map existing data and resources on sexual violence against women in the EU*, Vilnius: EIGE (www.eige. europa.eu/content/document/the-study-to-identify-and-map-existing-data-and-resources-on-sexual-violence-against-women-in-the-EU).

EIGE (2012b) *Review of the implementation of the Beijing Platform for Action in the EU Member States: Violence against women – Victim support* (www.eige.europa.eu/sites/default/files/Violence-against-Women-Victim-Support-Report.pdf).

EIGE (2014) *Administrative data sources on gender based violence in the EU*, Vilnius: EIGE (http://eige.europa.eu/gender-based-violence/administrative-data-sources).

Elliot, D. (2012) 'Anonymity for rape victims: should the rules change?', *Journalism Ethics Cases Online*, Bloomington, IN: Indiana University (http://journalism.indiana.edu/resources/ethics/naming-newsmakers/anonymity-for-rape-victims/).

Ellis, E.M., Atkeson, B.M. and Calhoun, K.S. (1981) 'An assessment of long-term reaction to rape', *Journal of Abnormal Psychology*, vol 90, pp 263-66.

Ellsberg, M., Arango, D.J., Morton, M., Gennari, F., Kiplesund, S., Contreras, M. and Watts, S. (2014) 'Prevention of violence against women and girls: what does the evidence say?', *The Lancet*, 21 November, pp 1-12.

Enloe, C. (1990) *Bananas, beaches and bases: Making feminist sense of international politics*, Berkeley, CA: University of California Press.

Enloe, C. (2007) 'Feminist readings on Abu Ghraib: Introduction', *International Feminist Journal of Politics*, vol 9, no 1, pp 35-7.

Equis: Justicia para las Mujeres (2012) 'Informe sobre la situación de acceso a la justicia para las mujeres en México', *CEDAW shadow report*, 52nd session, July (www2.ohchr.org/english/bodies/cedaw/docs/ngos/EquisSubmission_for_the_session.pdf).

Ertürk, Y. and Purkayastha, B. (2012) 'Linking research, policy and action: a look at the work of the special rapporteur on violence against women', *Current Sociology*, vol 60, no 2, pp 142-60.

Escobedo Shepherd, J. (2010) 'Swedish feminists defend Assange's accusers with twitter campaign', *AlterNet*, 18 December (www.alternet.org/newsandviews/article/400873/swedish_feminists_defend_assange's_accusers_with_twitter_campaign).

Estes, R. and Weiner, N. (2001) *Commercial sexual exploitation of children in the US, Canada, and Mexico*, Philadelphia, PA: University of Pennsylvania.

EU (European Union) (2007) 'Treaty of Lisbon', *Official Journal of the European Union* (http://eur-lex.europa.eu/legal-content/EN/TXT/PDF/?uri=OJ:C:2007:306:FULL&from=EN).

EU (2008) *EU guidelines on violence against women and combating all forms of discrimination against them*, General Affairs Council, 8 December (www.consilium.europa.eu/uedocs/cmsUpload/16173cor.en08.pdf).

EU Council (2010) *EU Council conclusions on the eradication of violence against women in the EU* (www.eu-un.europa.eu/articles/en/article_9553_en.htm).

EU (European Union) FRA (Agency for Fundamental Rights) (2014) *Violence against women: An EU-wide survey*, Vienna: EU FRA (www.fra.europa.eu/fraWebsite/research/projects/proj_eu_survey_vaw_en.htm).

European Commission (2010a) *New strategy on gender equality*, COM (2010) 491 final, Brussels: Employment, Social Affairs and Inclusion (http://ec.europa.eu/social/main.jsp?langId=en&catId=89&newsId=890&furtherNews=yes).

European Commission (2010b) *A strengthened commitment to equality between women and men: A women's charter*, Brussels: European Commission (http://ec.europa.eu/commission_2010-2014/president/news/documents/pdf/20100305_1_en.pdf).

European Commission (2010c) *Opinion on EU strategy on violence against women and girls*, Brussels: Advisory Committee on Equal Opportunities for Women and Men, Social Europe, December (http://ec.europa.eu/justice/gender-equality/files/opinions_advisory_committee/2010_12_opinion_on_eu_strategy_on_violence_against_women_and_girls_en.pdf).

European Commission (2010d) *Feasibility study to assess the possibilities, opportunities and needs to standardise national legislation on violence against women, violence against children and sexual orientation violence*, Brussels: European Commission, Justice.

European Commission (2015) *The Daphne Toolkit: An Active Resource from the Daphne Programme* (http://ec.europa.eu/justice/grants/results/daphne-toolkit/en/daphne-toolkit-%E2%80%93-active-resource-daphne-programme).

European Committee for the Prevention of Torture (2009) *Report to the Czech Government on the visit to the Czech Republic carried out by the European Committee for the Prevention of Torture and Inhuman or Degrading Treatment or Punishment (CPT) from 25 March to 2 April 2008*, Strasbourg.

European Committee for the Prevention of Torture (2010) *Response of the Czech Government to the report of the European Committee for the Prevention of Torture and Inhuman or Degrading Treatment or Punishment (CPT) on its visit to the Czech Republic from 21 to 23 October 2009*, Strasbourg.

European Committee for the Prevention of torture (2012) *Report to the German Government on the visit to Germany carried out by the European Committee for the Prevention of Torture and Inhuman or Degrading Treatment or Punishment (CPT) from 25 November to 7 December 2010*, Strasbourg.

European Court of Human Rights (2010) *European Convention on human rights: Convention for the protection of human rights and fundamental freedoms*, Rome 1950, as amended (www.echr.coe.int/Documents/Convention_ENG.pdf).

European Court of Human Rights (2015) *Factsheet – Violence against women* (www.echr.coe.int/Documents/FS_Violence_Woman_ENG.pdf).

European Parliament (2011a) *Resolution on priorities and outline of a new EU policy framework to fight violence against women* (www.europarl.europa.eu/oeil/popups/ficheprocedure.do?lang=en&reference=2010/2209(INI)).

European Parliament (2011b) *European Parliament Resolution of 7 July 2011 on the Democratic Republic of Congo (DRC) mass rape in the province of South Kivu* (www.europarl.europa.eu/document/activities/cont/201107/20110720ATT24508/20110720ATT24508EN.pdf).

EVAW (End Violence Against Women) Coalition (2011) *A different world is possible: A call for long-term and targeted action to prevent violence against women and girls*, Prevention Strategy, London: EVAW Coalition.

EVAW Coalition (2012) Factsheet for Schools on Violence Against Women and Girls, *Schools Safe 4 Girls* (www.endviolenceagainstwomen.org.uk/schools-safe-4-girls).

EVAW, Eaves, Equality Now and Object (2012) *'Just the women'. An evaluation of eleven British national newspapers' portrayal of women over a two week period in September 2012, including recommendations on press regulation reform in order to reduce harm to, and discrimination against, women* (www.endviolenceagainstwomen.org.uk/data/files/resources/51/Just-the-Women-Nov-2012.pdf).

Fajnzylber P., Lederman, D. and Loayza, N. (1998) *Determinants of crime rates in Latin America and the world: An empirical assessment*, World Bank Latin American and Caribbean Studies, Washington, DC: The World Bank (http://siteresources.worldbank.org/INTKNOWLEDGEFORCHANGE/Resources/491519-1199818447826/multi_page.pdf).

Fantini, A. and Hegarty, M. (2003) *Best practice guidelines for NGOs supporting women who have experienced sexual violence*, Galway: Rape Crisis Network Europe (http://ec.europa.eu/justice/grants/results/daphne-toolkit/en/file/1714/).

Farr, V., Myrttinen, H. and Schnabel, A. (eds) (2009) *Sexed pistols: The gender impacts of small arms and light weapons*, Tokyo: UN University Press.

Fay, K. and Medway, F. (2006) 'An acquaintance rape education program for students transitioning to high school', *Sex Education*, vol 6, no 3, pp 223-36.

FCO (Foreign and Commonwealth Office) (2014) *International protocol on the documentation and investigation of sexual violence in conflict: Basic standards of best practice on the documentation of sexual violence as a crime under international law*, London: UK FCO (www.gov.uk/government/uploads/system/uploads/attachment_data/file/319054/PSVI_protocol_web.pdf).

Fehler-Cabral, G., Campbell, R. and Patterson, D. (2011) 'Adult sexual assault survivors' experiences with sexual assault nurse examiners (SANEs)', *Journal of Interpersonal Violence*, vol 26, no 18, pp 3618-39.

Feist, A., Ashe, J., Lawrence, J., McPhee, D. and Wilson, R. (2007) *Investigating and detecting recorded offences of rape*, Home Office Online Report 18/09, London: Home Office (www.ncjrs.gov/App/publications/Abstract.aspx?id=246622).

Ferguson, C. (2012) 'Positive female role-models eliminate negative effects of sexually violent media', *Journal of Communication*, vol 62, no 5, pp 888-99.

Ferree, M.M. (2012) *Varieties of feminism: German gender politics in global perspective*, Stanford, CA: Stanford University Press.

Ferreira, S.T.G., Paula, K.A., Flávia, A.M., Svidzinski, A.E., Amaral, M.R., Diniz, S.A. and Moraes, A.V. (2013) 'A study of the first DNA database of biological evidence from sexual assaults and rapes in Brazil', *Forensic Science International: Genetics Supplement Series 4*, vol 4, no 1, e368-e369.

Fisher, B.S. (2009) 'The effects of survey question wording on rape estimates: evidence from a quasi-experimental design', *Violence Against Women*, vol 15, no 2, pp 133-47.

Flood, M. (2011) 'Involving men in efforts to end violence against women', *Men and Masculinities*, vol 14, no 3, pp 358-77.

Flores, S.A. and Hartlaub, M.G. (1998) 'Reducing rape-myth acceptance in male college students: a meta-analysis of intervention studies', *Journal of College Student Development*, vol 39, pp 438-48.

Foshee, V.A., Bauman, K.E., Ennett, S.T., Linder, G.F., Benefield, T. and Suchindran, P. (2004) 'Assessing the long-term effects of the Safe Dates program and a booster in preventing and reducing adolescent dating violence victimization and perpetration', *American Journal of Public Health*, vol 94, no 4, pp 619-24.

Frank, D.J., Hardinge, T. and Wosick-Correa, K. (2009) 'The global dimensions of rape-law reform: a cross-national study of policy outcomes', *American Sociological Review*, vol 74, no 2, pp 272-90.

Franzway, S. and Fanow, M.M. (2011) *Making feminist politics: Transnational alliances between women and labor*, Chicago, IL: University of Illinois Press.

Friedman, B. and Golding, S. (1997) *Guys talk too: Report of the Young Men and Acquaintance Rape Survey*, Adelaide, SA: Family Planning, South Australia.

Friedman, E.J. (2009) 'Re(gion)alizing women's human rights in Latin America', *Politics and Gender*, vol 5, no 3, pp 349-75.

G8 (2013) *Declaration on preventing sexual violence in conflict*, adopted in London on 11 April, London: Foreign and Commonwealth Office (www.gov.uk/government/uploads/system/uploads/attachment_data/file/185008/G8_PSVI_Declaration_-_FINAL.pdf).

García-Moreno, C. and Watts, C. (2011) 'Violence against women: an urgent public health priority,' *WHO Bulletin*, vol 89, no 2, pp 2-3 (www.who.int/reproductivehealth/publications/violence/bulletin_88_12/en/).

García-Moreno, C., Hegarty, K., d'Oliveira, A.F.L., Koziol-MacLain, J., Colombini, M. and Feder, G. (2014a) 'The health-systems response to violence against women', *The Lancet*.

García-Moreno, C., Zimmerman, C., Morris-Gehring, A., Heise, L., Amin, A., Abrahams, N., Montoya, O., Bhate-Deosthali, P., Kilonzo, N. and Watts, C. (2014b) 'Addressing violence against women: a call to action', *The Lancet*.

GBVIMS (Gender-Based Violence Information Management System) Global Team (2013) www.k4health.org/toolkits/rh-humanitarian-settings/gender-based-violence-information-management-system#

Gentlemen, A. (2010) 'Assange rape allegations: treatment of women unfair and absurd', *The Guardian*, 8 December (www.theguardian.com/media/2010/dec/08/julian-assange-rape-allegations).

Gill, A. and Anitha, S. (2011) *Forced marriage: Introducing a social justice and human rights perspective*, London: Zed Books.

Gill, A. and Rehman, A. (2004) 'Empowerment through activism: responding to domestic violence in the South Asian Community', *Gender and Development*, vol 12, no 1, pp 75-82.

Global Voices (2012) *Jordan: Campaign against 'rape-marriage' law* (http://globalvoicesonline.org/2012/05/14/jordan-campaign-launched-against-rape-marriage-law/).

Goetz, A.-M. (2008) *Women's participation in peace negotiations. Where are the numbers?*, UNIFEM Briefing Paper, New York: UNIFEM.

Golding, J.M., Stein, J.A., Seigal, J.M., Burman, M.A. and Sorenson, S.B. (1998) 'Sexual assault history and use of health and mental health services', *American Journal of Community Psychiatry*, vol 16, no 5, pp 625-44.

Government of South Australia (2013) *South Australian legislation*, Adelaide, SA: Government of South Australia (www.legislation. sa.gov.au).

Gray, S. (2011) 'Julian Assange case sparks rape "grey zones" debate among Twitter fans', news.com.au, 10 February (www. news.com.au/world/govts-fear-wikileaks-truths-rally-told/ story-e6frfkyi-1226003263888).

Greco, D. and Dawgert, S. (2007) *Poverty and sexual violence: Building prevention and intervention responses: A guide for counsellors and advocates*, Enola, PA: Pennsylvania Coalition Against Rape (PCAR) (www.pcar.org/sites/default/files/file/poverty.pdf).

Gregory, J. and Lees, S. (1999) *Policing sexual assault*, London: Routledge.

Grubin, D. and Beech, A. (2010) 'Chemical castration for sex offenders', *British Medical Journal*, vol 340, pp 433-4.

Hadley-Kamptz, I. (2010) 'Lite om sex, normer och civilisation' (http://isobelsverkstad.blogspot.se/2010/12/lite-om-sex-normer-och-civilisation.html).

Hagen, J. (2006) 'Fighting sexual exploitation and abuse by UN peacekeepers', *UN Chronicle Online News Coverage*, 13 December (http://unchronicle.un.org/).

Hager, D. (2011) *Provision of specialised domestic violence and refuge services for women who currently find it difficult to access mainstream services: Disabled women, older women, sex workers and women with mental illness and/or drug and alcohol problems as a result of domestic violence*, Auckland, New Zealand: Homeworks Trust (www.communitymatters.govt.nz/vwluResources/ WCMFReport10Hager/%24file/WCMFReport10Hager. pdf).

Hald, G.M., Malamuth, N.M. and Yuen, C. (2010) 'Pornography and attitudes supporting violence against women: revisiting the relationship in nonexperimental studies', *Aggressive Behaviour*, vol 36, no 1, pp 14-20.

Halder, D. and Jaishankar, K. (2009) 'Cyber socializing and victimization of women', *TEMIDA*, str 5-26.

Hamilton, C. and Maddison, S. (2007) *Silencing dissent. How the Australian government is controlling public opinion and stifling debate*, Sydney, NSW: Allen & Unwin.

Harkins, L., Flak, V.E., Beech, A.R. and Woodhams, J. (2012) 'Evaluation of a community-based sex offender treatment program using a good lives model approach', *Sexual Abuse: A Journal of Research and Treatment*, vol 24, no 6, pp 519-43.

Harrison, K. (2007) 'The high-risk sex offender strategy in England and Wales: is chemical castration an option?', *The Howard Journal of Criminal Justice*, vol 46, no 1, pp 16-31.

Haven, The, Paddington, and Westminster Mind (no date) *Specialist mental health independent sexual violence advisor* (www.thehavens.co.uk/).

Hearn, J. (2012) 'A multi-faceted power analysis of men's violence to known women: from hegemonic masculinity to the hegemony of men', *Sociological Review*, vol 60, no 4, pp 589-610.

Hearn, J. (2013) 'The sociological significance of domestic violence: tensions, paradoxes and implications', *Current Sociology*, vol 61, no 2, pp 152-70.

Heath, M. (2005) 'The law and sexual offences against adults in Australia', *Issues*, no 4, June, Australian Institute of Family Studies.

Heenan, M. (2004) *Just 'keeping the peace': A reluctance to respond to male partner sexual violence*, Melbourne, VIC: Australian Institute of Family Studies.

Heenan, M. and McKelvie, H. (1997) *The Crimes (Rape) Act 1991: An evaluation report*, Melbourne, VIC: Attorney-General's Legislation and Policy Branch, Department of Justice.

Heise, L.L. (1998) 'Violence against women: An integrated, ecological framework', *Violence Against Women*, vol 4, no 3, pp 262–90.

Helland, A. and Kristensen, A. (1999) *Women in peace operations, women and armed conflicts – A study for the Norwegian Ministry of Foreign Affairs*, Oslo: Norwegian Institute of International Affairs.

Hester, M. (2013) *From report to court: Rape cases and the criminal justice system in the North East*, Bristol: University of Bristol, in association with the Northern Rock Foundation.

HM Government (2009) *Together we can end violence against women and girls: A strategy* (www.wiltshire.gov.uk/hm-government-violence-against-women-girls-strategy.pdf).

HM Government (2010) *Call to end violence against women and girls* (www.gov.uk/government/uploads/system/uploads/attachment_data/file/97905/vawg-paper.pdf).

HM Government (2015) *A call to end violence against women and girls: Progress report 2010-15* (www.gov.uk/government/uploads/system/uploads/attachment_data/file/409510/VAWG_Progress_Report_2010-2015.pdf).

Hogg, R. and Brown, D. (1998) *Rethinking law and order*, Sydney, NSW: Pluto.

Holly, J., Scalabrino, R. and Woodward, B. (2012) *Promising practices: Mental health trust responses to domestic violence*, London: AVA (Against Violence and Abuse) (www.avaproject.org.uk/our-resources/reports--publications/promising-practices-mental-health-trust-responses-to-domestic-violence-(2012).aspx).

Holmes, M.M., Resnick, H.S., Kilpatrick, D.G. and Best, C.L. (1996) 'Rape-related pregnancy: estimates and descriptive characteristics from a national sample of women', *American Journal of Obstetrics and Gynecology*, vol 175, no 2, pp 320-4.

Holmes, R. and Bhuvanendra, D. (2014) *Preventing and responding to gender-based violence in humanitarian crises*, London: Humanitarian Practice Network (www.odihpn.org/hpn-resources/network-papers/preventing-and-responding-to-gender-based-violence-in-humanitarian-crises).

Home Office (2014) *Multi-agency working and information sharing project* (www.gov.uk/government/uploads/system/uploads/attachment_data/file/338875/MASH.pdf).

Horvath, M. and Brown, J. (eds) (2009) *Rape: Challenging contemporary thinking*, Cullompton: Willan.

Hsieh, C.-C. and Pugh, M. D. (1993) 'Poverty, income inequality and violent crime: a meta-analysis of recent aggregate data studies', *Criminal Justice Review*, vol 18, no 2, pp 182–202.

Hudson, H. (2000) 'Mainstreaming gender in peacekeeping operations: can Africa learn from international experience?', *African Security Review*, vol 9, no 4, pp 18-33.

Human Rights Watch (2001) *Scared at school: Sexual violence in South African schools* (www.hrw.org/reports/2001/safrica/).

IASC (Inter-Agency Standing Committee) (2005) *Guidelines for gender-based violence interventions in humanitarian settings: Focusing on prevention of and response to sexual violence in emergencies* (field test version), Geneva: IASC (www.humanitarianinfo.org/iasc/pageloader.aspx?page=content-subsidi-tf_gender-gbv).

IASC (2007) *IASC guidelines on mental health and psychosocial support in emergency settings*, Geneva: IASC (www.who.int/mental_health/emergencies/guidelines_iasc_mental_health_psychosocial_june_2007.pdf).

IASC GHC (Global Health Cluster) (2010) *Removing user fees for primary health care services during humanitarian crises*, GHC Position Paper, 24 March, Geneva: IASC GHC (www.who.int/hac/global_health_cluster/about/policy_strategy/EN_final_position_paper_on_user_fees.pdf).

IASC Reference Group for Mental Health and Psychosocial Support in Emergency Settings (2012) *Who is where, when, doing what (4Ws) in mental health and psychosocial support: Manual with activity codes* (field test-version), Geneva: IASC (www.who.int/mental_health/publications/iasc_4ws/en/).

IAWG (Inter-Agency Working Group) on Reproductive Health in Crises (2010) *Inter-agency field manual on reproductive health in humanitarian settings 2010, Revision for field review* (www.iawg.net/resources/field_manual.html#download).

ICM (2006) *UK poll of 16-20 years: End violence against women*, London: ICM (www.amnesty.org.uk/press-releases/uk-42-young-people-know-girls-whose-boyfriends-have-hit-them-new-survey).

Iconis, R. (2008) 'Rape myth acceptance in college students: a literature review', *Contemporary Issues in Education Research*, vol 1, no 2, pp 47-52.

iCOP (2013) http://scc-sentinel.lancs.ac.uk/icop/

International Alert (2002) *Gender mainstreaming in peace support operations: Moving beyond rhetoric to practice* (http://reliefweb.int/sites/reliefweb.int/files/resources/8129419C790A3288C1256C23002A447B-gendermainstreaming-jul.pdf).

International Association of Forensic Nurses (2011) *SANE checklist for disaster planning* (www.vawnet.org/summary.php?doc_id=2715&find_type=web_sum_GC).

International Association of Women Judges (2012) *Stopping the abuse of power through sexual exploitation: Naming, shaming and ending sextortion* (www.iawj.org/IAWJ_International_Toolkit_FINAL.pdf).

International Criminal Court (2011) *Rome Statute of the International Criminal Court* (www.icc-cpi.int/NR/rdonlyres/ADD16852-AEE9-4757-ABE7-9CDC7CF02886/283503/RomeStatutEng1.pdf).

IRC (2013) *Syria: A regional crisis*, The IRC Commission on Syrian Refugees (www.rescue.org/sites/default/files/resource-file/IRCReportMidEast20130114.pdf).

IRC (2014) *From harm to home: International Rescue Committee annual report* (www.rescue.org/sites/default/files/IRC_AR_2013.pdf).

ISIS (2013) *Protecting children in online social networks* (http://gow.epsrc.ac.uk/NGBOViewGrant.aspx?GrantRef=EP/F035454/1).

ISIS Forensics (2013) *Protecting children online* (www.isis-forensics.com/).

ITU (International Telecommunications Union) (2011) *The world in 2011: ICT facts and figures*, Geneva: ITU (www.itu.int/ITU-D/ict/facts/2011/).

Jacobs, S., Jacobson, R. and Marchbank, J. (eds) (2000) *States of conflict: Gender, violence and resistance*, London: Zed.

Järvinen, J., Kail, A. and Miller, I. (2008) *Hard knock life: Violence against women. A guide for donors and funders*, London: New Philanthropy Capital (http://eige.europa.eu/content/hard-knock-life-violence-against-women-guide-for-donors-and-funders).

Jewkes, R., Sen, P. and Garcia-Moreno, C. (2002) 'Sexual violence', in E.G. Krug, L.L. Dahlberg, J.A. Mercy, A.B. Zwi and R. Lozano (eds) *World report on violence and health*, Geneva: World Health Organization (www.who.int/violence_injury_prevention/violence/world_report/en/).

Jewkes, R., Sikweyiya, Y. and Jama-Shai, N. (2014) 'The art of medicine: the challenges of research on violence in post-conflict Bougainville', *The Lancet*, vol 383, pp 2039-40.

Jewkes, R., Sikweyiya, Y., Morrell, R. and Dunkle, K. (2009) 'Understanding men's health and use of violence: interface of rape and HIV in South Africa', MRC Policy Brief, June (www.svri.org/understanding.pdf).

JfA (Justice for Assange) (no date) 'Is national journalism prize-winning #Prataomdet a grassroots twitter phenomenon or an organised lobby campaign against Assange?' (www.swedenversusassange.com/).

Ji-hoon, K. (2012) 'Politicians seek surgical castration for sex offenders', *The Hankyoreh*, 6 September (www.hani.co.kr/arti/english_edition/e_national/550476.html).

Johns Hopkins School of Nursing (no date) *A microfinance intervention to improve health of rape survivors in the Democratic Republic of Congo* (http://nursing.jhu.edu/faculty_research/research/projects/pigs/index.html).

Johnson, H., Ollus, N. and Nevala, S. (2008) *Violence against women: An international perspective*, New York: Springer.

Johnson, T. (2012) *Mosaic* (www.mosaic.org.za/SMALL.pdf).

Jordan, J. (2002) 'Will any woman do? Police, gender, and rape victims', *Policing: An International Journal of Police Strategies and Management*, vol 25, no 2, pp 319-24.

Justice and Constitutional Department (2008) *Information sheet: Criminal law (sexual offences and related matters) Amendment Act No 32 of 2007* (www.justice.gov.za/docs/InfoSheets/2008%20 02%20SXOactInsert_web.pdf).

Karamé, K.H. (2001) 'Military women in peace operations: Experiences of the Norwegian battalion in UNIFIL 1978-98', *International Peacekeeping*, vol 8, no 2, pp 85-96.

Karl, M. (1995) *Women and empowerment: Participation and decision making*, London: Zed Books.

Karzi, S. (2013) 'State of the nation', *Frontline*, 25 January, pp 1-6 (www.frontline.in/cover-story/state-of-the-nation/article4282563.ece#test).

Keck, M.E. and Sikkinck, K. (1998) *Activists beyond borders: Advocacy networks in international politics*, Ithaca, NY: Cornell University Press.

Kelly, L. (1988) *Surviving sexual violence*, Cambridge: Polity Press.

Kelly, L. (2000) 'Wars against women: sexual violence, sexual politics and the militarised state', in R. Jacobson and J. Marchbank (eds) *States of conflict: Gender, violence and resistance*, London: Zed Books, pp 45-65.

Kelly, L. (2005) 'Promising practices addressing sexual violence', Expert paper prepared for the Expert Group Meeting on 'Violence against women: Good practices in combating and eliminating violence against women', UN Division for the Advancement of Women in collaboration with the UN Office on Drugs and Crime, 17-20 May, Vienna (www.un.org/womenwatch/daw/egm/vaw-gp-2005/docs/experts/kelly.sexualviolence.pdf).

Kelly, L. (2007) *Rape in the twenty-first century: Old behaviours, new contexts and emerging patterns*, Full research report, ESRC End of Award Report RES-000-22-1679, Swindon: Economic and Social Research Council (www.esds.ac.uk/doc/5827%5C mrdoc%5Cpdf%5C5827userguide.pdf).

Kelly, L. and Dubois, L. (2008) *Combating violence against women: Minimum standards for support services*, Strasbourg: Council of Europe, Directorate General of Human Rights and Legal Affairs (www.coe.int/t/dg2/equality/domesticviolencecampaign/Source/EG-VAW-CONF(2007)Study%20rev.en.pdf).

Kelly, L., Lovett, J. and Regan, L. (2005) *A gap or a chasm? Attrition in reported rape cases*, Home Office Research Study 293, London: Home Office (http://webarchive.nationalarchives.gov.uk/20110218135832/rds.homeoffice.gov.uk/rds/pdfs05/hors293.pdf).

Kelly, L., Lovett, J. and Regan, L. (2006) *Violence against women: A briefing document on international issues and responses*, Manchester: British Council (www.cwasu.org/publication_display.asp?type=2&pageid=PAPERS&itemkey=185).

Kelly, L., Hagemann-White, C., Meysen, T. and Römkens, R. (2011) *Realising rights: Case studies on state responses to violence against women and children in Europe*, London: CWASU (Child & Woman Abuse Studies Unit), London Metropolitan University (www.cwasu.org/publication_display.asp?pageid=PAPERS&type=1&pagekey=44&year=2011).

Kilonzo, N., Dartnall, E. and Obbayi, M. (2013) *Policy and practice requirements for bringing to scale sexual violence services in low resource settings*, Briefing Paper, Sexual Violence Research Initiative and LVCT (www.svri.org/ BriefingPaperPolicyPracticeRequirements.pdf).

Kim, J., Mokwena, L., Ntlemo, E., Dwane, N., Noholoza, A., Abramsky, T. and Marinda, E. (2007a) *Developing an integrated model for post-rape care and HIV post-exposure prophylaxis in rural South Africa*, Johannesburg: RADAR (Rural AIDS and Development Action Research Programme), School of Public Health, University of the Witwatersrand (http://pdf.usaid.gov/ pdf_docs/PNADK615.pdf).

Kim, J., Watts, C., Hargreaves, J., Ndhlovu, L., Phetla, G., Morrison, L., Busza, J., Porter, J. and Pronyk, P. (2007b) 'Understanding the impact of a microfinance-based intervention on women's empowerment and the reduction of intimate partner violence in South Africa', *American Journal of Public Health*, vol 97, no 10, pp 1794-802.

Kippenberg, J., Sawyer, I. and Stauss, K. (2009) *Soldiers who rape, commanders who condone: Sexual violence and military reform in the Democratic Republic of Congo*, New York: Human Rights Watch (www.hrw.org/reports/2009/07/16/soldiers-who-rape-commanders-who-condone-0).

Klein, A. (2006) *Sexual violence in disasters: A planning guide for prevention and response*, Baton Rouge, LA and Enola, PA: LaFASA (Louisiana Foundation Against Sexual Assault) and NSVRC (National Sexual Violence Resource Center) (www.nsvrc.org/sites/default/files/Publications_NSVRC_ Guides_Sexual-Violence-in-Disasters_A-planning-guide-for-prevention-and-response_0.pdf).

Knott, L. (2013) *Post-traumatic stress disorder* (www.patient.co.uk/ doctor/post-traumatic-stress-disorder-pro).

Kofaviv, M. (2012) *Struggling to survive: Sexual exploitation of displaced women and girls in Port au Prince, Haiti*, New York: NSVRC (National Sexual Violence Resource Center) (www. nsvrc.org/publications/struggling-survive-sexual-exploitation-displaced-women-and-girls-port-au-prince-haiti).

Koljonen, J. (2010) 'Dags att prata om det', *DN Debatt*, 18 December (www.dn.se/kultur-noje/debatt-essa/dags-att-prata-om-det).

Koss, M.P. (2006) 'Restoring rape survivors: justice, advocacy, and a call to action', *Annals of the New York Academy of Sciences*, vol 1087, pp 206-34.

Kristof, N. and WuDunn, S. (2010) *Half the sky: How to change the world*, London: Virago Press.

Krizsán, A. and Popa, R. (2010) 'Europeanization in making policies against domestic violence in Central and Eastern Europe', *Social Politics*, vol 17, no 3, pp 379-406.

Krug, E.G., Mercy, J.A., Dahlberg, L.L. and Zwi, A.B. (2002) 'The world report on violence and health', *The Lancet*, vol 360, no 9339, pp 1083-88.

Kulkarni, S., Bell, H. and McDaniel Rhodes, D. (2012) 'Back to basics: essential qualities of services for survivors of intimate partner violence', *Violence Against Women*, vol 18, no 1, pp 85-101.

Kushel, M., Evans, J., Perry, S., Robertson, M. and Moss, A. (2003) 'No door to lock: victimization among homeless and marginally housed persons', *JAMA Internal Medicine*, vol 163, no 20, pp 2492-9.

Lagarde, M. (2005) 'El feminicidio, delito contra la humanidad', *Feminicidio, justicia y derecho*, México: Comisión Especial para Conocer y Dar Seguimiento a las Investigaciones Relacionadas con los Feminicidios en la República Mexicana y a la Procuración de Justicia Vinculada.

Lagarde, M. (2006a) *Violencia feminicida en 10 entidades de la República Mexicana*, México: Cámara de Diputados, LIX Legislatura, Comisión Especial para Conocer y Dar Seguimiento a las Investigaciones Relacionadas con los Feminicidios en la República Mexicana y a la Procuración de Justicia Vinculada.

Lagarde, M. (2006b) *Violencia feminicida en la República Mexicana*, México: Cámara de Diputados, LIX Legislatura, Comisión Especial para Conocer y Dar Seguimiento a las Investigaciones Relacionadas con los Feminicidios en la República Mexicana y a la Procuración de Justicia Vinculada.

Lagarde, M. (2008) 'Antropología, feminismo y política: violencia feminicida y Derechos Humanos de las mujeres', in M. Bullen and C. Díez (eds) *Retos teóricos y nuevas prácticas*, Donostia: Ankulegi Antropologia Elkartea.

Lake, M. (1999) *Getting equal: The history of Australian feminism*, Sydney, NSW: Allen & Unwin.

Larasi, M. (2012) *Media as a site to prevent violence against girls and women*, Expert Paper prepared for UN Women in cooperation with ESCAP, UNDP, UNFPA, UNICEF and WHO Expert Group Meeting for the prevention of violence against women and girls (www.unwomen.org/~/media/headquarters/attachments/sections/csw/57/egm/egm-paper-marai-larasi%20pdf.pdf).

Larcombe, W. (2011) 'Falling rape conviction rates: (some) feminist aims and measures for rape law', *Feminist Legal Studies*, vol 19, pp 27-45.

Larsen, K.S. and Long, E. (1988) 'Attitudes toward rape', *Journal of Sex Research*, vol 24, pp 299-304.

Lawson, E. (2013) *Acute stress reaction* (www.patient.co.uk/health/acute-stress-reaction-leaflet).

Letourneau, E.J., Bandyopadhyay, D., Armstrong, K.S. and Sinha, D. (2010) 'Do sex offender registration and notification requirements deter juvenile sex crimes?', *Criminal Justice and Behavior*, vol 37, no 5, pp 553-69.

Letourneau, E.J., Levenson, J.S., Bandyopadhyay, D., Sinha, D. and Armstrong, K.S. (2009) 'Effects of South Carolina's sex offender registration and notification policy on adult recidivism', *Criminal Justice Policy Review*, vol 21, no 4, pp 435-58.

Leveson Inquiry (2012) *Culture proactive and the ethics of the press*, London: The Stationery Office.

Lievore, D. (2003) *Non-reporting and hidden recording of sexual assault: An international literature review*, Barton, ACT: Commonwealth Office of the Status of Women.

Littel, K., Malefyt, M.B., Walker, A.H. and Kuriansky, J.A. (1998) *Assessing the justice system response to violence against women: A tool for communities to develop coordinated responses*, Washington, DC: Minnesota Center Against Violence and Abuse, July (www.mincava.umn.edu/documents/promise/pp3/pp3.html).

Lockett, K. and Bishop, K. (2012) *A Practical Guide on Community Programming on Violence Against Women and Girls*, Department for International Development (www.gov.uk/government/uploads/system/uploads/attachment_data/file/67335/How-to-note-VAWG-2-community-prog.pdf).

Londono, P. (2007) 'Positive obligations, criminal procedure and rape cases', *European Human Rights Law Review*, vol 2, pp 128-71.

Lonsway, K.A., Banyard, V.L., Berkowitz, A.D., Gidycz, C.A., Katz, J.T., Koss, M.P., Schewe, P.A. and Ullman, S.E. (2009) *Rape prevention and risk reduction*, VAWnet (National Electronic Network on Violence Against Women), January, Harrisburg, PA: National Resource Center on Domestic Violence (www.vawnet.org/applied-research-papers/print-document.php?doc_id=1655).

Loots, L., Dartnall, L. and Jewkes, R. (2011) *Global review of national prevention policies*, Pretoria, South Africa: Sexual Violence Research Initiative and the South African Medical Research Council (www.svri.org/GlobalReview.pdf).

Lösel, F. (2010) 'What works in reducing reoffending: a global perspective offender rehabilitation', First European Seminar of the STARR Project, Cambridge and Erlangen, Germany: Institute of Criminology, University of Cambridge and Institute of Psychology, University of Erlangen-Nuremberg (www.cepprobation.org/uploaded_files/Pres STARR Cam 10 Loesel.pdf).

Lovett, J. and Kelly, L. (2009) *Different systems, similar outcomes? Tracking attrition in reported rape cases across Europe*, London: CWASU (Child & Woman Abuse Studies Unit), London Metropolitan University (http://kunskapsbanken.nck.uu.se/nckkb/nck/publik/fil/visa/197/different_systems_03_web(2).pdf).

Lovett, J., Regan, L. and Kelly, L. (2004) *Sexual assault referral centres: Developing best practice and maximizing potentials*, Home Office Research Study 285, London: Research Development and Statistics Directorate, Home Office (http://webarchive.nationalarchives.gov.uk/20100413151441/crimereduction.homeoffice.gov.uk/sexual/sexual22.htm).

Macdowall, W., Gibson, L.J., Tanton, C., Mercer, C.H., Lewis, R., Clifton, S., Field, N., Datta, J., Mitchell, K.R., Sonnenberg, P., Erens, B., Copas, A.J., Phelps, A., Prah, P., Johnson, A.M. and Wellings K. (2013) 'Lifetime prevalence, associated factors, and circumstances of non-volitional sex in women and men in Britain: findings from the third National Survey of Sexual Attitudes and Lifestyles (Natsal-3)', *Lancet*, vol 382, pp 1845-55.

MacKinnon, C.A. (1979) *Sexual harassment of working women*, New Haven, CT: Yale University Press.

MacKinnon, C.A. (2006) *Are women human? And other international dialogues*, Cambridge, MA: Harvard University Press.

McFarlane, J., Malecha, A., Watson, K., Gist, J., Batten, E., Hall, I. and Smith, S. (2005) 'Intimate partner sexual assault against women: frequency, health consequences, and treatment outcomes', *Obstetrics and Gynecology*, vol 105, no 1, pp 99-108.

McKimmie, B.M., Masser, B.M. and Bongiorno, R. (2014) 'What counts as rape? The effect of offense prototypes, victim stereotypes, and participant gender on how the complainant and defendant are perceived', *Journal of Interpersonal Violence*, vol 29, no 12, pp 2273-303.

McLennan, W. (1996) *Women's safety Australia*, Canberra, ACT: Australian Bureau of Statistics.

McMahon-Howard, J. (2011) 'Does the controversy matter? Comparing the causal determinants of the adoption of controversial and noncontroversial rape law reforms', *Law & Society Review*, vol 45, no 2, pp 401-33.

McNaughton Reyes, H.L., Billings, D.L., Paredes-Gaitan, Y. and Zuniga, K.P. (2012) 'An assessment of health sector guidelines and services for treatment of sexual violence in El Salvador, Guatemala, Honduras and Nicaragua', *Reproductive Health Matters*, vol 20, no 40, pp 83-93.

Machisa, M.T. and van Dorp, R. (2012) *The Gender Based Violence Indicators Study Botswana*, Gaborone: Gender Links (http://countryoffice.unfpa.org/botswana/drive/GBVIndicators Botswanareport.pdf)

Macy, R., Johns, N., Rizo, C., Martin, S. and Giattina, M. (2011) 'Domestic violence and sexual assault service goal priorities', *Journal of Interpersonal Violence*, vol 26, no 16, pp 3361-82.

Maddan, S., Miller, J.M., Walker, J.T. and Marshall, I.H. (2011) 'Utilizing criminal history information to explore the effect of community notification on sex offender recidivism', *Justice Quarterly*, vol 28, no 2, pp 303-24.

Maghri, A. (2012) *In Morocco, the rape and death of an adolescent girl prompts calls for changes to the penal code*, UNICEF (www.unicef.org/infobycountry/morocco_62113.html).

Mallios, C. and Markowitz, J. (2011) 'Benefits of a coordinated community response to sexual violence', *Strategies in Brief*, issue 7, December, Washington, DC: Æquitas.

Malo-juvera, V. (2012) 'The effect of young adult literature on adolescents' rape myth acceptance', DEd Thesis, Florida International University (http://digitalcommons.fiu.edu/etd/564).

Martin, P.Y. (2005) *Rape Work: Victims, Gender and emotions in organization and community context*, New York: Routledge.

Martin, P.Y. (2007) 'Coordinated community services for victims of violence', in L.L. O'Toole, J.R. Schiffman, and M.L. Kiter Edwards (eds) *Gender violence: Interdisciplinary perspectives* (2nd edn), New York: New York University Press, pp 443–51.

May-Chahal, C., Mason, C., Rashid, A., Walkerdine, J., Rayson, P. and Greenwood, P. (2014) 'Safeguarding cyborg childhoods: incorporating the on/offline behaviour of children into everyday social work practices', *British Journal of Social Work*, vol 44, no 3, pp 596-614. doi: 10.1093/bjsw/bcs121.

Mertus, J. (2004) 'Shouting from the bottom of the well. The impact of international trials for wartime rape on women's agency', *International Feminist Journal of Politics*, vol 6, no 1, pp 110-28.

Michau, L., Horn, J., Bank, A., Dutt, M. and Zimmerman, C. (2014) 'Prevention of violence against women and girls: lessons from practice', *The Lancet*.

Miller, T., Cohen, M. and Wiersema, B. (1996) *Victim costs and consequences: A new look*, NCJ 155282, Washington, DC: US Department of Justice, Office of Justice Programs, National Institute of Justice (www.ncjrs.gov/pdffiles/victcost.pdf).

Missing Link (2015) *Missing Link: Mental health and housing services for women* (www.missinglinkhousing.co.uk/).

Moghadam, V.M. (2005) *Globalising women: Transnational feminist networks*, Baltimore, MD: Johns Hopkins University Press.

Moreton-Robinson, A. (2002) *Talkin' up the white woman: Aboriginal women and feminism*, Brisbane, QLD: University of Queensland Press.

Morris, M. (2008) *Violence against women in Canada: Effective approaches and resources*, Ottawa, ON: MATCH International (http://matchinternational.org/docs/publications/match-gender-violence-against-women-in-canada.pdf).

Morrison, A., Ellsberg, M. and Bott, S. (2007) 'Addressing gender-based violence: a critical review of interventions', *The World Bank Research Observer*, vol 22, no 1, pp 25-51 (http://wbro.oxfordjournals.org/content/early/2006/12/31/wbro.lkm003.full.pdf+html).

Morrison, S., Hardison, J., Mathew, A. and O'Neil, J. (2004) *An evidence-based review of sexual assault preventive intervention programs*, Washington, DC: National Institute Justice, US Department of Justice.

Moser, C. and Shrader, E. (1999) *A conceptual framework for violence reduction*, Urban Peace Program Series, Latin America and Caribbean Region Sustainable Development Working Paper No 2, Washington, DC: The World Bank (www-wds.worldbank.org/external/default/WDSContentServer/WDSP/IB/1999/11/19/000094946_99110405534914/Rendered/PDF/multi_page.pdf).

Mossman, E., Jordan, J., MacGibbin, L., Kingi, V. and Moore, L. (2009) *Responding to sexual violence: A review of the research literature on good practice*, Wellington: Ministry of Women's Affairs (http://mwa.govt.nz/documents/responding-sexual-violence-review-literature-good-practice-2009).

Mouzos, J. and Makkai, T. (2004) *Women's experiences of male violence: Findings from the Australian component of the International Violence against Women Survey (IVAWS)*, Canberra, ACT: Australian Institute of Criminology.

MPS (Metropolitan Police Service) (2005) *A review of rape investigations in the MPS: Final report*, London: Deputy Commissioner's Command, Directorate of Strategic Development and Territorial Policing, Project Sapphire (http://content.met.police.uk/News/Review-of-Rape-Inve stigations/1260267633108/1257246745756).

Mullighan, T. (2008) *Children on Anangu Pitjantjatjara Yankunytjatjara (APY) Lands Commission of Inquiry: A report into sexual abuse*, Adelaide, SA: Children on APY Lands Commission of Inquiry.

Murray, C.J.L. and Lopez, A.D. (1999) 'On the comparable quantification of health risks: lessons from the global burden of disease study', *Epidemiology*, vol 10, no 5, pp 594-605 (http://cdrwww.who.int/quantifying_ehimpacts/methods/ en/murray.pdf).

National Council to Reduce Violence against Women and their Children (2009) *Time for action: The National Council's plan for Australia to reduce violence against women and their children, 2009-2021*, Canberra, ACT: National Council to Reduce Violence against Women and their Children, Commonwealth of Australia.

Neudorf, K., Taylor, T.M. and Thurman, T.R. (2011) *The Greater Rape Intervention Program (GRIP): A case study*, New Orleans, LA: Tulane University (http://tulane.edu/publichealth/ghsd/ upload/GRIP-case-study-122011.pdf).

NHS England (2013) *Securing excellence in commissioning sexual assault services for people who experience sexual violence* (www. england.nhs.uk/wp-content/uploads/2013/06/130613-sec- exc-cvsa.pdf).

nia (no date) *The Emma Project* (www.niaendingviolence.org. uk/refuge/index.html).

NICE (National Institute for Health and Care Excellence) (2013) *Post-traumatic stress disorder*, London: NICE (www.nice.org.uk/ guidance/cg26).

NPA (2012) *Strategic plan 2012-2017*, Pretoria: NPA (www.issafrica.org/crimehub/uploads/NPA-Strategic- Plan-2012-2017.pdf).

NSVRC (National Sexual Violence Resource Center) (2006) *Hurricanes Katrina/Rita and sexual violence: Report on database of sexual violence prevalence and incidence related to Hurricanes Katrina and Rita*, Enola, PA: NSVRC (www.nsvrc.org/).

NSVRC (2014) *Sexual assault awareness month: Prevention tips for medical professionals*, Enola, PA: NSVRC (www.nsvrc.org/publications/nsvrc-publications-sexual-assault-awareness-month-fact-sheets/prevention-tips-medical).

Nunes, M., (2006) *Cyberspaces of everyday life*, Minneapolis, MN: University of Minnesota Press.

Olle, L. (2005) *Mapping health sector and interagency protocols on sexual assault*, Canberra, ACT: Australian Centre for the Study of Sexual Assault.

Olsson, L. (1999) *Gendering UN peacekeeping: Mainstreaming a gender perspective in multidimensional peacekeeping operations*, Report 53, Uppsala, Sweden: Department of Peace and Conflict Research, Uppsala University.

O'Malley, P. and Sutton, A. (1997) *Crime prevention: Issues in policy and research*, Sydney, NSW: Federation Press.

ONS (Office for National Statistics) (2014) *Focus on violent crime and sexual offences, 2012-13*, Cardiff: ONS (www.ons.gov.uk/ons/rel/crime-stats/crime-statistics/focus-on-violent-crime-and-sexual-offences--2012-13/index.html).

ONU Mujeres, IN Mujeres, and LXI Legislatura Cámara de Diputados Comisión Especial para Conocer y Dar Seguimiento Puntual y Exhaustivo a las Acciones que han emprendido las Autoridades Competentes en relación a los Feminicidios registrados en México (2011) *Feminicidio en México. Aproximación, tendencias y cambios, 1985-2009*, México.

Organization of American States (1994) *Inter-American Convention on the prevention, punishment and eradication of violence against women* (Convention of Belem do Para) (www.oas.org/en/CIM/docs/Belem-do-Para[EN].pdf).

Panda, P. and Agarwal, B. (2005) 'Marital violence, human development and women's property status in India', *World Development*, vol 33, no 5, pp 823-50.

Patterson, D. (2009) *The effectiveness of sexual assault services in multi-service agencies*, Harrisburg, PA: VAWnet, National Resource Center on Domestic Violence/Pennsylvania Coalition against Domestic Violence (www.vawnet.org/assoc_files_vawnet/ar_dualprograms.pdf).

Payne, D.L., Lonsway, K.A. and Fitzgerald, L.F. (1999) 'Rape myth acceptance: exploration of its structure and its measurement using the Illinois Rape Myth Acceptance Scale', *Journal of Research in Personality*, vol 33, pp 27-68.

Peate, W.F. and Mullins, J. (2008) 'Disaster preparedness training for tribal leaders', *Journal of Occupational Medicine and Toxicology*, vol 3, no 2.

Peersman, C., Schulze, C., Rashid, A., Brennan, M., Fischer, C. (2014) iCOP: automatically identifying new child abuse media in P2P networks, IEEE Symposium on Security and Privacy Workshops, IEEE Publishing, pp 124-31 (www.ieee-security.org/TC/SPW2014/papers/5103a124).

Pence, E.L. and Shepard, M.F. (1999) (eds) *Coordinating community responses to domestic violence: Lessons from Duluth and beyond*, London: Sage.

Pettman, J. (1992) 'Gendered knowledges: Aboriginal women and the politics of feminism', *Journal of Australian Studies*, vol 35, pp 120-31.

Phillips, R. (2008) 'Feminism, policy and women's safety during Australia's "war on terror"', *Feminist Review*, vol 89, pp 55-72.

Powers, T.M. (2003) 'Real wrongs in virtual communities', *Ethics and Information Technology*, vol 5, pp 191-8.

Prata om det [Talk about it] (no date) *Prataomdet.Se*.

Pratt, T.C. and Cullen, F.T. (2005) 'Assessing macro-level predictors and theories of crime: A meta-analysis', *Crime and Justice*, vol 32, no 1, pp 373-450.

Quadara, A., Fileborn, B. and Parkinson, D. (2013) *The role of forensic medical evidence in the prosecution of adult sexual assault*, Melbourne, VIC: Australian Centre for the Study of Sexual Assault (http://aifs.gov.au/acssa/pubs/issue/i15/index.html).

Quast, S. (2008) 'Justice reform and gender', in M. Bastick and K. Valasek (eds) *Gender and security sector reform toolkit*, Geneva: Centre for the Democratic Control of Armed Forces (DCAF), UN-INSTRAW (www.peacewomen.org/assets/file/Resources/UN/dcaf_justicereformgender_2009.pdf).

Radford, A (2014) *Innovative community-based approaches to addressing access to sexual violence* (http://issuu.com/isglobal/docs/20_innovative_community_based?e=0/9897769).

Radford, L. and Tsutsumi, K. (2004) 'Globalization and violence against women: inequalities in risks, responsibilities and blame in the UK and Japan', *Women's Studies International Forum*, vol 27, no 1, pp 1-12.

Raitt, F.E. (2010) 'Independent legal representation for complainants in rape trials', in C. McGlynn and V.E. Munro (eds) *Rethinking rape law: International and comparative perspectives*, London: Routledge, pp 267-80.

Rambaree, K. (no date) 'The ecology of sexuality in a Mauritian internet chat room (ICR): an internet mediated research (IMR)', Department of Social Studies and Humanities, University of Mauritius (www.irfd.org/events/wfsids/virtual/papers/sids_krambaree.pdf).

Rape Crisis England & Wales (2014) 'Government announces £7 million funding boost for survivors of sexual violence', London: Rape Crisis England & Wales (www.rapecrisis.org.uk/news_show.php?id=136).

Rape Crisis Network Europe (2015) *Help is there for you, no matter where you are* (www.rcne.com).

Rape Crisis Scotland (no date) *Definition of rape in Scotland* (www.rapecrisisscotland.org.uk/facts/).

Rashid, A., Baron, A., Rayson, P., May-Chahal, C., Greenwood, P. and Walkerdine, J. (2013) 'Who am I? Analysing digital personas in cybercrime investigations', *Computer*, vol 46, no 4, pp 54-61.

Rasool, S. (2000) 'Sexual offences courts: do more courts mean better justice?', *Nedbank ISS Crime Index*, vol 4, no 2, pp 11-14.

Ray, L. (2011) *Violence and society*, London: Sage.

Regan, L., Lovett, J. and Kelly, L. (2004) *Forensic nursing: An option for improving responses to reported rape and sexual assault*, Home Office Online Report 28/04, London: Home Office (http://citeseerx.ist.psu.edu/viewdoc/download?doi=10.1.1. 183.8948&rep=rep1&type=pdf).

Regehr, C., Alaggia, R., Dennis, J., Pitts, A. and Saini, M. (2013) 'Interventions to reduce distress in adult victims of rape and sexual violence: a systematic review', *Research on Social Work Practice* (http://rsw.sagepub.com/content/early/2013/01/29/1049731512474103).

Rehman, Y., Kelly, L. and Saddiqui, H. (2013) *Moving in the shadows: Violence in the lives of minority women and children*, Farnham: Ashgate.

Rehn, E. and Johnson Sirleaf, E. (2002) 'Women, war, peace: the independent experts' assessment on the impact of armed conflict on women and women's role in peace-building', *Progress of the world's women 2002, Vol 1*, New York: UN Women (www.unwomen.org/en/digital-library/publications/2002/1/women-war-peace-the-independent-experts-assessment-on-the-impact-of-armed-conflict-on-women-and-women-s-role-in-peace-building-progress-of-the-world-s-women-2002-vol-1).

Rice, M.E. and Harris, G.T. (2011) 'Is androgen deprivation therapy effective in the treatment of sex offenders?', *Psychology, Public Policy, and Law*, vol 17, no 2, pp 315-32.

Riger, S., Staggs, S. and Schewe, P. (2004) 'Intimate partner violence as an obstacle to employment among mothers affected by welfare reform', *Journal of Social Issues*, vol 60, no 4, pp 801-18.

Robinson, A.L. (2009) *Independent sexual violence advisors: A process evaluation*, London: Home Office (www.cf.ac.uk/socsi/resources/isvareport.pdf).

Roggeband, C. (2014) 'Latin American advocacy on violence against women and the OAS convention', in A. van der Vleuten, A. van Eerdewijk and C. Roggeband (eds) *Gender equality norms in regional governance. Transnational dynamics in Europe, South America and Southern Africa*, Basingstoke: Palgrave, pp 139-164.

Roks (Riksorganisationen for Kvinnojourer och Tjejjourer i Sverige) (2012) *Våld mot äldre kvinnor*, Roks rapport 1/2012, Stockholm: ROKS (www.roks.se/sites/default/files/pdf/puffar/vald_mot_aldre_kvinnor_-_roks_rapport_1-2012.pdf).

Rothbaum, B.O., Foa, E.B., Riggs, D.S., Murdock, T. and Walsh, W. (1992) 'A prospective examination of post-traumatic stress disorder in rape victims', *Journal of Traumatic Stress*, vol 5, no 3, pp 455-73.

Rowley, E., Garcia-Moreno, C. and Dartnall, E, (2012) *A research agenda for sexual violence in humanitarian, conflict and post-conflict settings: Executive summary*, Geneva: World Health Organization, UN Action, Sexual Violence Research Initiative and Medical Research Council South Africa (www.svri.org/ExecutiveSummary.pdf).

Rowntree, M. (2010) '"Living life with grace is my revenge": situating survivor knowledge about sexual violence', *Qualitative Social Work*, vol 9, no 4, pp 447-60.

Roy, C. and Martin, N. (2002) *Improving services to sexual assault victims in Olmsted County, 2000-01 evaluation report of a Minnesota Model Protocol Project test site*, Saint Paul, MN: Wilder Research Center (www.idmarch.org/document/KTM/kG5V-show/Improving+services+to+sexual+assault+victims+in+Olmsted+County+2000-01+evaluation+report+of+a+Minnesota+Model+Protocol+Project+test+site).

Russell, W., Hilton, A., Peel, M., Loots, L. and Dartnall, L. (2011) *Care and support of male survivors of conflict-related sexual violence*, Briefing paper, Sexual Violence Research Initiative (www.svri.org/CareSupportofMaleSurviv.pdf).

SACT (Sexual Assault Crisis Team) (2013) http://sactvt.org/

Sadan, M., Dikweni, L. and Cassiem, S. (2001) *Pilot assessment: The Sexual Offences Court in Wynberg and Cape Town and related services*, Pretoria: Institute for Democracy in Africa (www.afrimap.org/english/images/documents/file434e4ac9d1f29.pdf).

Sandler, J.C., Freeman, N.J. and Socia, K.M. (2008) 'Does a watched pot boil? A time-series analysis of New York State's sex offender registration and notification law', *Psychology, Public Policy, and Law*, vol 14, no 4, pp 284-302.

Sawer, M., (2002) 'The representation of women in Australia: meaning and make-believe', *Parliamentary Affairs*, vol 55, pp 5-18.

Schmucker, M. and Lösel, F. (2008) 'Does sexual offender treatment work? A systematic review of outcome evaluations', *Psicothema*, vol 20, no 1, pp 10-19.

Schram, D.D. and Milloy, C.D. (1995) *Community notification: A study of offender characteristics and recidivism*, Olympia, DC: Washington State Institute for Public Policy (www.wsipp. wa.gov/rptfiles/chrrec.pdf).

Scutt, J.A. (1998) 'Legal activism', in B. Caine (ed) *Australian feminism: A companion*, Melbourne, VIC: Oxford University Press.

Shepherd, L.J. (2006) *Gender, violence and security: Discourse as practice*, London: Zed.

Short, L., McMahon, P., Chervin, D., Shelley, G., Lezin, N., Sloop, K. and Dawkins, N. (2000) 'Survivors' identification of protective factors and early warning signs for intimate partner violence', *Violence Against Women*, vol 6, no 3, pp 272-85.

Simić, O. (2012) *Regulation of sexual conduct in UN peacekeeping operations*, Berlin, Heidelberg: Springer Berlin Heidelberg.

Skinner, T. and Taylor, H. (2009) '"Being shut out in the dark": young survivors' experiences of reporting rape and sexual assault', *Feminist Criminology*, vol 4, no 2, pp 130-50.

Skjelsbaek, I. (2001) 'Sexual violence in times of war: A new challenge for peace operations?', *International Peacekeeping*, vol 8, no 2, pp 69-84.

Smith, O. and Skinner, T. (2012) 'Observing court responses to victims of rape and sexual assault', *Feminist Criminology*, vol 7, no 4, pp 298-326.

Soothill, K. and Walby, S. (1991) *Sex crime in the news*, London: Routledge.

South African Law Commission (2001) *Conviction rates and other outcomes for crimes reported in eight South African police areas*, Research Paper 18 (www.justice.gov.za/salrc/rpapers/rp18. pdf).

Southampton Rape Crisis (2011) *Annual report 2011 Southampton*, Southampton Rape Crisis & Sexual Abuse Counselling Service.

Spangaro, J., Zwi, A., Adogu, C., Ranmuthugala, G., Davies, G.P. and Steinacker, L. (2013) *What is the evidence of the impact of initiatives to reduce risk and incidence of sexual violence in conflict and post-conflict zones and other humanitarian crises in lower and middle-income countries? A systematic review*, London: EPPI-Centre, Social Science Research Unit, Institute of Education, University of London (http://eppi.ioe.ac.uk/cms/Default.aspx?tabid=3405).

Sphere Project, The (2011) *The Sphere handbook: Humanitarian charter and minimum standards in humanitarian response*, Rugby: Practical Action Publishing (www.sphereproject.org/).

St Mary's Centre SARC (2013) *St Mary's SARC Annual Report: April 2012-April 2013* (www.stmaryscentre.org/wp-content/uploads/2013/11/12-19544-SARC-Annual-Report-2013.pdf).

St Mary's Sexual Assault Referral Centre (no date) www.stmaryscentre.org/

Stark, E. (2007) *Coercive control: How men entrap women in personal life*, Oxford: Oxford University Press.

Statistics South Africa (2000) *Quantitative research findings on rape in South Africa*, Pretoria: Statistics South Africa (www.statssa.gov.za/publications/rape/rape.pdf).

Stiehm, J. (1997) 'Peacekeeping and peace research: men's and women's work', *Women and Politics*, vol 18, pp 27-51.

Stubbs, J. (2003) 'Sexual assault, criminal justice and law and order', *Women Against Violence: An Australian Feminist Journal*, vol 14, pp 10-21.

Stubbs, J. (2004) 'Restorative justice, domestic violence and family violence', *Issues*, no 9, pp 1-15, Australian Domestic and Family Violence Clearinghouse.

Suarez, E. and Gadalla, T.M. (2010) 'Stop blaming the victim: a meta-analysis on rape myths', *Journal of Interpersonal Violence*, vol 25, no 11, pp 2010-35.

Sugar, N.F., Fine, D.N. and Eckert, L.O. (2003) 'Physical injury after sexual assault: findings of a large case series', *American Journal of Obstetrics and Gynecology*, vol 190, no 1, pp 71-6.

Sullivan, C.M. and Bybee, D.I. (1999) 'Reducing violence using community-based advocacy for women with abusive partners', *Journal of Consulting and Clinical Psychology*, vol 67, no 1, pp 43-53.

Summers, A. (2003) *The end of equality: Work, babies and women's choices in 21st century Australia*, Melbourne, VIC: Random House Australia.

SVRI (Sexual Violence Research Initiative) (2011) *Mental health responses for victims of sexual violence and rape in resource-poor settings*, Briefing paper (www.svri.org/MentalHealthResponse.pdf).

SVRI (Sexual Violence Research Initiative) (2013) *Emergency contraception for rape survivors: A human rights and public health imperative* (www.cecinfo.org/custom-content/uploads/2014/03/ICEC_EC-For-Rape-Survivors_March-2014.pdf).

Swedish Grand Journalism Award (2011) (www.storajournalistpriset.se/#year2011)

Temkin, J. and Krahé, B. (2008) *Sexual assault and the justice gap: A question of attitude*, Portland, OR: Hart Publishing.

Templeton, D.J., Williams, A., Healey, L., Odell, M. and Wells, D. (2008) 'Letter to the Editor: Male forensic physicians have an important role in sexual assault care. A response to Chowdhury-Hawkins et al. Preferred choice of gender of staff providing care to victims of sexual assault in Sexual Assault Referral Centres (SARCs)', *Journal of Forensic Legal Medicine*, vol 17, no 1, pp 50-2.

Tewksbury, R. and Jennings, W.G. (2010) 'Assessing the impact of sex offender registration and community notification on sex-offending trajectories', *Criminal Justice and Behavior*, vol 37, no 5, pp 570-82.

Tewksbury, R., Jennings, W.G. and Zgoba, K. (2012) 'A longitudinal examination of sex offender recidivism prior to and following the implementation of SORN', *Behavioral Sciences and the Law*, vol 30, no 3, pp 308-28.

Thomas, C., Young, L. and Ellingen, M. (2011) *Working with the justice sector to end violence against women and girls*, New York: UN Women (www.endvawnow.org/uploads/modules/pdf/1325624043.pdf).

Tickner, J.A. (1992) *Gender in international relations: Feminist perspectives on achieving global security*, New York, NY: Columbia University Press (www.ces.uc.pt/ficheiros2/files/Short.pdf).

Tolman, R. and Raphael, J. (2000) 'A review of research on welfare and domestic violence', *Journal of Social Issues*, vol 56, no 4, pp 655-82.

Toon, C. and Gurusamy, K. (2014) 'Forensic nurse examiners versus doctors for the forensic examination of rape and sexual assault complainants: a systematic review', *Campbell Systematic Reviews*, vol 10, issue 5, p 5.

Towers, J. and Walby, S. (2012) *Measuring the impact of cuts in public expenditure on the provision of services to prevent violence against women and girls*, Newcastle upon Tyne and London: Northern Rock Foundation and Trust for London (www.trustforlondon. org.uk/VAWG%20Full%20report.pdf).

Tryggestad, T.L. (2010) 'The UN peacebuilding commission and gender: a case of norm reinforcement', *Journal of International Peacekeeping*, vol 17, no 2, pp 159-71.

UN (1979) *Convention on the elimination of all forms of discrimination against women* (www.un.org/womenwatch/daw/cedaw/text/ econvention.htm).

UN (1992) *Convention on the elimination of all forms of discrimination against women*, General Recommendation 19 (www.un.org/ womenwatch/daw/cedaw/recommendations/recomm.htm).

UN (2000) *Report of the Panel on UN peace operations: The Brahimi report*, New York: UN.

UN (2006a) *Report of the Special Committee on peacekeeping operations and its working group at the 2006 Substantive Session* (A/60/19), New York: UN.

UN (2006b) *Ending violence against women: From words to action: Study of the Secretary-General*, Geneva: UN.

UN (2007) *New challenges, new horizons*, Year in Review, 2006, UN Peace Operations, New York: UN Department of Public Information, Peace and Security Section (www.un.org/en/ peacekeeping/publications/yir/2006/YIR2006.pdf).

UN (2010a) *Handbook for legislation on violence against women,* New York: UN Division for the Advancement of Women, Department of Economic and Social Affairs (www.un.org/ womenwatch/daw/vaw/handbook/Handbook%20for%20 legislation%20on%20violence%20against%20women.pdf).

UN (2010b) *Ten-year impact study on implementation of UN Security Council Resolution 1325 (2000) on women, peace and security in peacekeeping,* Final report to the UN Department of Peacekeeping Operations, Department of Field Support, New York: UN.

UN (2011) *UN Strategic results framework on women, peace and security: 2011-2020,* New York: UN (www.un.org/womenwatch/ ianwge/taskforces/wps/Strategic_Framework_2011-2020. pdf).

UN (2012) *Year in review 2011,* UN Peace Operations, New York: Peace and Security Section of the United Nations Department of Public Information (www.un.org/en/ peacekeeping/publications/yir/yir2011.pdf).

UN (2013) *Why do some men use violence against women and how can we prevent it? Quantitative findings from the United Nations multi-country study on men and violence in Asia and the Pacific,* Geneva: UN Development Programme, UN Population Fund, UN Women and UN Volunteers.

UN Action Against Sexual Violence in Conflict (2015) UN Action Against Sexual Violence in Conflict: Progress Report 2013-2014, UN Action, Stop Rape Now, New York, NY: UN Action Against Sexual Violence in Conflict (www.stoprapenow. org/uploads/docs/UN_Action_Progress_Report_2013-2014. pdf).

UNDP (2009) *Final Report. Drafting a Strategic Platform for Community Coordination against Domestic Violence in Albania,* Prepared by: Trisha Gentle and Monika Kocaqi. Albania: United Nations Develop Program.

UN Economic and Social Council (2010) *Resolution 15/2010, Strengthening crime prevention and criminal justice responses to violence against women,* 45th plenary meeting (www.un.org/en/ecosoc/ docs/2010/res%202010-15.pdf).

UN General Assembly (1993) *Declaration on the elimination of violence against women*, A/RES/48/104 (www.un.org/documents/ga/res/48/a48r104.htm).

UNHCR (United Nations High Commissioner for Refugees) (2003) *Sexual and gender-based violence against refugees, returnees and internally displaced persons: Guidelines for prevention and response*, London: UNHCR (www.unhcr.org/refworld/pdfid/3edcd0661.pdf).

UNICEF (2009) *Thuthuzela Care Centres* (www.unicef.org/southafrica/hiv_aids_998.html).

UNIFEM (2010) *Formulating National Action Plans (NAPs) to end violence against women and girls*, New York: UNIFEM, part of UN Women (www.un.org/womenwatch/daw/vaw/egm/nap2010/EGM.GPNAP.2010.SP.02.pdf).

UNISDR (International Strategy for Disaster Reduction) (2009) *UNISDR terminology on disaster risk reduction*, Geneva: UNISDR (www.unisdr.org/files/7817_UNISDRTerminologyEnglish.pdf).

UNiTE (2011) *UNiTE to end violence against women* (www.un.org/en/women/endviolence/).

UN Office for the High Commissioner of Human Rights (2013) 'UN rights chief praises groundbreaking report on violence against women in India', UN News Centre (www.un.org/apps/news/story.asp?NewsID=44000&Cr=India&Cr1=rights#.UQZXovImTp8).

UN Secretary-General (2004) *Women, and peace and security* (S/2004/814), New York: UN.

UN Secretary-General (2006) *In-depth study on all forms of violence against women*, Report to UN General Assembly (www.un.org/womenwatch/daw/vaw/SGstudyvaw.htm).

UN Security Council (2000) *Resolution 1325 on women, peace and security* (www.un.org/womenwatch/osagi/wps/).

UN Security Council (2001) *Resolution 1325 on women, peace and security* (S/RES/1325), New York: UN.

UN Security Council (2008) *Resolution 1820 on women, war and peace* (www.un.org/ga/search/view_doc.asp?symbol=S/RES/1820%282008%29).

UN Security Council (2009) *Resolution 1889* (www.peacewomen.org/assets/file/BasicWPSDocs/scr1889.pdf).

UN Security Council (2010) *Resolution 1960* (www. securitycouncilreport.org/atf/cf/%7B65BFCF9B-6D27-4E9C-8CD3-CF6E4FF96FF9%7D/WPS%20SRES%201960. pdf).

UN Security Council (2013a) *Resolution 2106* (http:// peacemaker.un.org/sites/peacemaker.un.org/files/SC_ ResolutionWomen_SRES2106%282013%29%28english%29. pdf).

UN Security Council (2013b) *Resolution 2122* (http://unscr. com/en/resolutions/doc/2122).

UN Women (2011) '16 steps policy agenda', New York: UN Women (www.unwomen.org/en/news/in-focus/end-violence-against-women/2011/16-steps-policy-agenda).

UN Women (2012a) *Handbook for national action plans on violence against women*, New York: UN Women (www.un.org/ womenwatch/daw/vaw/handbook-for-nap-on-vaw.htm).

UN Women (2012b) *High-level panel: Strong commitment and actions imperative for the prevention of sexual violence and gender-based crimes in conflict and for securing justice for survivors*, New York: UN Women (http://comms-authoring.unwomen.org/en/news/ stories/2012/9/high-level-panel-strong-commitment-and-actions-imperative-for-the-prevention-of-sexual-violence-an).

UN Women (2014) *Safe Cities Global Initiative*, Brief update, September, New York: UN Women (www.unwomen. org/~/media/headquarters/attachments/sections/library/ publications/2014/un%20women%20safe%20cities%20brief-us-web.pdf).

US Department of Health and Human Services, Office of Minority Health (no date) *Cultural competency curriculum for disaster preparedness and crisis response* (https://cccdpcr. thinkculturalhealth.hhs.gov/).

Valenti, J. (2010) 'Misogyny and the backlash against Assange's accusers', *Feminist Frequency*, 16 December (www. feministfrequency.com/2010/12/misogyny-backlash-against-assanges-accusers/).

Vasquez, B.E., Maddan, S. and Walker, J.T. (2007) 'The influence of sex offender registration and notification laws in the United States: A time-series analysis', *Crime & Delinquency*, vol 54, no 2, pp 175-92.

VAWnet.org (2011) *Special collection: Disaster and emergency preparedness and response* (www.vawnet.org/special-collections/DisasterPrep).

Vetten, L. (2001) 'While women wait (2): can specialist sexual offences courts and centres reduce secondary victimisation?', *Nedbank ISS Crime Index*, vol 5, no 3.

Vetten, L. and Bhana, K. (2001) *Violence, vengeance and gender: A preliminary investigation into the links between violence against women and HIV/AIDS in South Africa*, The Centre for the Study of Violence and Reconciliation (www.csvr.org.za/old/docs/gender/violence.pdf).

VicHealth (2014) *Australians' attitudes to violence against women. Findings from the 2013 National Community Attitudes towards Violence against Women Survey (NCAS)*, Melbourne, VIC: Victorian Health Promotion Foundation.

Walby, S. (2004) *The cost of domestic violence*, London: Department of Trade and Industry, Women and Equality Unit (www.devon.gov.uk/de/text/cost_of_dv_report_sept04.pdf).

Walby, S. (2005a) 'Gender mainstreaming: productive tensions in theory and practice', *Social Politics*, vol 12, no 3, pp 321-43.

Walby, S. (2005b) 'Improving the statistics on violence against women', *Statistical Journal of the United Nations Economic Commission for Europe*, vol 22, no 4, pp 193-216.

Walby, S. (2009) *Globalization and inequalities: Complexity and contested modernities*, London: Sage.

Walby, S. (2011) *The future of feminism*, London: Polity Press.

Walby, S. (2013a) 'Violence and society: introduction to an emerging field of sociology', *Current Sociology*, vol 61, no 2, pp 95-111.

Walby, S. (2013b) *The European added value of a directive on combating violence against women: Legal perspectives for action at EU level*, Research paper for European Union Value Added Unit, Brussels: European Added Value Unit.

Walby, S. (2015) *Crisis*, Cambridge: Polity Press.

Walby, S. and Allen, J. (2004) *Domestic violence, sexual assault and stalking: Findings from the British Crime Survey*, Home Office Research Study 276, London: Home Office.

Walby, S. and Myhill, A. (2001) 'New survey methodologies in researching violence against women', *British Journal of Criminology*, vol 41, no 3, pp 502-22.

Walby, S. and Olive, P. (2014) *Estimating the costs of gender-based violence in the European Union*, Vilnius: European Institute for Gender Equality.

Walby, S., Armstrong, J. and Strid, S. (2012) 'Developing measures of multiple forms of sexual violence and their contested treatment in the criminal justice system', in J. M. Brown and S.L. Walklate (eds) *Handbook on sexual violence*, London: Willan, pp 90-114.

Walby, S., Towers, J. and Francis B. (2014) 'Mainstreaming domestic and gender-based violence into sociology and the criminology of violence', *The Sociological Review*, vol 62, no S2, pp 187-214.

Walby, S., Olive, P., Towers, J., Francis, B., Strid, S., Krizsán, S., Lombardo, E., May-Chahal, C., Franzway, S., Sugarman, D. and Agarwal, B. (2013) *Overview of the worldwide best practices for rape prevention and for assisting women victims of rape*, Brussels: European Parliament.

Walden, I. and Wall, L. (2014) *Reflecting on primary prevention of violence against women: The public health approach*, Melbourne, VIC: Australian Centre for the Study of Sexual Assault and the Australian Family and Domestic Violence Clearinghouse (www.aifs.gov.au/acssa/pubs/issue/i19/index.html).

Wall, L. and Quadara, A. (2014) *Acknowledging complexity in the impacts of sexual victimisation trauma*, Melbourne, VIC: Australian Centre for the Study of Sexual Assault (http://aifs.gov.au/acssa/pubs/issue/i16/index.html).

Wall, L. and Stathopoulos, M. (2012) *A snapshot of how local context affects sexual assault service provision in regional, rural and remote Australia*, Melbourne, VIC: Australian Centre for the Study of Sexual Assault (http://aifs.gov.au/acssa/pubs/wrap/wrap13/index.html).

Wang, S.K. and Rowley, E. (2007) *Rape: How women, the community and the health sector respond*, Geneva: Sexual Violence Research Initiative, World Health Organization (www.svri.org/rape.pdf).

Ward, C.A. (2013) 'Significance of wartime rape', *Gendered Perspectives on Conflict and Violence: Part A*, pp 189-212.

Ward, T. (2002) 'Good lives and the rehabilitation of offenders: promises and problems', *Aggression and Violent Behavior*, vol 7, pp 513-28.

Ward, T. and Maruna, S. (2007) *Rehabilitation: Beyond the risk paradigm*, London: Routledge.

Ward, T. and Stewart, C.A. (2003) 'The treatment of sex offenders: risk management and the good lives model', *Professional Psychology: Research and Practice*, vol 34, pp 353-60.

Ward, T., Yates, P.M. and Willis, G.M. (2012) 'The Good Lives Model and the Risk Need Responsivity Model: a critical response to Andrews, Bonta, and Wormith (2011)', *Criminal Justice and Behavior*, vol 39, no 1, pp 94-110.

Wasco, S., Campbell, R., Howard, A., Mason, R., Staggs, S.L., Schewe, P. and Riger, S. (2004) 'A state wide evaluation of services provided to rape survivors', *Journal of Interpersonal Violence*, vol 19, no 2, pp 252-63.

Washington State Institute for Public Policy (2005) 'Sex offender sentencing in Washington State: has community notification reduced recidivism?', Olympia, WA, December (www.wsipp. wa.gov/rptfiles/05-12-1202.pdf).

Watts, C. and Zimmerman, C. (2002) 'Violence against women: global scope and magnitude', *The Lancet*, vol 359, pp 1232-7.

Weeks, W. (1994) *Women working together. Lessons from feminist women's services*, Melbourne, VIC: Longman Cheshire.

Weinberger, L.E., Sreenivasan, S., Garrick, T. and Osran, H. (2005) 'The impact of surgical castration on sexual recidivism risk among sexually violent predatory offenders', *The Journal of the American Academy of Psychiatry and the Law*, vol 33, no 1, pp 16-36.

Weldon, S.L. (2002) *Protest, policy, and the problem of violence against women: A cross-national comparison*, Pittsburgh, PA: University of Pittsburgh Press.

Weldon, S.L. and Htun, M. (2012) 'The civic origins of progressive policy change: combating violence against women in global perspective, 1975-2005', *American Political Science Review*, vol 106, no 3, pp 548-69.

Westmarland, N. and Alderson, S. (2013) 'The health, mental health, and well-being benefits of rape crisis counseling', *Journal of Interpersonal Violence*, vol 28, no 17, pp 3265-82.

Whitaker, D., Morrison, S., Lindquist, C., Hawkins, S.R., O'Neil, J.A., Nesius, A.M. Mathew, A. and Reese, L. (2006) 'A critical review of interventions for the primary prevention of perpetration of partner violence', *Aggression and Violent Behavior*, vol 11, pp 151-66.

WHO (World Health Organization) (2002) *World report on violence and health*, Geneva: WHO (prepared by E.G. Krug, L.L. Dahlberg, J.A. Mercy, A.B. Zwi and R. Lozano (www.who.int/violence_injury_prevention/violence/world_report/en/full_en.pdf).

WHO (2003) *Guidelines for medico-legal care for victims of sexual violence*, Geneva: WHO (www.who.int/violence_injury_prevention/publications/violence/med_leg_guidelines/en/index.html).

WHO (2004a) *The economic dimensions of interpersonal violence*, Geneva: Department of Injuries and Violence Prevention, WHO.

WHO (2004b) *Clinical management of rape survivors: Developing protocols for use with refugees and internally displaced persons* (revised edn), Geneva: WHO (http://whqlibdoc.who.int/publications/2004/924159263X.pdf).

WHO (2005a) *Multi-country study on women's health and domestic violence against women: Initial results on prevalence, health outcomes and women's responses*, Geneva: WHO.

WHO (2005b) *Violence and disasters*, Geneva: WHO (www.who.int/violence_injury_prevention/publications/violence/violence_disasters.pdf).

WHO (2007) *Ethical and safety recommendations for researching, documenting and monitoring sexual violence in emergencies*, Geneva: WHO (www.who.int/gender/documents/OMS_Ethics&Safety10Aug07.pdf).

WHO (2011a) *mHealth: New horizons for health through mobile technologies*, Geneva: WHO (http://apps.who.int/iris/bitstream/10665/44607/1/9789241564250_eng.pdf?ua=1).

WHO (2011b) *The interagency emergency health kit 2011: Medicines and medical devices for 10,000 people for approximately three months*, Geneva: WHO, Department of Medicines and Pharmaceutical Policies (www.who.int/medicines/publications/emergencyhealthkit2011/en/index.html).

WHO (2012a) *Understanding and addressing violence against women: Sexual violence*, Geneva: WHO (http://apps.who.int/iris/bitstream/10665/77434/1/WHO_RHR_12.37_eng.pdf).

WHO (2012b) *Mental health and psychosocial support for conflict-related sexual violence: Principles and interventions*, Geneva: WHO (http://apps.who.int/iris/bitstream/10665/75179/1/WHO_RHR_HRP_12.18_eng.pdf).

WHO (2012c) *'Do's and don'ts in community-based psychosocial support for sexual violence survivors in conflict-affected settings*, Geneva: WHO (www.who.int/reproductivehealth/publications/violence/rhr12_16/en/).

WHO (2013a) *Responding to intimate partner violence and sexual violence against women: WHO clinical and policy guidelines*, Geneva: WHO (http://apps.who.int/iris/bitstream/10665/85240/1/9789241548595_eng.pdf).

WHO (2013b) *Global and regional estimates of violence against women: Prevalence and health effects of intimate partner violence and non-partner sexual violence*, Geneva: WHO (http://apps.who.int/iris/bitstream/10665/85239/1/9789241564625_eng.pdf).

WHO (2013c) *Humanitarian health action definitions: Emergencies*, Geneva: WHO (www.who.int/hac/about/definitions/en/).

WHO (2013d) *Violence against women: The health sector responds*, Geneva: WHO (http://apps.who.int/iris/bitstream/10665/82753/1/WHO_NMH_VIP_PVL_13.1_eng.pdf).

WHO (2014a) *Evidence-informed policy-making: What is evidence?*, Geneva: WHO (www.who.int/evidence/library/en/).

WHO (2014b) *Global status report on violence prevention 2014*, Geneva: WHO, United Nations Office on Drugs and Crime and United Nations Development Programme.

WHO and LSHTM (London School of Hygiene and Tropical Medicine) (2010) *Preventing intimate partner and sexual violence against women: Taking action and generating evidence*, Geneva: WHO (http://whqlibdoc.who.int/publications/2010/9789241564007_eng.pdf).

Wild, R. and Anderson, P. (2007) *Little children are sacred, Ampe Akelyernemane Meke Merkale, Report of the Northern Territory Board of Inquiry into the protection of Aboriginal children from sexual abuse*, Report to the Northern Territory Government, Darwin.

Wille, R. and Beier, K.M. (1989) 'Castration in Germany', *Annals of Sex Research*, vol 2, no 2, pp 103-33.

Willett, S. (2010) 'Introduction: Security Council Resolution 1325: Assessing the impact on women, peace and security', *Journal of International Peacekeeping*, vol 17, no 2, pp 142-58.

WNC (Women's National Commission) (2010) *A bitter pill to swallow: Report from WNC focus groups to inform the Department of Health Taskforce on the health aspects of violence against women and girls* (http://wnc.equalities.gov.uk/work-of-the-wnc/violence-against-women/news-and-updates/309-a-bitter-pill-to-swallow-report-from-the-wnc-focus-groups.html).

Women's Budget Group (2014) *2014 assessments* (http://wbg.org.uk/2014-assessments/).

Women's Resource Centre (2008) *The crisis in Rape Crisis: A survey of Rape Crisis (England and Wales) Centres*, London: Women's Resource Centre (http://thewomensresourcecentre.org.uk/).

Xenos, S. and Smith, D. (2001) 'Perceptions of rape and sexual assault among Australian adolescents and young adults', *Journal of Interpersonal Violence*, vol 16, no 11, pp 1103-19.

Zaidi, Y. (2002) *Violence against women in South Asia: A regional scan of efforts to end violence*, New York: UNIFEM.

Zgoba, K., Witt, P., Dalessandro, M. and Veysey, B. (2008) '*Megan's Law*': Assessing the practical and monetary efficacy*, Trenton, NJ: New Jersey Department of Corrections.

Zimmerman, C., Hossain, M., Yun, K., Roche, B., Morison, L. and Watts, C. (2006) *Stolen smiles: A summary report on the physical and psychological health consequences of women and adolescents trafficked in Europe*, London: London School of Hygiene & Tropical Medicine (www.lshtm.ac.uk/php/ghd/docs/stolensmiles.pdf).

Index

SORN (sex offender registration
and notification) 146
Austria 51, 121, 132, 137
awareness raising 97, 195, 206, 208
Aydin v Turkey 115

B

Baillot, H. 130
Balagopal, G. 166
Bandy, R. 149
Baños Smith, M. 134, 200, 201,
202, 203
Bedford, K. 211
Beech, A. 141
Behrendt, L. 42
Beier, K.M. 140
Beijbom, A. 206, 207
Beijing Platform for Action (UN)
22, 24
Bein, K. 52, 54, 55
Belem do Para Convention 114,
152, 154, 234
Belgium 122, 137
Bell Bajo campaign 199
Bhana, K. 129
Bhuvanendra, D. 89, 90, 91, 97,
198
Bishop, K. 198, 199
Black, M.C. 64, 80
BME (black and minority ethnic)
women 94
Boba, R. 138
body parts 12, 122–3
Bohner, G. 193
Bonnes, S. 192
Borzacchiello, E. 152, 154, 155,
157
Bosnia-Herzegovina 16, 68, 117,
175, 180–1
Bouhours, B. 44, 45
Bourke, J. 63
Brazil 87, 88
Brecklin, L.R. 197
Breiding, M.J. 64, 196
Bridges, D. 177, 181
Brierley, G. 86
British Crime Survey 14, 15
Bronfenbenner, U. 9
Brown, D. 43
Brown, J. 132
Brown, J.M. 35, 206
Brown, M. 212
Brownmiller, S. 35, 175
Buerkle, H. 167
Buiten, D. 193
Bulgaria 121

Bumby, K.M. 197
Bumiller, K. 28, 129
Burnett, G. 167
Burt, M.R. 192
Burundi 182
Bybee, D.I. 132
bystander projects 53, 195, 198,
199, 200

C

Callander, I. 138
Cambodia 123, 175
Campbell, J.C. 63, 80
Campbell, R. 26, 73, 91
Canada
anonymity in court 194
mental health services 83
Risk-Need-Responsivity Model
141, 143
SARCs (sexual assault referral
centres) 66, 94
SORN (sex offender registration
and notification) 145
capable and care conducive
environment 70–8, 105, 107
capacity-building 177, 182, 186
Care project 220
Care Rooms 34–5
Carey, H.F. 177, 180, 181
Carmody, M. 41
case studies
#talkaboutit campaign 205–9
Australian coordinated and
integrated services 39
coordinated community responses
in US and other countries
48–51
EU cyberspace identification case
study 167–71
International Rescue Committee
(IRC) 185–9
Mexican law 152–8
South African specialised sexual
offences courts 158–67
Southampton Talking About
Relationships (Star) 200–5
St Mary's case study 100–4
US SACT (Sexual Assault Crisis
Team) case study 52–7
Cassim, F. 170
castration of sex offenders 139–42
Cawson, P. 200
CBT (cognitive behavioural
therapies)
for sex offenders 142–3
for victim-survivors 82, 84